THE JOY OF GEOCACHING

JoyOfGeocaching.com

THE JOY OF GEOCACHING

HOW TO FIND HEALTH, HAPPINESS AND CREATIVE ENERGY THROUGH A WORLDWIDE TREASURE HUNT

Paul and Dana Gillin (PnD)

Quill Driver Books
Fresno, CA

The Joy of Geocaching
©2010 Paul and Dana Gillin
All photos are by the authors unless noted differently.
Visit **http://bit.ly/JOGphotos** to view/download the photos in the book.

Published by Quill Driver Books,
an imprint of Linden Publishing.
2006 S. Mary, Fresno, California, 93721
559-233-6633 / 800-345-4447
QuillDriverBooks.com

Quill Driver Books and Colophon are trademarks of
Linden Publishing, Inc.

Quill Driver Books' titles may be purchased in quantity at special
discounts for educational, fund-raising, business, or promotional use.
Please contact Special Markets, Quill Driver Books, at the
above address or at 559-233-6633.
To order another copy of this book, please call
1-800-345-4447

ISBN: 978-1-884956-99-7
135798642
Printed in the United States of America on acid-free paper.

Library of Congress Cataloging-in-Publication Data

Gillin, Paul.
The joy of geocaching : how to find health, happiness and creative energy
through a worldwide treasure hunt / by Paul and Dana Gillin.
    p. cm.
Includes bibliographical references and index.
ISBN 978-1-884956-99-7 (pbk. : alk. paper)
1. Geocaching (Game) I. Gillin, Dana. II. Title.
GV1202.G46G55 2010
796.5--dc22

2009053699

To Dana's parents,
who taught us by example
to rejoice in lifelong learning

CONTENTS

INTRODUCTION

In early 2003, Ed Manley decided to kill himself.

Life couldn't have been much worse for the then 49-year-old war veteran. A series of mishaps resulting in forty-two surgeries over almost thirty years, featuring bone grafts, chronic bone infection, amputation, and repeated prolonged recoveries had left him with one leg and an irreparable broken neck, not to mention in severe chronic pain that would never go away. Finally unable to work, he sold his business and began a long slide into depression.

By 2003, Manley was nearly bedridden, in constant pain, addicted to massive amounts of the pain medicine Fentanyl, and ashamed of himself and of the burden he believed he was to his family. "I saw no hope for a functional life. I wanted out of here," he says. "Whatever was next had to be better than this."

Manley planned to go fishing, his favorite hobby. He would drive his pontoon boat to the center of Lay Lake near his Birmingham, Alabama, home, where he would stage a realistic-looking fall from the boat. This plan would not only relieve his pain, but would also spare his family of the burden of caring for him while leaving them with sufficient life insurance to carry on.

As he was loading his boat on the chosen morning, the postman arrived with a package. Inside was a Garmin eTrex global positioning satellite receiver. Manley had forgotten that he had ordered the gadget months earlier in a mail-order promotion. Even in his hour of darkness, the gadget freak in him was intrigued. What was the new toy good for? Manley stopped loading the boat and went to his computer, where Google led him to **Geocaching.com**, a website dedicated to a new kind of global treasure hunt in which people pointed each other to hidden objects by sharing latitude-longitude coordinates. He saw that one of these so-called geocaches was near his old high school. The listing description for "The Mountie Cache" mentioned a hole in the fence as a landmark. "I knew that hole very well, because we used to go there to smoke," he says. "I wanted to see if this GPS thing could navigate me to that place."

Although wheelchair-bound and in what he terms "seriously sorry shape," Manley struggled out to find the treasure: an ammunition can full of toys. "Found it! Cool!" For the first time in years he was excited about something. And the website said geocaches were hidden all over!

Arriving home exhausted, Manley was faced with a decision: "Do I kill myself or get healthy? Killing myself really didn't sound too appealing, so that left getting healthy." Geocaching would be his road to recovery. The goal: "Higher Than a Hawk," a cache placed at the top of a nearby mountain. Finding that cache would prove that he still had the power to recover. The first step was to get off drugs, so Manley threw away $1,600 worth of painkillers. Withdrawal was agonizing, but at least there was a goal. Four months of withdrawal sickness yielded to six months of geocaching-driven physical therapy: a couple of easy caches a day at first and then harder ones as his emotional and physical stamina rebuilt.

Then came the day Ed Manley scaled the mountain and found the treasure. "I had been a successful businessman for 28 years, raised a fine family, and accomplished many things," he says, "but finding that cache was one of my greatest accomplishments. It proved I could take my life back."

Six years later, Ed "TheAlabamaRambler" Manley's life has been transformed by geocaching. He has found more than 2,500 caches in 28 states, met thousands of people at geocaching events, and helped found the Alabama Geocachers Association and its DixieCachers.com forum, which are among the largest and most active geocaching enthusiast groups in the country. In 2008, he launched The Online Geocacher (TheOnlineGeocacher.com), a free Web magazine dedicated to assembling the best stories, news, and advice from cachers around the world.

"Geocaching literally saved my life," he says, "and I use that experience to promote a 'Just Do It' attitude. When life bears down hard, don't reach for drugs, whine or quit. Go find a geocache; it will make a positive difference!"

Ed Manley is only one of the many people whose lives have been touched by the global game of geocaching. In the course of researching this book and interviewing scores of veteran geocachers, we met many others. One of them is Brad Simmons, who goes by the online handle "MonkeyBrad." The Chapel Hill, Tennessee, owner of a gourmet foods provider shed 150 pounds and quit smoking on the path to logging more than 10,000 cache finds. Like many of the cachers we interviewed, geocaching has changed Brad's life. He peppers his frequent business travels with excursions to local treasure troves and dines weekly with a group of local geocaching enthusiasts. "The wait staff thinks it's a family reunion," he laughs. Like hunters on a camping expedition, they find bonds in geocaching that the uninitiated can't fathom.

Love at First Byte

We still remember our own introduction to geocaching. Dana had read an article that described this increasingly popular high-tech treasure hunt that had people crashing through woods and scrambling over sand dunes following signals on

Can you say "addicted?" Dana searches for a geocache during our 2007 honeymoon in France.

a handheld Global Positioning Satellite receiver (GPSr).

She thought it was kind of neat. Paul didn't agree. "This sounds sooooo geeky," he said, rolling his eyes.

Much as we try to deny it, though, we're both pretty geeky. A few months later, Paul was listening to a podcast produced by a local newspaper. The reporter followed a geocacher as he made the rounds of Boston Harbor, uncovering tiny treasures as he went and explaining the basics of the game. The prospect of acquiring a new consumer electronics gadget was too strong for us to resist. A couple of weeks later, armed with a Garmin GPSmap 60C we had purchased on eBay, we set out to search for our first cache.

Our search took us to a nature preserve less than a mile from our home. Wandering through the woods, we marveled that we had lived in the area for years and had never known that such a beautiful spot existed. While Dana drank in the flora and fauna, Paul kept his nose buried in the GPS, expecting it to take us directly to our destination. We were surprised to find out that GPS receivers aren't all that precise; it took us 20 minutes of poking around before we discovered the ammunition box filled with trinkets.

We were hooked. In the following weeks, we discovered about a dozen new parks and recreation areas just minutes from our home. We began to explore **Geocaching.com** and discovered that the community had invented all kinds of variations on the basic search that involve elaborate puzzles, multi-staged mysteries, and exotic destinations.

Why We Wrote this Book

That was in 2006. Since then, the global population of geocachers has more than doubled. A game that began with just 75 hidden treasures in 2000 surpassed one million in early 2010. That's a compound annual growth rate of nearly 320 percent! Each week, some 6,500 new geocaches are placed and 1.4 million log entries filed at **Geocaching.com**. Geocaching.com operator Groundspeak estimates that more than 3 million people worldwide now geocache, and that number is likely to grow rapidly as the location technology in smart phones begins to rival that of costlier dedicated devices. What's remarkable is that this growth has been achieved with no marketing or advertising. Geocaching awareness grows entirely through word-of-mouth.

In looking for books to help guide us, we found that the available how-to guides—*Geocaching for Dummies* and *The Complete Idiot's Guide to Geocaching*— were both more than four years old. With technology changing so quickly and groups springing up all over the globe, it seemed that a new guide was appropriate. Shortly before we finished writing this book, a new version of the *Complete Idiot's Guide* was published, but that field manual lacks the rich human stories that make geocaching such a magnet of enthusiasm.

We thought we could contribute to the community by gathering the knowledge of veteran geocachers and by presenting the secrets we learned from true enthusiasts. We also wanted to tap into the human element and tell lots of stories. We contacted and interviewed more than 40 of the world's 50 most prolific cachers, as well as people who specialize in camouflage, puzzles, and a physically taxing variation of the game called extreme geocaching.

We also interviewed dozens of people in other corners of the geocaching world: experts in container design, group organizers, equipment vendors, professional educators, and even public officials who see rich new opportunities to improve public health and ecology.

Different Strokes

We asked nearly everybody we interviewed why they geocache. The answers are all over the, er, map. Some people enjoy the thrill of the hunt. Others find it an excellent way to get outdoors. Some do it for exercise and others for the thrill of discovery. We talked to experienced geocachers who find almost nothing but puzzles. For them, geocaching is a way to exercise their mind. We also met many senior geocachers who have found the game to be a wonderful way to renew their energy and meet new friends after retirement.

"I have three kids and all like it for different reasons," says Michael Jacobus, former publisher of *Geocacher* magazine, which succumbed to the media downturn in 2009. "One likes the numbers. One likes the puzzles and the difficult terrain. A third is all about trackables and coins." Geocaching really does seem to have something for everyone.

Perhaps what surprised us most was the number of people who told us they do it for camaraderie. Although geocaching is basically a solo venture, it turns out

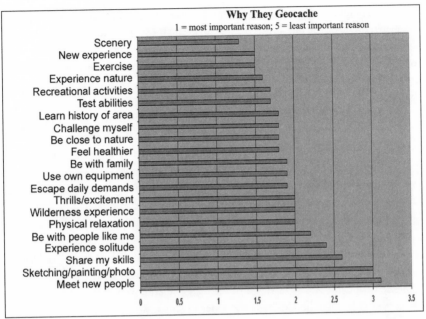

Why They Geocache
1 = most important reason; 5 = least important reason

Source: *The Social-Psychology of a Technology Driven Outdoor Trend: Geocaching in the USA.* Chavez, D., I. Schneider, and T. Powell, 2003.

that many people wouldn't think of caching alone. For them, the experience of sharing an adventure with a group of good friends is an essential appeal of the game. Perhaps that's why geocaching clubs have sprung up in all 50 states and many of the more than 100 countries around the world where geocachers can be found.

We set out to write a how-to manual, but along the way we discovered that geocaching is much more than a game. To the community of avid practitioners, it is a passion that energizes their spare hours, defines their social groups, and connects them with nature. It is a paradox in our high-tech world. To paraphrase a common refrain, geocaching is a game that uses billions of dollars' worth of satellite technology to find Tupperware in the woods.

This book is a collection of the experiences and secrets that enthusiasts shared with us. It is intended for the novice to intermediate geocacher as a companion to the technical how-to manuals. Experienced geocachers may enjoy and relate to the stories told here. While there's plenty of practical advice, our goal was also to communicate the passion, fun, and memorable experiences that enthusiasts shared with us.

We were awarded access to some of the best geocachers in the sport—from Alamogul, who has over 36,000 logs to his name; to Sandy and Sunny, the duo of

Podcacher fame; to master hiders and extremists. Some are ranked number one in their own niche of the game, but they are also the most approachable people in the world. This sense of camaraderie, of helping people less experienced, and of learning from those same relative newbies, made the year-long process of researching and writing this book such a joy. We've made friends the world over and hope that this is just the beginning of that process.

A note about the statistics in this book: One of the hazards of writing a book with any sort of cumulative statistics is that they're outdated by the time the book is published. All of the cache tallies for specific geocachers were correct as of late 2009, but the numbers have no doubt changed since then.

Conventional wisdom is that cowriting a book with a good friend is stressful enough to ruin a relationship. Doing it with a spouse? Forget it. We found the opposite was true. Connecting with so many passionate people inspired passion in us, too. Our dinner conversations were animated by sharing what great stories we heard that day and discussing the tips other cachers had shared. We learned together as a couple and that fueled our own enthusiasm. When we started this project, we cached once or twice a month. By the end, we were doing so at every opportunity, all the while loving each other's company.

This book is full of human stories ranging from hilarious to hair-raising. We recorded most of our interviews and will make audio excerpts available on our website, JoyOfGeocaching.com. There you can also see photos contributed by the people we met and read our constantly updated list of geocaching-related resources.

The Joy of Geocaching is a how-to manual for the modern game, but it is also an account of the life-changing force of this remarkable activity. The Internet is sometimes perceived to be a magnet for seclusion, a medium that forces people indoors to waste time in front of their screens. But in the case of geocaching, the Internet has enabled millions of people to get back into touch with the environment, make new friends, and rediscover the joy of the outdoors. We hope this book conveys some of the thrill we got from uncovering their stories and helps you gain new insights about yourself and the undiscovered world around you.

Paul & Dana Gillin
Framingham, MA
January, 2010

How to Use this Book

The *Joy of Geocaching* is a little different from other how-to guides because it's about people as much as it's about tips and tactics. Therefore, this book is organized somewhat differently from other books.

There are four main sections: **Preparing to Geocache, In the Field, Taming Technology,** and **Beyond the Game.** The first two are intended to get you out the door as quickly as possible with the best tactics in hand for maximizing found caches and minimizing frustration.

We put the technical stuff at the back of the book. There's some really useful material in the Taming Technology section on how navigation works, how to select a GPSr, and about great software and Internet tools you can use to make your outings more productive, but we know that stuff isn't for everyone. It's back there if you're interested, though.

The final section is about groups, outings, and how to use geocaching to promote your organization or business.

Throughout the book, we've included geocachers' online handles in parentheses when we introduce them, and refered to them by their handles thereafter. This is in keeping with the semi-anonymous culture of the game.

Looking chapter-by-chapter:

The **Quick Start Guide** gets you kicked off with step-by-step instructions for finding your first geocache. If we did our job right, it should be all you need to experience that initial rush of success.

The **Joy of Geocaching (Chapter 1)** is about the way geocaching changes people's lives. There are lots of good stories here, and you will learn why people get so crazy enthusiastic about this global game.

Getting Around Geocaching.com (Chapter 2) and **Planning Your Outing on Geocaching.com (Chapter 3)** acquaint you with the comprehensive but quirky website that powers the game.

In **Finding a Geocache (Chapter 4)**, we take you out into the field, providing you with advice from the world's most prolific geocachers on how to find what you're looking for—and how to find it fast.

Hiding a Geocache (Chapter 5) turns the tables by teaching you how to stash your own geocache, which is as much fun as finding one. You're going to want to do this at some point, believe us.

In **Caching to the Limits (Chapter 6)**, it's back to people stories as we explore the motivations of cachers who take the game to its limits. These folks dangle from bridges to nab a cache or deprive themselves of sleep in the name of finding containers in all 50 U.S. states in just 10 days. They're amazing—and a little nuts.

Navigation Basics (Chapter 7) explains how knowledge and technology have evolved to make it possible to pinpoint any place on earth with three-meter accuracy, which is pretty incredible when you think about it.

Choosing a GPSr (Chapter 8) is about, well, choosing a GPS receiver. We tested several units and asked experts for their advice so you can sort through the many options and avoid over-paying.

Software Goodies for Geocachers (Chapter 9) should satisfy your inner geek, because it's all about cool software tools for geocaching. It certainly satisfied Paul's inner geek to write it.

The Social Side (Chapter 10) is about camaraderie, friendship, and having pizza together, which are three things geocachers do very well.

Geocaching in Education and Business (Chapter 11) discusses how people are using the game to teach Shakespeare, attract customers and build management teams.

There's also a cool **Glossary** section that we adapted from the nice people at GeoLex.

Throughout this book, you'll find mini-chapters we call **Waypoints**. These are a mix of fun and fascinating facts. There are also, sprinkled throughout, profiles of several of the experts we interviewed for this book and collections of the stories we gathered. Mostly, Waypoints and the profiles are just fun. Which is what geocaching is. So have fun!

Quick Start Guide

First find for CurleyKids—who happen to be Dana's parents!

If you've never gone geocaching before, there are some steps you can take to make sure your first outing is a successful one. There is an extended glossary at the end of this book (Appendix A), but here are just a few terms that you need to know to get started.

A **geocache** is defined simply as "a hidden container that includes, at minimum, a logbook for geocachers to sign." That's it. Containers come in all shapes and sizes and there's nothing about the game that specifies what they must contain other than the logbook. The log is simply a written record of your visit. It may correspond to an online record posted at **Geocaching.com**, but the physical logbook is all that counts.

Geocaching.com is the website of record for geocaching. It contains the world's largest collection of geocaches and related destinations, such as virtual and event caches. **Geocaching.com** isn't the only website of its kind; others include **Earthcache.org, Gcinfo.no, Navicache.com, TerraCaching. com** and **GPSgames.org**. There are also several country-specific versions of **Geocaching.com**. However, nothing else comes close to this site in its scope and importance to the community.

GPSr is shorthand for global positioning system receiver. You need one to play the game, although some masochists do play without these gadgets. Like almost every aspect of geocaching, how you play is up to you. GPSr models range in price from less than $100 to several hundreds of dollars. You can buy them used and online these days at very low cost.

Coordinates are intersecting points of longitude and latitude that specify a unique location on Earth. For the purposes of this game, coordinates are provided by satellite signals and are interpreted by the GPSr.

A **waypoint** is a coordinate that has some significance. It may be the location of a geocache, a parking area, a nearby business, or just a location you want to remember. GPSr units store designated locations as waypoints.

GC is the prefix used to designate waypoints that are geocaches. Every registered geocache on **Geocaching.com** is assigned a unique code that begins with these letters.

A **log** is a written record of a visit to a geocache. A geocache is considered found once the player signs the physical logbook at the site. However, the find (or the fact that the player wasn't able to make the find) isn't added to a player's online tally until it is entered at **Geocaching.com**.

A **trackable** is an item placed in a geocache for the purpose of being moved from one location to another. Its whereabouts can be tracked online.

That's really all you need to know. You will encounter many other terms and geocaching slang throughout this book, but the basic concepts are pretty simple.

Hit the Trail

Here's a step-by-step guide to finding your first geocache:

1 **Purchase a handheld GPSr (Chapter 8)**. Used and low-end units can be found for under $100 on eBay and Internet retail sites. Read the user manual, become familiar with the way the device displays your location, and learn how to navigate to a destination or "waypoint."

2 **Register at Geocaching.com (Chapter 2).** Tell the site where your home coordinates are so you'll have a starting point. You must also choose a username when you register. More on this later. The next seven steps are accomplished on the website.

3 **Look for caches in your area (Chapter 3)** by searching your ZIP code or address. The search results page gives you high-level summaries and links to detailed descriptions.

4 **Choose basic, single-stage caches** that have a difficulty and terrain rating of 1 or 1.5. We also recommend you look for "small" or "regular" cache sizes so you aren't frustrated searching for a tiny container, called a "micro."

5 **Choose a convenient location.** You may have to return to search more than once. Select a park rather than a busy shopping center because you're less likely to endure the gaze of bystanders. You'll get used to curious onlookers over time, but it can be a little disconcerting at first.

6 **Look for terms like "easy," "simple", "fast" and "park and grab"** in the descriptions. You don't want to be too ambitious your first time out!

7 **Check the log summaries** and look for geocaches with a high ratio of "Found" to "Did Not Find" results. A good candidate looks like this:

A poor one looks like this:

😁17 😵22 📖14 💧1 ❄1 ➖1 ✅2 ◯1 ➕1

Those little frown faces are logs of people who did not find the cache. If more than about one in four people failed to find the cache, it's probably a poor candidate for a first-time search.

8 **Decrypt and check the hint.** Geocachers love to play word games. If the hint looks confusing, it probably won't do you much good. On the other hand, a hint like "under rock, behind large maple tree" is intended to help you get to your destination.

9 **Read the most recent logs.** Beware of any recent "Did Not Finds." These could indicate that a cache is missing. Conversely, logs may contain valuable information that can help you in your search. An expression like "I've never seen a hide like this!" tips you off to an unusual container or placement. For your first time out, look for language that indicates the cache is a quick and easy find.

10 **Check your GPSr.** Make sure you have fresh batteries and that you're getting a good satellite signal (all units have a feature that conveys signal strength). You'll want to check signal strength again when you get to your location. If your GPS accuracy is greater than 30 feet, it will complicate the find.

11 **Consult a topographic map** if you have one, or look up the location on Google Earth. This will show you surrounding terrain and help you find the easiest approach route. Remember that coordinates don't discriminate by elevation. Your GPSr may say your destination is 50 feet in front of you, but it won't tell you about the sheer rock wall you have to climb to get there! In addition to free services like Google Maps and Google Earth, you can purchase topographic software like DeLorme's Topo USA (**delorme.com**) or GeoBuddy (**geobuddy.com**).

12 **Calibrate your GPSr's compass.** Non-magnetic compasses of the type found in most GPSr units are notorious for getting out of alignment. A poorly calibrated compass can send you on a wild goose chase. Calibrating is usually a simple setup procedure that's described in the manual.

13 **Drive or walk to your destination (Chapter 4).** Many descriptions will guide you to appropriate parking.

14 **Don't rely too much on your GPSr when you reach your destination.** It's easy to make the mistake of thinking that electronics will lead you directly to the treasure. Even the best handheld GPSr units are only accurate to within a 15-foot radius. Let your eyes guide you from there.

15 **Leave the shovel at home.** It is against the rules to bury a cache, so digging won't be necessary.

16 **Look for items that are out of place.** Rock piles or branches that don't look like they were placed by the hand of nature are a good bet. If the hide has a low difficulty rating, you can probably catch at least a glimpse of the container without probing. Large containers are generally easier to find because there are fewer places to hide them.

17 **Find the cache and sign the log book** with your **Geocaching.com** username and the date. Include a comment if you'd like. Be sure to note that it's your first find!

18 **Take something/leave something.** You may discard this practice after your first few finds, but this is one of the fun parts of discovering the game. Leave a toy, trinket, or personal item like a key chain. The value of an item you leave should be at least as great as the value of anything you take.

19 **Snap a photo.** You do have a digital camera, right? Take a shot of yourself or of the surroundings, being careful not to give away the actual location of the cache. Upload this to **Geocaching.com** when you get home.

20 **Log your find on Geocaching.com** via the "Log Your Visit" link in the description. Be sure to note that this is your first cache. Cache owners are always delighted to hear that they've helped introduce someone to the game, and you may even get a welcome message from the owner.

THE JOY OF GEOCACHING

JoyOfGeocaching.com

CHAPTER ONE
The Joy of Geocaching

Deermark balances on top of the world near GCVZ2W. *Scott Wilcoxson (kepnfit)*

MonkeyBrad was talking with a friend one evening in 2005 about the famous "BoB" geocache series in Chicago. BoB stands for "bottles of beer," a play on the popular "99 Bottles of Beer on the Wall" drinking song. The series of 99 identical caches was placed all over Chicago in 2004 and archived two years later.

MonkeyBrad and his friend agreed they'd enjoy the challenge of seeing how fast they could complete the series. "We were curious, so we went to the computer and found $40 fares on Southwest Airlines," he says. "The next weekend we were on a plane." They completed the challenge in less than eight hours.

Darrell Smith (Show Me The Cache) also found all caches in the BoB series during a day when there was a foot of snow on the ground. The total for the day was 104 caches, his personal record. He drove with a friend from Louisville to Chicago, did the complete series, and returned home by 10 P.M. that evening. The intense caching portion of the trip netted the 99 BoB finds in just over five hours.

What is it that motivates otherwise normal people to do this? It's the same passion that inspires Doug Eyre (DE_Cryptoman) of Hewitt, Texas, to pick his way through the woods in the middle of the night. An insomnia sufferer, DE_Cryptoman is often awake late at night when the volunteer cache reviewers at **Geocaching.com** are posting the most recent submissions. His computer is set to alert him immediately when a new cache has been approved in his area. Then he's out of the house like a shot. He's been known to log a first-to-find at 2 A.M.

Julie Perrine (Mrs. Captain Picard) can relate. With over 18,000 logged finds to her name, she spends at least part of most weekends geocaching. Julie is relentless. A short day for her is 30 finds and she's logged as many as 233 in 13 hours. But she doesn't only seek big numbers. She loves the clever treasures and tries to hide those, as well. "I put caches out there that make people smile," she says.

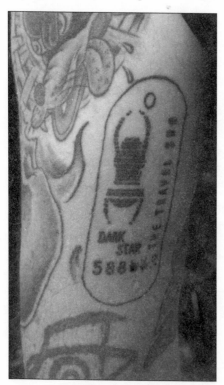

Committed. Dark Star (Robert Bruton) sports a travel bug on his heavily tattooed left arm.

Magnificent Obsession

The original name of this book was *Geocaching Secrets*, but halfway through our research we changed the title to something we thought was more appropriate to describe the emotional commitment we found in avid geocachers. This isn't a game, it's a love affair. It's an obsession.

Most players start geocaching more or less the same way: A friend drags them along on an outing. Most people remain casual geocachers, but a few become deeply involved in the game. To them, geocaching becomes a social circle, an exercise regimen, a journey of discovery, and a tool to satisfy their innate curiosity. When they're not geocaching, they spend their free time planning outings or devising clever new hides. They build geocaching time into their business travel. They organize vacations around the game. In fact, in our survey of 142 geocachers, more than 70 percent said they had gone on a vacation for the primary purpose of geocaching.

Restless Urge

"Geocaching has given me an outlet to allow my imagination and creativity to flow," says Scott Veix (InfiniteMPG). "It's also kind of a 'secret society,' operating under the noses of the general public. It brings back that rush of fun that we tend to lose as we grow older."

"This sport was custom-made for me," says MonkeyBrad. "Whenever I'd travel on business, I'd wander around and try to find interesting corners of the city or oddball attractions. I later found that most caches were placed in these out-of-the-way places. It's not what the tourism office thinks you should see; it's what people in the community think you should see."

Part of geocaching's appeal is its grounding in nature. At a time when more than 80 percent of the U.S. population is packed into urban zones, caching is an escape to simplicity.

Geocachers talk of their surroundings in almost poetic terms. "The Blue Ridge Mountains cannot be matched for uninterrupted joy of life," says Ken Alexander (Granpa Alex) of Sanford, North Carolina. "The flora, the fauna, the bird songs, the peace; it's almost like being in the Garden of Eden. Surely, it is closer to unblemished creation than anywhere on earth."

It's ironic, yet somehow fitting in the twenty-first century, that we need so much technology to get us out of the house. After all, geocaching wouldn't exist if it weren't for computers, satellites, the Internet, and sophisticated personal gadgets. We've managed to combine these high-tech conveniences into a game whose low-tech goal is to lead us to an ammunition can hidden in a tree trunk.

"Geocaching demonstrates that individuals who are both technologically sophisticated and environmentally engaged can and do use an extended communications network and a highly developed navigational system not to supplant a formerly physical engagement but rather explicitly to promote [it]," Margot Anne Kelley wrote in her 2006 book, *Local Treasures: Geocaching Across America*.

The game of geocaching dovetails nicely with several other hobbies. As Show Me The Cache says, "Whether it is photography, hiking, backpacking, bicycling, leisure

Kepnfit geocaches the Grand Canyon. *Mark Wilcoxson (Deermark)*

travel, fishing, bird watching, business trips, or whatever your other interests are, adding a few geocaches to the agenda can add to the adventure."

There's no question that avid geocachers tend to be geeks. They'll be the first to admit it. Get a few of them together at a local meeting and the talk will quickly turn to the merits of one GPSr versus another or whether they prefer Google Maps or Google Earth for planning geocaching runs.

Avid geocachers also tend to be restless and inquisitive. They can't be content sitting in a hotel room; any visit to a new city is a chance to explore. In a 2003 study entitled *The Social-Psychology of a Technology Driven Outdoor Trend: Geocaching in the USA*, researchers Deborah Chavez, Ingrid Schneider, and Todd Powell found that geocachers cited scenery, exercise, and adventure as their most important motivators (see chart on next page). Clearly, these are not the type of people who are inclined to lounge at the beach.

One day, Guy Aldrich (graldrich) and Ray King (Peasinapod) were in the middle of nowhere in the desert, hunting around some rocks, when the gravel gave way and Peasinapod dropped ten feet onto his back and broke six ribs. En route to

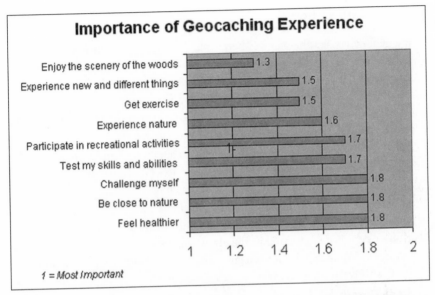

Importance of Geocaching Experience

Enjoy the scenery of the woods	1.3
Experience new and different things	1.5
Get exercise	1.5
Experience nature	1.6
Participate in recreational activities	1.7
Test my skills and abilities	1.7
Challenge myself	1.8
Be close to nature	1.8
Feel healthier	1.8

1 = Most Important

Source: Chavez, Schneider, and Powell, *The Social-Psychology of a Technology Driven Outdoor Trend*, 2003.

the hospital, he stopped to grab six more caches. "We weren't gonna drive right by them!" he said in self-defense.

Paradoxes

Geocaching is also a game of paradoxes. Players curse owners who subject them to the humiliation of a "Did Not Find," while at the same time cheering the owners' inventiveness. They risk injury and even death in extreme cases for a prize that has no practical value. They hunt their quarry cooperatively in packs even as individuals compete against each other for the find. They walk through some of the most beautiful scenery on earth with their noses buried in a satellite receiver. Geocachers are driven, competitive, inquisitive, and restless. Enthusiasts don't take leisurely strolls; they power-walk. For them, walking has to have a purpose to be fun.

"Ask me if I want to walk around the block and my answer is no. Ask me if I want to walk a mile to find a box in the woods full of stuff I don't want and I am ready to go," wrote Jerry and Karen Smith (Team J&K) in response to our online survey.

Caching with Others

Many geocachers say the game is better played with friends than alone. There's a practical reason for this: Woods and mountain caching can be dangerous, and hiding places have a nasty habit of existing out of the range of cell phone service. But there's also a social reason. Why would you not want to discover new places and unravel mysteries with people you like? It's not surprising that respondents to our survey said they geocache with others more than half the time.

"It gets our whole family together and gets us out doing some exercise and getting fresh air," wrote Bill Waller (Derby City Searchers) in response to our survey. "When we all get together, there are 15 of us caching."

Geocachers seem to congregate naturally into groups. Even when they're not with their colleagues in the field, they're hanging out with members of their local geoclub or even just conversing in the always-active Groundspeak forums. Some regional geocaching organizations count their membership in the thousands and organize outings as often as every week.

Steve O'Gara (who, along with his girlfriend, Sandy Gude, makes up ventura_kids) of Malibu Beach, California, loves to cache in the California desert with his Jeep and a group of friends, who also take their own Jeeps. The pack has a leader, FishPOET, who figures out the route, which caches they'll seek, and what materials each person needs to pack, as they're often gone for several days at a time. Another member of the tribe takes care of the Jeeps themselves and packs everything the group will need to fix a broken-down Jeep in the middle of the desert; he also determines when and where the troop gets gas. Each member pitches in for some task.

The game is also a great equalizer. Its enthusiasts come from all professions, economic classes, and walks of life. It doesn't matter how many degrees you have or how big your house is; if you can nab that Lock & Lock in a tree before anybody else, you deserve their respect.

MonkeyBrad caches with a group that ranges in size from four to 12 people, depending on who's available on any given day. "Every person in the group I met through geocaching," he says. "We've got two doctors, a couple of computer programmers, a welder, a plumber, a guy who does concert lighting, a teacher, a mailman, and a hospital worker. Their ages range from 7 to 66."

"All my great and memorable finds have involved other cachers," says Larry Lemelin (Stressmaster). "The fun is being able to share the experience, the time, the camaraderie, and the friendship."

"I can literally drive from Alabama to Kansas, pull up to some guys sitting around the campfire, and within minutes I'm accepted," says TheAlabamaRambler.

The Outlaw and TreyB prove that they found The Picard Nuptials (GCJG9B). *Candy Lind*

Part of the appeal is shared trust. Geocaching couldn't work without it. Owners expect that visitors will take care of the containers they place, respect the contents, and carefully re-hide them just as they were found. In fact, many geocachers go one step further by notifying owners when maintenance is needed or by simply making the repairs themselves.

Some geocaches have been in the field for more than eight years with hundreds of logged finds. While containers do disappear sometimes, cachers tend to chalk up that disruption to the Muggles who don't understand the game. (Geocachers refer to the uninitiated as "Muggles," a reference to ordinary mortals in the Harry Potter fantasy book series.) In reality, there's no way of knowing why some containers disappear. Geocache owners post the coordinates of their hides on a public forum that's visible to anyone. They wouldn't do that if they didn't trust that others would respect their work.

Geocachers seem to instinctively cluster into groups that share an unspoken bond. Even though they know each other's names, many prefer to refer to each other by their handles. We've met Blackstone Val, a legendary eastern Massachusetts geocacher, several times and still don't know his last name. We're also friendly with Michael Babcock, who's a legendary FTF hunter (meaning he specializes in being the first person to find a newly hidden geocache, a rare skill that often involves sleep deprivation since many caches are first published in the wee hours). But why call him Mike when Ether Bunny is more fun? The handle is appropriate; Michael is an anesthesiologist.

And, if you're in a strange city for a day and need someone to pal around with, contact the local geocaching group. Mrs. Captain Picard did that one weekend in Toronto. She and four business colleagues arrived on a Sunday morning. Mrs. Captain Picard wasn't about to subject her fellow travelers, who weren't geocachers, to a day of waiting in the car for her, so before leaving Texas she looked up the Toronto caching group, alerted them of her arrival, and asked if anyone wanted to pick her up at the airport for a day of caching.

The community responded in less than 20 minutes, and when Mrs. Captain Picard landed at Pearson International Airport, there was a car waiting.

"Hi, I'm Julie," she said, climbing in. "I'm Dan," the driver responded. And off they went.

Tips from the Experts

"When you plan to cache in a new town while you're on vacation, write ahead and find cachers who can give you advance information. Tell them exactly what type of caching experience you're going for, how much time you have, whether you have transportation or not, if you're in it for the numbers, or just want *the one* cache you shouldn't miss. That's a great way to plan ahead, plus local cachers may offer to take you to places or show you things that will blow you away." —*Mrs. Captain Picard*

"Now, you may be thinking, 'What on Earth was she thinking? A single woman in a strange city; this guy could have been anyone!'" says Julie with a laugh. But she knew Dan was okay. He was a geocacher.

Inveterate puzzle cacher Jim Wellington (pghlooking) sums it up nicely: "I can go anywhere in the United States and I'll have friends to hang out with and have fun." But the talk isn't just about the game. "I have a friend in California I met through geocaching and we talk three times a week," he says. "We spend more time talking about friends and family than anything else."

In order to make the most of group geocaching, veterans recommend you fine-tune your outing to the needs and expectations of the members. Many hard-core players belong to several groups that favor different experiences. Dave Grenewetzki (dgreno) advises, "If you're going with a group, make sure everyone has the same goal for the trip. If someone wants to try to get the most caches possible and another person wants to be a tourist between finds, your group could see some friction. Better to hash these things out when the pressure's not on."

Dave's tip for making caching with partners or groups more fun: Cache with other people who have a GPSr. Having a navigation device involves each finder more directly in the game and has the practical benefit of helping to verify readings.

Kids dig geocache treasures. *Laura Goodwin (thrifty-chick)*

Family Time

Geocaching is a healthy and inexpensive way to get the whole family outdoors, energized, and pulling together toward a common goal. Many cachers told us delightful stories about how the opportunity for adventure had pried their kids away from video screens and out into the woods.

Graeme McGufficke (OzGuff) said his most memorable caching experience was "in Australia, when three generations climbed to the top of Mount Beerburrum in the Glasshouse Mountains to find a cache. And the view was amazing! My wife, kids, dad, sister (and her family) had a great time!"

Geocaching has special appeal to kids because of the fantasy factor (it's the closest they'll get to a real search for pirate treasure), gadget appeal, and the chance to find some really cool toys. Time and again, cachers of all experience levels told us that the game had reconnected them with children who had previously seemed lost in a video haze. It was almost like transplanting a computer game to the outdoors: Everyone got something out of the experience. For gamers who don't want to part with their fantasy, specialized games like Wherigo duplicate the experience in the great outdoors, with the GPSr substituting for the game controller.

When Laura Goodwin (thrify-chick) started caching with her kids, she thought she'd be the one doing the finding and her kids would be into the trinkets. Her ten-year-old daughter Sydney has attention deficit disorder, so Laura wasn't expecting her to focus on the task of actually looking for the target. But after showing Sydney how to find a few simple caches, she has found something that not only keeps her daughter focused, but Sydney typically won't stop until she's found the treasure, no matter how long it takes. Even DNFs (Did Not Finds) are simply future possibilities—Sydney always wants to go back another day and look again. One day, Sydney's teacher asked her to find what was wrong on her paper. Sydney replied, "Give me a moment. I know it's there in plain sight!" Laura says, "Funny how your words often come back to you like a boomerang! Geocaching is helping her to approach life issues in the right way."

Think of Your Health

After spending a day geocaching in our home area of eastern Massachusetts, we frequently download the track logs from our GPSr to find we'd walked six to eight miles, usually over hilly terrain. The experience is equivalent to a vigorous two-hour workout at the gym, yet somehow we barely seem to notice. Exercise isn't an ordeal when it's fun, and in the pursuit of an ammo can, we often forget that we're tired and sweaty or haven't eaten all day.

Geocaching is great exercise. Time and time again the veterans we interviewed brought up the health benefits of the game. MonkeyBrad says it helped him lose 150 pounds and quit smoking. TheAlabamaRambler says geocaching pulled him back from the brink of suicide, broke a debilitating painkiller habit, and helped him rediscover his health. In our travels to various geocaching groups and events, we met many seniors who said geocaching had reinvigorated them and given them a reason to "get up off the couch." That phrase seems to resonate with other players, too; in 142 responses to our survey, ten people mentioned getting "off the couch" as a significant benefit of the game.

In Cachers' Own Words

What, exactly, is the joy of geocaching? We'll let the respondents to our survey sum it up. Here are some of our favorite comments from the many they submitted (some people asked us not to publish their full names):

> I find geocaching to be very good for my mental health. It allows me to gather my thoughts, relieve stress, get exercise, and learn about new places and things that I would never think of or even consider going to without geocaching!
> —*Carol Patterson (Adventurousgrandma)*

With This Cache I Thee Wed

Geocaching brought Kim and Duane Gorenflo together, so it only made sense that it would be included as part of their wedding. Even by the standards of dedicated cachers, though, the Gorenflos' nuptials were extreme.

Kim (Kimbyj), a medical biller from Cincinnati, and Duane (nolefan9399), an aircraft mechanic, first met in an America Online geocaching forum. There was clearly good chemistry, so Kim visited Florida on a geocaching trip and made it a point to meet the man who would become her husband. "Sparks flew and he came up to visit, interviewed and found a job," she says. The couple was married in February 2007.

Geocaching actually runs in Kim Gorenflo's family. She caught the bug from her parents, who have together found more than 7,000 caches, so it's no surprise the family was so keen on making the sport part of the wedding ceremony. Everyone joined in the fun.

Invitations bearing the coordinates of the ceremony site were sent to their friends and fellow members of the Ohio-Kentucky-Indiana Geocachers. In fact, about 30 of the 150 wedding guests were geocaching buddies. We'll let Kim describe the scene:

> The cake had an outdoor theme. There were trees on top and a camping scene with a plastic tent. On one side was a waterfall. On the other side there was a Jeep with a popup trailer. When my husband went to get the garter, there was a bison tube cache attached to it. The DJ stopped the ceremony because he had never seen such a thing. We gave him a little rundown, like what you would tell a Muggle.

> Our friends placed a wedding cache in our honor for the day and there were people caching in the parking lot during our wedding. Afterwards, we left on our honeymoon and cached in Las Vegas, the Grand Canyon, and Utah. That wasn't what it was all about, though. We probably only logged about 50 finds.

It all sounds like great fun and very appropriate for the situation, but Kim notes that there was one risk: "Our geocaching friends were trying to tear up our cake," she says. "They thought there was a cache in it."

Cachers are some of the most creative and smart people we've ever met. Just when you think you've seen every way possible to hide a cache, someone will do something totally unexpected, tricky, and devious. It's like being in school again; we've learned about light wave lengths, Morse code, stars, Caesar ciphers, computer languages, and Latin—all so we could hunt for a cache.
—*Greg & Aleesa Drennen (Team Itchy & Scratchy)*

Most geocachers are people I never would have met otherwise, because we come from such diverse backgrounds. Most are generous, caring, interesting people who would do anything for you or for geocaching.
—*Sherri Abromavage (Neos2)*

It's about the journey and the friends you meet along the way. We laugh from the moment the day begins, until we separate at the end of the day.
—*Jim & Jackie*

We've adopted a very large circle of friends through geocaching. Some we've never physically met.
—*Paul & Karen Sandvick (Jug & Roon)*

Caching is a great leveler....You can be caching with a bank president or a ditch digger ... it doesn't matter.
—*Don & Jacqi Liddiard (Rock & Crystal)*

It stirs a passion in me that no other hobby has before. It has dimensions of camaraderie, competition, mental stimulation, fitness, and creativity that I've never found elsewhere.
—*Dean Powell (J5 Crew)*

We're doing a lot more as a family now. Instead of doing yard work around the house on weekends, you'll find us on trails, on lakes, on our bikes, or discovering unique aspects of our community.
—*Monika Riedel (tmkbk)*

I feel the weight of the world lifting from me when I'm tramping through the woods.
—*billandlore*

We find places we would never have found/seen otherwise. Did you know that there is a pet cemetery on Catalina Island? I know now.
—*Keira Palmer (C.A.K.E. UNIT)*

Final Stages

No story was more sadly heartwarming than the one told to us by Kathy Markham about her parents, Ben and Grace Johnson (Ben & Grace) of Louisville, Kentucky.

Ben took up geocaching at the age of 70. At a time when many people fear the loss of their social circle, Ben and Grace found a new one among geocachers. Ben loved to regale members of the local geocaching club with his stories and the game was a perfect excuse to get outside with friends and breathe a little fresh air. "They knew way more about Louisville than I did," Kathy says. "They cached in every corner of the city. When we traveled together, we always looked up caches to find. We cached in Aruba, Alaska, Panama, and places they would never have seen otherwise."

Sadly, Ben was stricken with lung cancer at the age of 72. As his health deteriorated, he continued to go to local meetings of InKy, a loose confederation of Southern Indiana and Louisville geocachers. "They were a great support group for him," Kathy remembers. Ben became thin and weak, but he still managed to summon the strength to get out of the house to cache now and then. He knew he was dying, but the hope of reaching the milestone of finding 1,000 caches was one of the incentives he used to keep going.

He wouldn't get there on his own. In May 2008, Ben Johnson suffered a stroke that put him in the hospital. He had logged his 967th geocache find just two days earlier, but he was still 33 short of his goal. Friends and family knew he would never leave the hospital.

"One thousand is a big deal in the club," Kathy says. "So their friends decided they had to get him there." Members fanned out and gathered 33 caches, which they brought to the hospital. "My mom signed all the logs," Kathy remembers. "She cried and cried because it was such a wonderful thing to do." Ben logged his 1,000th cache on June 3, 2008. He died two days later.

But that wasn't the end. After the funeral, members of InKy presented Grace with an ammunition box they had painted gold and labeled "Ben & Grace's 1,000 cache" (GC1CZHM). It's hidden in the cemetery where Ben Johnson is buried. "Without geocaching, my dad probably would have sat at home and been depressed," Kathy says. "Geocaching got him out of the house and doing things."

What We Love About Geocaching

By Sonny & Sandy Portacio
Podcacher.com

Why are people nuts about geocaching? (And believe us, they're nuts!) After almost four years of interacting with the geocaching community via our podcast at **Podcacher.com**, we've seen many expressions of the passion that this game/hobby/sport seems to inspire.

What makes it so appealing? So captivating? So… addictive?

We think there are a number of reasons, based on the common threads we've observed in the lives of the many geocachers we've been privileged to meet.

Although the treasure hunting aspect has some level of appeal to all of us —especially children—we think it's the sense of adventure that draws people in. Whether you're planning a two-day hike to the top of a glacier or jumping in the car to rush a couple of miles down the road for a "first-to-find" attempt, it's the spirit of discovery and newness that pulls at you. We've had the pleasure of interviewing many geocachers on our show and it's not unusual to find that they have a love for adventure in other aspects of their lives as well. There was the sword-swallower, the hot-air balloonist, the missionary living in Ecuador, the mountain climber, and the guy who left everything behind to travel the country to accomplish his bucket list. Even for those of us who can't imagine doing any of those things, the game of geocaching gives us a taste of the adventure we crave.

We've found that gecocachers are generally creative, curious, helpful, and gadget-loving. They also appreciate the outdoors and the environment. Geocaching is an opportunity to fan the flame of these interests. We know cachers who spend weeks on a complicated puzzle cache or an amazingly designed cache container. Their creativity has found the perfect outlet. There are others who prefer to be out hiking the trails and mountains every week. They'd go whether or not there were geocaches to find, but the game makes their outdoor time even more fun and meaningful.

And then there's the competitive aspect of the game. Some people are inspired to geocache for the sake of the numbers of caches found, their ranking, and other bragging rights. Many geocachers call into our "PodCacher hotline" to share a first-to-find attempt or a milestone with the rest of the world. Challenging oneself and meeting that challenge is reason enough to fuel the passion for some of us.

A Life Changer

We've also heard from many geocachers about the positive impact this game has had on their lives. Some are now spending more quality time with their kids and talking to their teenagers as they hike to a cache, something that might not happen otherwise. Others have lost weight, become more active, and improved their physical fitness. For some, geocaching is a healthy alternative to other, less virtuous activities.

We *love* to share stories on our show because we've found that everyone loves a good story and geocachers are no exception. Stories inspire, mesmerize, and tantalize us. Some of these stories have an obvious connection with the adventurous nature of geocaching: *Treasure Island, Raiders of the Lost Ark, Lord of the Rings, 20,000 Leagues Under the Sea* and *The Chronicles of Narnia*, just to name a few. They tease us with tales of hidden treasures that everyday people like you and me could find if only we looked a little harder, searched a little more, rounded one more corner, or turned over one more stone. Most people are naturally inclined to be curious, to seek out things that are hidden, to solve puzzles and mysteries. Geocachers realize that inclination and take action!

Finally geocachers are social. This hobby is enjoyed in nearly every corner of the Earth, and the Internet allows us to share our passion with a global community. Whether geocachers meet face-to-face at a local event or connect online, they're eager to share their adventures, stories, tips, and gadgets with other GPS treasure hunters all around the world. We're proud to be part of this worldwide community and we love to help geocachers make those connections that inspire them to keep on caching.

So there you have it: the sense of adventure, curiosity, creativity, gadgetry, exploration, competition, positive life changes, storytelling, and socializing. These are just a few reasons to be nuts about geocaching!

---

*Sonny and Sandy Portacio, a geocaching team from California, host the popular PodCacher podcast (**podcacher.com**), which has been nominated for multiple awards and featured on iTunes. PodCacher has produced more than 250 family-friendly shows. Sonny is a high school district IT Director. Sandy cares for their baby boy, Sean.*

CACHER PROFILE
Alamogul

Geocaching.com handle: Alamogul
Name: Lee van der Bokke
Claim to fame: Leads the game of geocaching by number of finds. Alamogul is the Michael Jordan of geocaching.
Location: Alamo, California
Caching since: October 27, 2002
Total finds: 36,157
Total hides: 498
Preferred GPSr: Garmin 60 CSx, which he has to replace approximately every 10 months because he wears them out.

Favorite Cache Types

Alamogul likes Earthcaches, puzzles, virtuals, and hiking, but he's famous for power caching, which is how he really loads up his count. He admits that days spent geocaching are typically half hiking and half caching. He likes to go out about once a week with Fisherwoman. Ironically, he doesn't like inner city caches or caches hidden in bushes.

Special Equipment

- Logs and extra containers for caches that need maintenance
- Palm Treo
- Pen
- Tweezers
- Hiking stick
- Extendable pole, the type used to change lightbulbs
- Something to stand on—he's not a tall man
- Bug spray
- Toilet paper

- Extra socks
- Diet Pepsi
- Tecnu, for washing off poison oak

Great Caching Story

To many GeoWoodstock VII attendees, it was a day trip. To others, the event was a weekend that included a couple of plane trips. But to the dedicated—the obsessed—it was a 19-day journey that allowed a team of three men to rack up at least 1,550 finds. The team consisted of Alamogul, Lil Devil (owner of the truck and camper they drove across the country from California to Tennessee and back), and Materus (who began the trip ranked 46th in the world and ended it ranked 26th). One day near Jefferson, Texas, the trio nabbed 212 geocaches and had to DNF between 50 and 75 because two enormous storms had just ransacked the landscape and the ensuing cleanup crew had unknowingly obliterated several caches in the area. They power cached the whole way with no difficult caches, no long hikes, no difficult terrain, just massive strings of caches each day. We talked to Alamogul when the group was just southeast of Abilene, Texas, on their way back to California on day 16 of their trip. They had already logged about 1,313 caches on the journey. We let Alamogul off the phone to defend himself from a cow that was staring him down on his way to GC1KN57, Cattle Pens. This would be a great story for any normal geocacher, but Alamogul does this sort of thing all the time.

Most Memorable Find

One of Alamogul's favorite caches (and ours, too) is a virtual in San Antonio, Texas, called Barney Smith's Toilet Seat Museum (GCB6A8). Barney is an artist who only works with wooden toilet seats. He has engraved and decorated more than 700 of them. They're all on display and they all have a story to go with them, which Barney will happily tell you at length during your visit. Barney Smith is a huge part of the equation. Loquacious and entertaining, he lives for the audience he gets every day at his garage-turned-museum. He's been on every major TV talk show and has amassed a huge library of press clippings. Allow plenty of time for this stop, Alamogul warns, as he was there for an hour and a half.

Words of Wisdom

"Play the game your own way. Find what's fun and do that. Keep it light and remember it's a game."

"If you're in the middle of the woods and you just can't find the cache, poke every nook and cranny with a stick. Climb up things, look down into broken trees, change your perspective. If all else fails, whip out the phone to call a lifeline."

When power caching, Alamogul makes no left turns. Left turns require waiting, which takes time, and time is what he always lacks, not caches to find.

What Drives Him

Alamogul started caching to provide himself with a destination for his hikes. He stuck with it because caching is a competition against two other people—the person ahead of you and the person behind you. According to Alamogul, "Megacaching (pursuing big numbers) by yourself isn't fun. At all."

Alamogul cares less about his numbers than he does about the challenges and first-to-finds he's nabbed lately. His personal record for finds in a day is 216.

SECTION I

Preparing to Geocache

CHAPTER TWO
Getting Around Geocaching.com

O ne of the beauties of the Internet is its abundance of choice. There are websites devoted to almost every topic, and because new sites are so easy to start, someone is always coming up with a new idea and a pitch to build an audience.

That's not the case with geocaching.

Astonishingly, a game played with passion by millions of people around the globe has only one website that matters. It's called **Geocaching.com**, and it is the place you have to go if you want to hide or find a geocache.

Founded by **Geocaching.com** creator Jeremy Irish in 2000 and operated by his Seattle-based company Groundspeak, **Geocaching.com** is both a phenomenal resource and a frustrating bottleneck. On the positive side:

- Its database of members, caches, trackables, and events is exhaustive and far-reaching. Nearly every geocache placed anywhere in the world can be found there.

- The presentation format is consistent and flexible. The person who places a cache can include HTML in the online description, which gives him or her considerable creative latitude.

- The site is geographically oriented, meaning that it is designed to deliver information about caches near any location you specify.

- Basic membership is free, although Groundspeak is increasingly limiting its most useful features to paid memberships ($30 annually as of this writing).

- Very little of the site is hidden behind registration walls, meaning that its content is well-indexed by search engines. In fact, Google is the best way to search **Geocaching.com** (type in <searchterm> site:**Geocaching.com**).

- There is some nice integration with Google Maps, including a feature that shows caches on a map around a designated point. Groundspeak is constantly improving **Geocaching.com**'s integration with Google Maps.

- It's pretty easy to find and contact other members using the "Hide & Seek a Cache" page, if you know their handle. If you don't know the precise name, though, finding people can be a nightmare. **Geocaching.com**'s search engine doesn't comprehend text strings, only complete names. To search for a partial name, use Google to search the site.

- Rudimentary social networking features provide for basic friending.
- Paid members can upload an unlimited number of photos, although not videos.
- The site's tutorials and online resources provide a good introduction to geocaching.
- Forums are busy and content-rich.
- Each cache can be downloaded to a Garmin or DeLorme GPSr that is connected to your computer directly from the cache description page on **Geocaching.com**. (This is what that "Send to GPS" button does.)

Monopolies, however, have their downsides, and **Geocaching.com** is no exception. While the veteran cachers we interviewed admire the site's scope and utility, they also have their share of complaints and we have a few of our own. Here are some of the downsides that existed as of the writing of this book (note that these weaknesses may have been improved by the time you read this):

- For a site that collects so much information about geocaches, it's remarkable how limited **Geocaching.com**'s search features are. The site's basic "Hide & Seek a Cache" offers very few options to narrow your search. For example, you can search for a multi-stage cache within 25 miles of a ZIP code, but that's about the limit of complexity. The pocket query function is more robust, but it's confined to paying members. Third-party software like Geocaching Swiss Army Knife (GSAK) are a big help here (more on GSAK in Chapter 9).
- Groundspeak makes changes slowly and doesn't always do a good job of explaining its decisions. For example, a 2008 design tweak inexplicably removed global search from the home page. Fortunately, by using the Google query format <*searchterm*> *site:Geocaching.com*, you can still run searches against the site.
- The site does surprisingly little to enable offline use. It supports the information-rich GPX files that can be downloaded into GPSr devices and third-party software applications, but you're on your own figuring out what to do with them. Fortunately, some very good third-party software is available to help you, including an iPhone application from Groundspeak (see Chapter 9). You can also download descriptions in PDF format, but you can't customize the output.

- Social networking features are weak at best. Users can't form groups on the site or get news feeds about their geocaching friends. Photo tagging is limited and the site isn't open to third-party applications. There's also no video support.
- The approval process for new cache placements is policed by a group of volunteers who are very knowledgeable and committed, but whose decisions can sometimes appear arbitrary.
- It's difficult to find other geocachers using the site's search engine unless you have the precise username spelling and spacing. Google does a better job than **Geocaching.com** of searching for users.
- RSS isn't currently supported, although you can set up notifications of new caches in your area.
- If you navigate with a Magellan (or any other maker that isn't a Garmin or a DeLorme brand), you can't download a cache's information directly from the description page.

The Terracaching Alternative

Members of **Terracaching.com** might dispute the statement that there's only one geocaching site that matters. Terracaching, which isn't affiliated with Groundspeak, is a members-only club for high-quality geocaching, or at least that's how it describes itself. Registration is free, but to become a full member, you need to find two other members to sponsor you. The site makes this fairly easy via a bulletin board system. Terracaching "employs a complex, dynamic rating system which learns from members and actively encourages a focus on the quality, not quantity, of caches that members post," the site says. "If you'd like to spend more time outdoors on fun, memorable, and challenging cache hunts and less time online wading through hundreds of questionable cache listings, you've come to the right place!" Terracaching doesn't list nearly as many geocaches as **Geocaching.com**—we counted just 14 within a 10-mile radius of Dallas-Fort Worth airport, compared to more than 1,100 on **Geocaching.com**—but it says the quality of its listings are much higher. Anyone can place a cache, but the ones that withstand the test of time are those that are rated by other members as being particularly creative or devilish.

Groundspeak says some of these shortcomings, such as the lack of group support, are a conscious policy decision. Also, basic **Geocaching.com** services are free, and considering all it offers, it's a pretty good deal. In any case, this is the site that you're going to use. So let's talk about how to get the most out of the time you spend on it.

Getting Registered

Geocaching.com is free to use, and that makes it a great resource for the casual cacher. If you're planning to pursue the game actively, though, you'll want to invest in a **premium membership**. The most valuable premium features are the ability to download listings in GPX format, to upload photos, and to create pocket queries. You can also create multiple bookmark lists and tell the site to notify you instantly when new caches that meet the criteria you specify are posted. Frequent geocachers will quickly become frustrated with the site's basic features, so you can probably expect to upgrade at some point. You can sometimes find money-saving coupons by searching "geocaching discounts" on a search engine.

As we mentioned, **Geocaching.com** has rudimentary social networking features, the most important of which is your user profile. Here's where you can post a photo of yourself, some biographical material, and a record of your activities.

Set Up an Account

This is easy, but give some thought to how public you want to be. Specifying a public e-mail address (instead of the site's standard contact alias) makes it easy for people to contact you, but also for spambots to hijack you. If you have a blog or website, list it here. Choose an e-mail address that you monitor regularly, because cachers expect quick response to their messages.

Also, apply some creativity to your "handle." Geocachers rarely refer to each other by their given name, even if they're good friends. Pick a name that feels good and says something about yourself. Our alias, PnD, says that we are, well, P and D. But you might do better. Here are some of the creative names we encountered in our interviews:

- **Mrs. Captain Picard**—Wouldn't any woman dream of being married to the commander of the starship *Enterprise*? Julie Perrine of Austin, Texas, indulged a bit of her own fantasy with this choice. "If you could be anyone in the world, who would you be?" she asks, challenging newbies to be creative.

The Campbells prove that the family that names together stays together.

- **Mondou2**—Bill Lopez named himself after his favorite coffee shop. Now *that* is devotion.
- **WE4 NCS**—Bert Carter is all for North Carolina State. His handle, which is also his amateur radio call sign, says so.
- **Peasinapod**—U.S. Airways pilot Ray King chose this handle because when he was dating his wife-to-be, "Everyone said we were just like two peas in a pod, so the name stuck."
- **Alamogul**—Originally, Lee van der Bokke was VDB Alamo, after his surname's initials and the California town in which he lives. But when his wife started geocaching with him, he dropped his initials and added the "Team." Well, it turns out the missus didn't like geocaching very much—although she still loves the events—and he was getting tired of the question, "How many are in your team?" So after Lee bought another house in Mogul, Nevada, he combined the two to create his newest handle.
- **Bikely**—Lee Campbell (above left) started a trend. The cycling enthusiast named himself Bikely, and wife Cookie joined in as Wifely. Daughter Bethy, who's a psychology major, became Psychly and future son-in-law Casey paid tribute to his favorite science fiction adventure by becoming Trekly. Psychly and Trekly were planning a geocaching wedding as we wrote this and hoped to nab their 1,000th find on their honeymoon.

After you choose a username and decide how much information about yourself you'd like to expose to the geocaching world at large, the account setup asks you for your home coordinates. Be sure to be as specific as possible. This is as simple as entering your home address on the "Hide & Seek a Cache" page and copying and pasting the coordinates at the top of the results page. This will make it easy for you to find caches in your area.

Dress Up Your Public Profile

Besides having the option of putting your e-mail address, location, and occupation in your public profile, you can also show people which states, countries, and provinces you've cached, your best geocaching story, what other hobbies you enjoy, and even include a bio, if you'd like. Many members have fun with their identities, posting funny or mysterious photos or hiding behind pseudonyms. Pretty

much anything goes, as long as it's in good taste. You don't have to reveal who you really are on **Geocaching.com**, although you should make it possible for members to contact you. This is particularly important if you own a cache and someone needs to tell you it's been compromised.

If you search around other people's profiles a little bit, you may see charts and graphs of data that resemble baseball stats. These are created by third-party websites that collect statistics about your geocaching activities based upon your publicly available information. These sites give you bits of HTML code that you can copy and paste into your public profile. So you can share, for example, how many days in a row you neglected the game (that happens to us, for example, during our frigid winters). You can also dress up this page with maps that track your finds. Some of the more popular sites are:

- **It's Not About The Numbers** (**www.itsnotaboutthenumbers.com**)—Organizes your statistics and has a map capability to show where you've picked up caches.
- **World66** (**world66.com**)—Creates maps of the places you've cached.
- **GCStatistic** (**www.macdefender.org/products/GCStatistic/**)—Displays detailed specifics about caches you've found and places you've visited.

Your public profile isn't the only thing that other players (and search engines) can view. There are four other tabs to your profile:

Geocaches—This tab in a player's public profile neatly and automatically collects all the geocaches found and hidden (sorted by type) in one page. If you'd like to see details, just click on the link above each list. It's fun to watch your total increase.

Trackables—We've devoted a section to trackables following Chapter 4. In this section of a profile, you can check which travel bugs and geocoins a user has moved or owns.

Gallery—The gallery stores photos of yourself and others from your geocaching adventures. This is a handy all-in-one collection of all the photographs a user has uploaded to the site. That is, if you post a picture of an owl in a tree near GCXXXX in your online log, that picture will automatically get added to the gallery in your profile. You cannot, however, add a picture directly or exclusively to the gallery. Oddly, **Geocaching.com** doesn't support geotagging of photos, but we trust that feature will be added eventually. With photos, as with online logs, be careful not to include "spoiler" information, which reveals details the cache owner didn't intend to reveal. Many owners fiercely protect their hiding places and containers, and they don't appreciate their work being compromised.

Bookmarks—One of the little-known gems of **Geocaching.com**'s premium membership is its bookmark feature. Any cache description page gives you a simple way to store caches you want to revisit later ("bookmark listing"). You can also create bookmarks of groups of caches under a common theme. Search results can be saved this way, as well as caches that meet special criteria such as proximity to a route. Bookmark lists can be exported as GPX files.

As a premium member, you can create as many bookmark lists as you like and add to them over time. For example, you could bookmark a list of caches with low difficulty for an easy outing with the kids, while maintaining a separate list of puzzle or high-difficulty targets when caching with other enthusiasts. You can also share your bookmark lists with others by making them public.

Navigating the Site

Because **Geocaching.com** is unique, its features and navigation schemes can be quirky. Let's take a look at some of its more important features. Designs and individual elements shift all the time, so we'll focus on the three major sections: **My Account, Hide & Seek a Cache,** and **Individual Cache Pages.** We'll discuss

What's a GC Number?

Every geocache comes with an associated six-or seven-digit code beginning with the letters "GC," which is prominently displayed at the top of
the description page. This is simply a unique identifier—a serial number,
in effect—that is assigned by Groundspeak when you register a geocache.
GC1351F is an example. These numbers are necessary because many caches
may have the same name, even though they are distributed around the world.
When caching as a group, members find it less confusing to refer to these
shorthand codes instead of names given by the cache owners. GC codes also
are a convenient way to display unique information on the limited screen
space of handheld devices and to cross-reference that information to a map
or documents with complete descriptions stored on paper or a PDA.

the first two sections here and talk about cache pages themselves in Chapter 3,
"Planning your Outing on Geocaching.com."

My Profile

This section lists all of your recent activity, as well as features available only to premium members. Tabs along the top enable you to easily navigate between caches
you're watching, hides and finds, trackables, and friends. The profile page is a convenient way to jog your memory if you need to hunt down a memorable cache
from your past or one that you didn't find and want to revisit. This page is also the
only way to get to certain premium features, such a finding caches along a route
or building pocket queries.

Hide & Seek a Cache

This is where you can find geocaches within a designated area by searching by
address, ZIP/postal code, state, cache name, and other variables. Unless you have
a very specific latitude and longitude in mind, you'll probably find yourself using
address or postal code. We don't know why anyone would want to use the default
100-mile radius, but it's simple enough to change. You also have the option of
searching by keyword, but that's not the same as a full-text search. Keywords are
limited to precise terms within the cache name. If you want to search full-text,
use Google.

Results are sorted by geographic proximity to the location specified. There is
no way to change that. If you want to limit your results to locations north of you,
for example, you have to figure that out manually or use a third-party application

like Geocaching Swiss Army Knife (GSAK). The site has an "Advanced Search" feature, but there's nothing very advanced about it.

One of the more useful features of this page is buried in the small print. That's the "Search with Google Maps" option, which opens a page containing a Google Maps mashup with geocaches imposed upon it. For some reason, this map does not default to your home coordinates but rather to the middle of a lake near Groundspeak headquarters. No matter: You can easily see the results of any query as a Google Map by clicking a link on the results page.

As of this writing, the map could only display a maximum of 500 waypoints, which can actually be a problem if you're trying to identify clusters of caches across a wide geographic area. The Google Maps mashup is also clearly a work-in-progress. Depending on the browser you use, it tends to hang or deliver an error message. We trust this will improve with time. For standard weekend geocaching, however, the Google Maps option is a fast and visually appealing way to plan your adventure. For a more detailed discussion of Google Maps and other online tools, see Chapter 9.

The "Found by Username" and "Hidden by Username" options are often used by experienced cachers to identify the work of friends or people whose skills they admire. Many cache owners, for example, specialize in puzzles, devilish hides, or exotic locations. Some cache owners, like Kandy and Dann McWilliams (Wheeler Dealers) of Palm Springs, California, develop substantial followings of people who keep up with their work.

As you develop your geocaching skills, you'll probably find that you spend less and less time on the **Geocaching.com** site and more time using pocket queries and tools like GSAK to plan your trip.

Geocache Types

In planning your outing, be aware of the kinds of caches you'll be looking for. The time requirements can vary dramatically. There are several variations on the basic geocache, but the following are the types you should know about.

Traditional—The most common geocache container ranges in size from a capsule about the size of the head of the pencil ("nano cache") to a large storage bin. Almost anything can be a cache container as long as it is waterproof, but the most common objects are ammunition boxes, plastic food containers, film canisters, pill bottles, and small metal cylinders called bison tubes (named after their manufacturer). However, cache owners have devised some truly devious ways to disguise treasures. We cover some of these in Chapter 5.

The bare minimum requirement for a geocache is a waterproof container holding a sheet of paper upon which cachers record their handle and date of visit. The purpose of this exercise is to document that the finder physically handled the cache. It's also an easy way for subsequent visitors to know the last time a cache was discovered. Technically, a cache isn't considered found unless the log book is signed. (There is no requirement to log it online.) In reality, few people ever check, but some owner purists do check the logs and will delete your online log if a paper match can't be found.

A traditional cache can usually be found near the coordinates specified in the description, although the inherent accuracy limitations of GPSr devices make this an inexact science. A difficult hide or a small container may make your search long and frustrating.

One of dgreno's favorite finds was in a huge public park: "There's a tree in this park that has an electrical conduit running up the trunk and at the top of the wire is a light fixture. Looks innocent enough, right? But when you open the junction box, you find a fishing reel. If you wind the fishing line, the light comes down the tree. Unscrewing the bulb reveals the cache."

Multi-Cache or Offset Cache—Finding a multi-stage cache usually involves searching for several caches, each of which contains clues that lead to the next stage. Multis can be as simple as two stages (sometimes called offset caches), or as complex as a dozen or more. In general, we budget at least a half hour to find a multi-cache, although we have encountered some examples that demanded two or more hours of searching.

Not surprisingly, the line between multis, offsets, and puzzles has become blurred over time. For instance, if you need to solve a puzzle to find a hint, you've got a puzzle cache. Multis can provide a great adventure, but they can also take up a lot of time. If you're trying to run up your numbers, it's best to avoid them. There's also the frustration of finding the first two or three stages of a multi-cache and then being unable to find the final stage. Multi-caches are more prone to loss or theft because there are more stages to maintain. But there's also greater satisfaction in finding a multi-cache and that smiley when you log a really arduous multi can feel like a frozen Popsicle on a hot summer day when you're standing in the middle of a desert dressed in a fur coat.

Mystery or Puzzle Caches—This popular variation requires the seeker to unravel a puzzle or cipher either before or during the hunt. This may take hours or 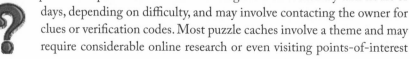 days, depending on difficulty, and may involve contacting the owner for clues or verification codes. Most puzzle caches involve a theme and may require considerable online research or even visiting points-of-interest to obtain clues. Some experienced cachers who get bored with traditionals devote their time almost exclusively to puzzles, some of which are very time-consuming.

You might ask what's the distinction between puzzles and multis? Technically, in a multi-stage cache, each stage provides specific coordinates for each subsequent stage. A puzzle cache requires you to twist your brain a little or a lot. You may need to research, calculate, assemble, decipher, or otherwise figure out the solution to a problem in order to find the next or final stage. A puzzle can also be a multi with a riddle.

Virtual—Virtual caches have no container, but merely consist of a location or attraction that must be visited before a log can be filed. Usually, the visitor has to note some information that can only be obtained by visiting this site and e-mail it to the cache owner in order to log the find. In reality, not all owners respond to these e-mails, so it's usually okay to file the log and retain the record of the e-mail in case anyone asks.

Our Best-Laid Plans Undone

Having placed seven park-and-grabs and one fairly easy Internet-based puzzle, we were ready to challenge ourselves and the local cachers we had come to respect and like. We decided to make a tricky puzzle cache and called it Evil Framingham Tour, as it is a tour of our town and all the landmarks and historic places to visit. The goal was to have people drive all over town (and create a nifty zig-zag track log) to find all 12 stages—without skipping any—and end up at one of our favorite places in town, where there awaited for the persistent cacher an ammo box with goodies, including two movie tickets for the first-to-find (FTF).

Dana thought up this beauty and did the legwork to create the puzzle. Paul tested it the next day in a cold rain that approached a downpour at times. Time to complete: four hours, along with 46 miles of driving.

The cache was published on a Monday at 1:06 P.M. We debated how quickly the maniacal cachers in our area would log the FTF, with Paul setting the over/under at midnight.

When we went to sleep that night, no finds had been logged. We were surprised because there are two or three cachers in our town who vie with each other to log FTFs. We checked e-mail constantly to see which of our picks would win.

As it turned out, it was neither of them. Two resourceful and observant cachers used their CSI-like geosense to find the last stage, while skipping most of the intermediate stages. One of them got to stage 11 with just a little bit of Internet searching and deductive reasoning. In their logs, both admitted to skipping a good number of the steps.

What was the weakness in our puzzle? In designing a cache that was meant to be impossible without the completion of each preceding step, we neglected to really look at the numbers we were using for the puzzle. Here are the original coordinates for stage nine in the cycle (not the real ones):

N 42 R9.008
W 71 23.(R+3)0(R−1)

The letter "R" is supposed to be derived from visiting a spot on the tour. But the first two finders knew that R must equal 1, in order for the cache to be within the town of Framingham. This enabled them to skip the first eight stages altogether and start the cycle at stage nine. What should have been a four-hour journey became a relatively easy one-hour jaunt.

We were actually grateful for these two finders to have pointed out the shortcuts. We also learned a few things from the experience:

- If you have what you think is a challenging puzzle, give it to a few friends to test. Ask them to "cheat" to see if it's really as difficult as you think it is.
- Never underestimate the craftiness and resourcefulness of a veteran cacher. Don't let an over-obvious hint undermine your careful planning.
- Cachers are amazingly fair and honest people. Both of our FTFs declined to take the movie tickets, choosing instead to leave them for the first person who ran the gauntlet.

Geocaching.com no longer supports newly placed virtual caches, having created a new website called **Waymarking.com** to gather and organize similar categories of landmarks in groups. Waymarking is a process similar to geocaching in that players look for sites using coordinates. However, the project has a bigger goal of collating collections of similar landmarks into a kind of catalog. Members join groups and can submit new waymarks for consideration and approval by the group. More details on geocaching variations follow this chapter.

There are still plenty of virtuals left under a grandfathering provision that Groundspeak created. Virtual caches are the only type allowed on facilities run by the National Park Service, which ensures their continued popularity. Virtuals

What's with the National Park Service?

If you think geocaching would be a great way to get out and explore America's national parks, you're in for disappointment. The National Park Service (NPS) banned geocaching in 2002, saying that the sport was too disruptive to the environment and potentially dangerous, too. There have been numerous grassroots campaigns to convince the NPS to reverse its decision, but so far it's no dice. "Stashing and leaving property unattended for a certain time period is illegal. The activity in itself will appear suspicious to bystanders and staff alike who might misinterpret what the individual is doing," reads the official rule.

Virtual caches or waymarks are the only permitted form of geocache on National Park Service property. The good news is that the NPS's prohibitions don't apply to National Forest Service lands, state parks, or wildlife management areas, many of which have embraced geocaching eagerly as a way to bring people through their gates. (See Chapter 11.)

are often the fastest and easiest caches to find. In some cases, you can log them without even leaving your car.

Letterboxes and Letterbox Hybrids—Letterboxing predates geocaching by more than 100 years and involves a combination of maps, clues, and compasses to search for containers. Players record their finds using personalized rubber stamps. There are an estimated 20,000 letterboxes in North America and many more in the United Kingdom, where the game was invented. Letterbox coordinates are posted online, but are also shared through a network of written notes and via word-of-mouth.

Letterbox hybrids are a twenty-first century variation in which the containers function as both a letterbox and conventional geocache. We don't discuss letterboxing very much in this book, but the **Letterboxing.org** site has plenty of information if you are interested, and there is more detail in the Waypoints sidebar following Chapter 5.

Event—Whenever geocachers get together as a group, they can submit the meeting as an event cache. These are listed on **Geocaching.com** as ordinary waypoints, although there's no container and the cache is archived after the meeting ends. This is a quick and easy way to add to your find total. There are many types of events that we explain in Chapter 10. As with all things geocaching, events can be quite creative in their design and execution.

Wherigo Cache—Wherigo is a geographic adventure game created by some of the same people who invented geocaching. It's essentially a fantasy role-playing game akin to Doom or Zork, only navigation doesn't require a GPSr, only following a set of instructions. However, there are variations of Wherigo that take place in specific locations and involve finding a cache. These hybrids are beginning to proliferate in popularity as Wherigo gains a following. For more, see the Waypoints section following this chapter.

Webcam cache—This comes under the heading of "grandfathered" caches, meaning that no new ones are allowed on **Geocaching.com**. Webcam caches are maintained on **Waymarking.com**, however. There's no container involved here; players have to get their photo taken in front of a designated webcam in order to log a find. The trick is finding someone to take the photo, since the player is not at a computer at the time. This brand of geocache appears to be declining in popularity.

Earthcache—This relatively recent variation has grown in popularity with concerns about the health of the planet. An Earthcache is a variation on a virtual cache, but the purpose is to teach players about the Earth. Most Earthcaches have a geological theme, but any natural formation is fair game. Players typically are required to e-mail the owner some facts about the location to receive credit for the find, as these locations, too, typically do not have containers with log books.

Now that you know the basics, the next chapter will look at how to find the cache of your dreams.

WAYPOINTS
Geocaching Variations

Benchmark found in Puerto Rico. *Gary Hobgood (Gary & Vicky)*

G eocachers aren't lacking in creativity, so it's not surprising that numerous variations on the game have emerged. Here are summaries of a few of the more popular ones.

Benchmarking

In your daily travels, you may occasionally come across brass disks embedded in the ground that bear odd sequences of letters and numbers. These markers are so common that most people barely even notice them, but they serve a vital public purpose: They help people like land surveyors, builders, engineers, map makers, and others whose work depends upon accurate geographic positioning to know to a precise level of accuracy where on the Earth they are.

They're called benchmarks, and they have been in use in the United States for about 200 years. Many of them are now part of a database currently maintained by the National Oceanographic and Atmospheric Administration's (NOAA's) National Geodetic Survey (NGS). No one knows how many benchmarks there are in the United States, in large part because coordinating bodies didn't exist until just a few decades ago. This makes them an exciting target for geocachers. After all, how often do you have the chance to find a government asset that even the government doesn't know about?

The United States has cataloged only a small percentage of the benchmarks that are out there. Geocachers are part of an informal network of citizens who help out by cataloging the markers they find. It's a kick to find one that's in the government database, but an even bigger thrill to find one that isn't.

Benchmarking isn't anything like geocaching. Instead of working from defined coordinates, players must hunt in wide areas and often scrape the ground to find disks that have been buried over the years. Also, since the government doesn't know where all its benchmarks are, you may stumble upon one quite by accident. **Geocaching.com** has instructions for how to add these to the NGS database. In fact, Geocaching.com maintains a voluminous amount of information about the topic at **Geocaching.com/mark**. If you're serious about benchmarking, start there.

Benchmarks are a lot harder to find than geocaches. Most were placed before the invention of global positioning systems, so coordinates were plotted from a map. If the benchmark page on **Geocaching.com** says the location is "adjusted," then its location has been updated with GPS data.

If you stumble upon one in the course of your activities, take a photo, capture the coordinates and note whatever information you can read from the often badly worn surface. You may be contributing to a body of public knowledge!

Bookcrossing

This literary treasure hunt combines some of the best elements of geocaching and trackables, but with a literary twist. Players share books with each other by dropping them off in public places and designating them as "released" on the BookCrossing.com website. Each book has a unique identification number that is obtained from the site. Users can search for particular titles or books within their immediate area. People log found books on the website, read them, and later release them again into "the wild." Players also may attend events at which books are discussed. More than 750,000 people have registered at **BookCrossing.com**.

Waymarking

This direct geocaching descendant grew out of the popular virtual caches on Geocaching.com and now supports its own website, **Waymarking.com**. Its basic function is to pull together information about interesting places using a crowd-sourcing approach. Members submit places to visit in categories like "medieval castles" or "giant balls of string." Subsequent visitors can then contribute their own observations and background information. Everything is bunched into categories, and members can join groups related to those categories.

Although the site originally shared profile information with **Geocaching.com**, it's now been separated into a stand-alone operation that carries its own membership fee. Members can log finds just like they do when geocaching, but GPS coordinates aren't always required.

The Little Church of the West wedding chapel in Las Vegas is an example of a waymark (WM284A).

Geodashing

Each month starts a new game in this appropriately named frantic global race. Geodashing.com announces the new waypoints at the outset of each game. The locations are chosen randomly by computer and are spread all over the world. Players compete to see who can visit the most "dashpoints" before the deadline. Up to five players can compete as a team. There's no container or treasure. The objective is simply to visit a waypoint, take a photo, and log it to the website. Players contribute detailed accounts of their visits to the site, and a leaderboard tracks the top performing individuals and teams. This game may seem overwhelming at first because each new month brings thousands of waypoints. However, everyone has more or the less the same handicap because of the random selection of locations, so the limitations work out about evenly, at least for players on large continents. New Zealanders definitely have a harder time of it.

Letterboxing

Geocaching was actually derived from this sprawling treasure hunt that has been played for more than 150 years. Instead of using coordinates, players figure out the location of containers from clues left by the owner. Navigation is primarily through compass bearing, and distance is measured in paces. Letterbox owners will spend a great deal of time writing clues and often embed them in stories or puzzles. When players find a letterbox, they stamp the container's logbook with a personal stamp and also their own logbook with a stamp that stays with the container. Players create their own unique stamp designs. Naturally, letterboxing has found a home on the Web. You can find more information at **Letterboxing.org**.

Letterbox hybrids are an increasingly popular variation on geocaches. The containers are usually larger than standard geocaches, which makes them somewhat easier to find. In addition to rubber stamps, letterboxes also often contain treasure troves of trackables and gifts. While still relatively uncommon (there are 325 placed within a 500-mile radius of Nashville), they're a nice reminder of where geocaching started.

Degree Confluence Project

The goal of this project is to visit each of the 64,442 points in the world where latitude and longitude integer degrees intersect. In other words, the geocoordinates have no minutes or seconds. For example, 43.00.000°S 69.00.000°W is 29.1 miles south of Colelache, Chubut, Argentina, and it looks like a desert. Visitors take photos at each location and post them, along with their stories, at **Confluence. org**.Visitors are asked to take an additional photo of their GPS screen to prove that they stood at the precise intersection. On April 20, 2005, a record 470 people stood at the confluence of 48 degrees north and 9 degrees east near a small village called Buchheim above the Danube Valley in southern Germany.

Orienteering

This sport predates geocaching by many years, having been practiced since the mid-19th century as a military training regimen. Participants use a map and compass to navigate between points over unfamiliar terrain. The instructions are coded as a series of symbols and numbers and players compete either on foot, mountain bike, skis or over trails. Competitions can be quite intense and demand a high level of physical conditioning. Players log finds on punch cards and each "control point" is assigned a different point level based upon difficulty. The International Orienteering Federation (**Orienteering.org**) oversees rules and competitions organized by regional federations spanning 70 countries. The federation has recently lobbied to make orienteering an Olympic event, so far without success. The sport has, however, been part of the World Games since 2001.

Opisy punktów							
M16		4,1 km		120 m			
▷			⤢✗				
1	40	↘	∩			⎪•⎪	
2	53		⟍⋰Y				
3	46	↓	V				
4	57		)(				
5	32		)⟩				
6	58	▲					
7	47	↙	∩	⌣			
8	48	✦			⌐		
9	49	▬		>·			
10	100		⤢	⤢✗			
○---180 m--⤳◉							

An example of an orienteering control description sheet from an event in Poland.

Wherigo Cache

This fascinating variation on geocaching is the equivalent of an online adventure game played in real life. It requires special software called a "cartridge" that usually includes an adventure story built around a set of coordinates (the term "cartridge" is a nod to the plastic cartridges used in console games). While playing the game, players may meet with many odd characters who may do different things based upon decisions the players make.

If you've ever played an adventure game classic like Zork or Doom, imagine transferring that experience to the real world. Only instead of navigating with a mouse or keyboard, you're walking a route defined by the author. Wherigo experiences don't necessarily have to be played in any one location and they don't require a GPSr. In fact, most Wherigo games are played on PDAs. That being said, players can download a cartridge to some newer GPSr units and play with them as game controllers.

Naturally, there's a version of Wherigo for geocachers. The only difference from standard Wherigo is that the adventure ends at a container. Wherigo caches are still relatively rare. There are fewer than 50 within a 500-mile radius of Nashville. However, these hybrids are a relatively new invention, so expect that number to grow.

Webcam Cache

This comes under the heading of "grandfathered" caches, meaning that no new ones are listed on **Geocaching.com**. Webcam caches are maintained on **Waymarking. com**, however. There's no container involved; players have to get their photo taken in front of a designated, remote webcam in order to log a find. The trick is finding someone to take the photo, since the player usually cannot be both online on a computer and in front of the webcam at the same time.

Geocaching without a GPSr

If your reaction to this idea is "Why on earth would you want to do that?" then you're not a candidate for this pursuit. Some people derive joy from complicating things, however, and geocaching without a GPSr certainly does that. A few years ago, this type of activity would have been almost impossible, but innovations like Google Maps' Street View, Google Earth, and Microsoft Multimap (**Multimap. com/maps**) have changed the equation. These services now provide strikingly detailed satellite and aerial imagery that can serve as a visual guide to a cache's location. Street View is part of an ambitious Google effort to create street-level images of major population areas in the United States. Web-savvy phones like the iPhone are making this form of visual geocaching more practical, but it's still likely you'll have to print or download maps and then navigate your way to the destination by sight.

CHAPTER THREE
Planning Your Outing on Geocaching.com

With so many geocaches in the world, your natural inclination might be to grab a fistful of waypoints and head out the door. There's nothing wrong with that, but you'll get more satisfaction if you plan your outing.

Your geoadventure should fit your mood, since there are so many options available to you. Do you want rural or urban? Easy or difficult? Are you willing to spend the entire afternoon pursuing that one evil hide that has eluded you in the past or do you just want to get outside and increase your total by a few? Are you looking to learn something about the local area? Will you be caching with children? Do others in your group have differing interests for the outing? Are you looking to explore a new location? How far from home would you like to drive before you start looking? All these factors and more enter into your planning.

Different types of geocaches serve different needs. For example, virtual and puzzle caches can educate about local history or folklore, whereas park-and-grabs are all about logging a lot of finds in a short time. Some caches are only available at certain times of the day, while others may be disabled because they've gone missing. It's best to find out that a cache is unavailable before you arrive at the destination. Good planning saves time.

Mapping Your Adventure

Geocaching.com's Google Maps mashup is a good way to visualize a possible journey. Icons quickly distinguish between traditional caches and the more time-consuming multis and puzzles. Click any of the icons to get a summary description and bookmark good candidates. You can later edit your bookmarks and download the results as a GPX file to be loaded into your handheld device (much more on that in Chapter 9).

Tabbed browsing is a great time-saver. By holding down the control key and clicking on a link, you automatically open each page in a separate tab. This lets you continue browsing while other pages load in the background. You can then visit them when you're good and ready. Most major browsers now support tabs.

Read descriptions carefully before deciding what to pursue. Some caches can take hours to find, particularly if they involve multiple stages, puzzles, or extraordinary geography. Difficulty ratings can give you a clue. As a rule of thumb, a "3" rating involves 15 to 30 minutes of searching, whereas a "5" may take an hour or more. Descriptions also yield valuable insight on extraordinary conditions that you may encounter, such as an area's opening and closing hours and seasonal variations. You want to know these things before you get started because it's a drag to drive five miles and then discover that the park you're looking for closed at 3:00 (not that we would know).

One useful strategy is to plan your trip around one challenging find and then fit in a few easier stops along the way. Or, cache along the route if you're taking a road trip. Geocaching.com has a great tool for this called (obviously enough) "Find Caches Along a Route." Many people have contributed their own maps to this collection, and you can create and save your own route, showing caches that lie, for example, within a half-mile of either side of the road. (See more on how to use this feature in Chapter 9.)

Amazing Adventures

Picture, if you will, a two-and-a-half mile, pitch black tunnel with barely a pinprick of light at the end. As you start your journey, you feel odd whiffs of freezing cold air blow at you from the darkness. You start on your way and as you are gradually robbed of your vision, you recall nightmares you've had your whole life— you realize you are walking along what used to be a railroad track. Your ears play tricks on you—is that a train coming? the ocean? a baby crying? a woman screaming?—as you feel your way along completely blind. You lose any sense of equilibrium. You feel cold water dripping on you from above—at least you hope it's water.

This is the kind of adventure people build entire vacations around (in fact, elmbaek flew in from Denmark just to do this cache). This is a mentally and physically challenging geocache not meant for the weak-hearted. The infamous Tunnel of Light (GC1169) in Washington state is the only remaining APE cache in North America (APE is a series of caches hidden in conjunction with a *Planet of the Apes* promotion in 2001). Are you up for the challenge?

The good news is that if you make it through the tunnel with your sanity intact, you're treated to a blooming mountainside of wildflowers bathed in sunlight. The bad news: You have to go back through the tunnel again to get home.

The start of the Tunnel of Light cache involves a 2.5-mile-long tunnel. Looks daunting, but 1,571 out of 1,573 people who have visited have logged the find. *Richard Bennett*

Understanding Descriptions

Geocache descriptions are a literary art form in themselves. At their best, they contain inventive clues, wordplay, and double meanings that can simplify your quest, or make it much more difficult. At their worst, they can be frustratingly vague and misleading. And here's the catch: Cagey owners sometimes use vague and confusing descriptions to intentionally mislead their pursuers!

In this section, we cover some of the finer points of descriptions. Whether you're a newbie or a veteran, an owner or a finder, you can learn from the experts.

Works of Art

Graeme McGufficke (OzGuff) loves hiding geocaches. In fact, he has more than 1,400 concealments to his credit. Graeme has an engineer's mind, so many of his descriptions contain miniature math or logic puzzles. Part of the fun, he says, is to "sell" his hides to prospective visitors. He says, "I try to make it sound appealing. How can I get somebody to want to have this experience? It helps to explain or provide a picture of what people are going to see along the way, especially if it's a cool spot. I make use of white space in the description. It's like laying out a magazine."

OzGuff is a master of the art of writing descriptions and he hides all kinds of clues in unexpected places. For his 300th hide, he embedded a numeric clue as a series of Roman numerals hidden in the cache title. Another series he adopted from Elaine Arpin (Laineybug) in honor of Disney's *101 Dalmatians* movie required seekers to log 100 finds in the series before being let in on the coordinates for the final. As an added twist, only four of the 100 caches contained the clues that were needed to reach the goal.

In interviewing veteran geocache owners, we were surprised to find how much attention they pay to descriptions. Some said they actually spend more time working on the description than they do placing the container. While most descriptions are straightforward, in the hands of a master they can be tools of deception or devious sources of redemption.

InfiniteMPG says it's not unusual for him to spend a full day thinking up a title and description. It's all about delivering a quality experience to the player. "The webpage is your sales tool. You're trying to entice the cacher to find your cache," he says. For a veteran owner like him, the reward is in the log books. A string of unremarkable "TFTCs" (Thanks for the Cache) is a sign that players don't think much of the hide or the container. "If you want them to go after more of your caches, you'd better have what you're selling," he says. "Don't give them a pretty webpage and then send them to a junky piece of Tupperware."

He's proud of a hide called "Alfred's Birds" (GC1DHMA) that he placed not far from his home. "It's a little island that's covered with birds, just like in the Alfred Hitchcock movie," he says. "The text is almost all drawn from Hitchcock movie quotes." He's got another hide called "None Shall Pass" (GC1351F), located near a wooden bridge. The inspiration (and key parts of the description) comes from the bridge scene in *Monty Python and the Holy Grail.*

Almost anything goes with a description, as long as it's in good taste and doesn't promote commercial interests. Personal stories are always popular, and many owners like to concoct fictional narratives that weave together elements from a complicated find. Word games can be great places to hide clues. One description we liked embedded numbered coordinates in words within a story. For example, "17" would be encoded as "All in all, *seven teen*agers joined us on the trip" (emphasis added).

We also love caches that teach us something. One multi we sought in New York City took us on a tour of Revolutionary War landmarks in lower Manhattan. We were fascinated to learn about all the important events that happened there. In areas frequented by tourists, descriptions can provide a history lesson or lead visitors to a landmark that they'll want to tell others about.

Dgreno discovered a favorite while on a cross-country trip with Alamogul and bthomas in 2005. Dgreno says the cache hints, "Report to this location, find the desk with the artwork behind it, and tell the person you're there to geocache." The location was a security desk of a 40-story office building (we won't tell you which city; we don't want to spoil the adventure). The players did as requested and were politely told to have a seat; someone would be with them in a minute. A building maintenance man guided them to the top of the building, then to a service elevator. They got off onto the roof of the building, overlooking the city. There they found a huge treasure chest filled with local swag. It turned out the cache owner was the chief engineer for that office building, who, upon learning that cachers were leafing through his treasure chest on the roof, took them to his office and showed them all the best places to go caching, where to eat, and what to do in the city.

Name that Cache

Names often provide clues about the cache's whereabouts. For example, "Knot Up Here" refers to a cache we hid in the knot of a tree several feet off the ground. One cache we sought bore a name that turned out to be the description of the container spelled backwards.

Many descriptions rely upon clues hidden in images, and this is another reason to scrutinize them on screen or print them before heading out into the field. If you're going paperless with a PDA or geocaching GPSr, be aware that your device may not display images that show up just fine on the website. Owners are increasingly opting for shorter descriptions to accommodate paperless caching, but many descriptions still use photos and drawings.

Descriptions can be as personal as fingerprints. Some owners like to disguise clues in seemingly innocuous phrases or mislead with clues that are actually deceptions. The more experienced the owner, the more likely it is that the description isn't what it seems. Our advice is to become familiar with owners in your area. Each has a unique style, and you will learn to identify their techniques over time.

When you encounter vague or baffling descriptions, a good practice is to Google them. Results can lead you to sources that clear up the confusion. Look for word play in hints as well. Homonyms and indirect language disguise clues. We suspended one cache from a wire and hung it from the top of a metal fence post. Our hint— "Why're you looking up here?"—was a dead giveaway to the location, if spoken aloud.

Puzzles and Riddles

Puzzles may involve watching movies, reading books, or unscrambling complicated ciphers. We can't begin to describe the innovation that goes into these complex riddles. One tip is to check out the cipher listings on **Wikipedia.org** (**en.wikipedia.org/wiki/Cipher**) for a link to pages that can help you unscramble particularly gnarly codes.

Before trying to untangle a puzzle cache, check the difficulty rating. A low difficulty indicates a puzzle that can be easily solved online or onsite. A high difficulty indicates that the puzzle language itself is meant to mislead. One of the toughest puzzles we encountered was in Philadelphia. The cache owner recommended that we watch the movie *National Treasure* before searching for letters in a famous document related to Benjamin Franklin. We knew *National Treasure* was about the Declaration of Independence, so we figured we could skip watching the film. But the clues made no sense. It was only after watching the movie that we figured out that the document in question was an obscure series of essays that we'd never heard of. Solving the puzzle was straightforward from there.

Mistakes in puzzle caches often aren't mistakes at all. If the clues seem a little off, there's probably a reason. Check the logs. If previous visitors have found the cache, then the typo or inconsistency is part of the deception.

Some owners like to play games with the HTML markup language in their descriptions, concealing clues in hidden tags or even in text that is displayed in invisible white type. Whether hiding or finding, be sure to consider the HTML as a factor. The "View Source" option on your menu bar is an asset. See "A Puzzle Cache Revealed" below for an example of how this works.

Some puzzles require the use of a field reference, often combined with the need to visit several stops in order to assemble the clues to the final destination. Take this one from "Whitin 'Tree' Park" (GCVF7A) in Massachusetts:

Clue 1:   Locate the Cercidiphyllum japonicum. Find the fourth letter in its common name.

Clue 2:   *Locate the American Yellowwood. Find the eighth letter in its botanical name.*

Clue 3:   *Locate the Fagus sylvatica 'Pendula.' Find the letter with the most occurrences in the 2-word common name.*

Clue 4:   *Locate the Liriodendron tulipfera. Find the fifth letter in the common name.*

Clue 5:   *Locate the Acer saccharinum. Find the first letter of the common name.*

Easy, huh? Fortunately, most owners specify any expertise a player needs to unravel the clues. So, in the case above, the trees were labeled. If they weren't, an owner would probably tell a seeker to bring along a guide to native vegetation. Of course, this portion can also be solved on the Internet, but then you have to do something with the resulting word once you get to the park.

Getting It Wrong

There is nothing more embarrassing for a cache owner than discovering that the solution to his puzzle leads to the wrong coordinates or that multiple solutions exist. Hopping mad players will let owners know in no uncertain terms about the disruption this causes. Geochecker (**geochecker.com**) is a great online resource for owners and seekers alike. It enables players to quickly and easily check their solutions against the intended one. The service doesn't reveal the answer to the puzzle, only whether the player has the correct one. The service saves players from heading up blind alleys and covers owners against accusations of deceit. Of course, it only works if the owner of the puzzle cache submits the answers first.

The Geocachers of the Bay Area created a great list of guidelines for San Francisco Bay Area puzzle caches. You can find it at **tinyurl.com/me5mf4**; scroll down one page to see it. You'll find the most valuable information at the top of each listing. This includes the name, the owner, size, difficulty, terrain, and various download options. There's also a wealth of information on the right side of the page.

Reading Descriptions

In the example below, the traditional container icon immediately tells us this is a conventional cache without puzzles or multiple stops. With three stars, the terrain is going to be a challenge, but the one-and-a-half difficulty rating tells us the cache itself should be relatively easy to find. A small cache is approximately the size of your hand, whereas a micro might be a film container. Any cache that is not wheelchair-accessible must be rated above difficulty 1, so we can assume that this one won't be very difficult to retrieve once we get there.

Learn to use the attributes section on the right side of the page. For example, these icons tell us that the owner believes it will take more than an hour to find the treasure, there are likely to be people around, and our search may involve

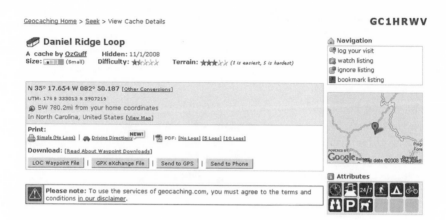

wading through some water. There are dozens of other attributes that will give you an indication of what you're in for. The small map also indicates that the cache is not near a major roadway, which means some hiking is probably involved.

Another cache along the Daniel Ridge Loop trail

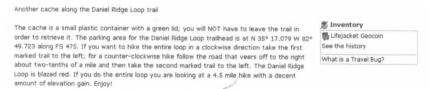

Scrolling down, we find that the owner has provided us with great detail. A particularly valuable bit of advice is that we will not have to leave the trail to find the cache. This is useful because trails often wind around crazily in the woods. Your GPSr may indicate that your goal is 300 feet dead ahead, when suddenly the trail takes a sharp turn to the left. Novice geocachers may be tempted to dive into the underbrush at that point to start "bushwhacking" their way to the target (and believe us, bushwhacking 300 feet through dense vegetation is no fun), but veterans know that the vast majority of woods caches lie within 30 feet of the trail. Unless the description tells you to go off trail (it's considered a courtesy to provide such information), you should stick to the path and you'll eventually come around.

This owner has even done us the favor of telling us that we're in for a 4.5-mile hike. This is useful to know if all you've got is an hour in your schedule.

Most geocaches come with one or more hints. Since not everyone wants this much help, **Geocaching.com** helpfully encrypts these using a simple letter substitution technique that can be decoded with a pen and paper in the field by using the key provided in the description or by clicking the "Decrypt" link on the web

Additional Hints (Decrypt **)**

Oruvaq gur ebpxf

```
Decryption Key
A|B|C|D|E|F|G|H|I|J|K|L|M
-------------------------
N|O|P|Q|R|S|T|U|V|W|X|Y|Z
(letter above equals below,
and vice versa)
```

Additional Waypoints

		Prefix	Lookup	Name	Coordinate
🧭	🔁	PK	PKING	GC1HRWV Parking (Parking Area)	N 35° 17.079 W 082° 49.723
Note:					

page. The experts we interviewed almost always decode hints because they believe the fun of geocaching is visiting lots of new places. But if you choose to make the process that much more difficult, that's your decision.

"Additional Waypoints" provides useful information about parking, trailheads, and other ancillary locations that may be useful. Having this information handy can save time. Additional waypoints are usually downloaded as a separate file that can be loaded into your GPSr.

Owners Share Their Favorites

Puzzles bring out the most playfule side of cache owners. One of dgreno's puzzle caches uses a YouTube video as the key. All you have to do to get the key to the puzzle is Google the name of the cache, then click on the first result (a YouTube video) and watch it. The video isn't dgreno's, but he loves the way it meshes with his objective. "I think it's clever to have found some guy who wasted so much of his life creating the key for my geocache," he told us. Incidentally, as far as dgreno knows, the creator of the video doesn't know about the cache.

Dgreno also has a somewhat twisted side. One of his hides requires the player to watch an actual video of dgreno's knee surgery and take numbers from the screen to solve a puzzle. The final cache is hidden inside the knee of a statue, which completes the theme. We've watched the video and can say that while it isn't bloody, it is weird.

Puzzle caching takes time, creativity, and a little bit of sadism. Pghlooking is addicted to puzzles. Like many advanced geocachers, he got bored with the basics: "Anybody can hit 5,000 guard rails. I wanted to put something out there to make people enjoy it a little more." For one cache, pghlooking filled a 2.5-gallon bucket with more than 150 film canisters. But that wasn't hard enough. To make sure visitors couldn't detect the right canister by sound or touch, he inserted small pieces of paper scribbled with random quotations in every canister. The only way to find the real clue was to keep popping tops.

Mining Logs

Cache Logs

☺ January 4 by Nuwati (1728 found)
Another nice hide along the trail. Thanks for the hide.

Nuwati
[view this log on a separate page]

☺ November 3, 2008 by whoamax (139 found)
This is one of the family's favorite trails. I'll have to bring them back soon for that dang ejmg. Thanks Whoamax
[view this log on a separate page]

At the end of each description page are the logs filed by earlier seekers. *You should always check these notes before beginning your search.* Here's a good reason:

☹ November 23, 2008 by ghettomedic (65 found)
Found #1 after a few minutes of scratching head. Once I punched in coordinates and seeing general location of #2 it made sense. But was unable to find final.
[view this log on a separate page]

☹ October 17, 2008 by Upshot (1022 found)
Not sure about this one. Will try again.
[view this log on a separate page]

☹ October 17, 2008 by Jazzbaby (1037 found)
It was very difficult to be inconspicuous in this very busy spot. We had to walk away empty handed. Another time!!
[view this log on a separate page]

See all those frowny faces that indicate DNFs (DNF means "did not find" in geocaching lingo)? They're not encouraging. What you're looking for is a string of recently posted yellow smiley faces. These log entries above tell us a very important thing, which is that the cache is probably gone (or incredibly difficult). Most caches have a few DNFs, particularly the difficult ones, but if you suddenly see a string of them turn up on a cache with a difficulty rating of between 1 and 3, it's a safe bet the object of your affection has disappeared. Don't waste your time with this one.

By default, **Geocaching.com** shows five logs for each entry, but you can expand that list to see every log that has ever been filed. Generally speaking, only the most recent entries will be useful to you. Everyone is expected to file a log entry, regardless of the result, and DNFs can be more helpful to you than the finds because they reveal strategies that didn't work. "A DNF is not a disgrace," Show Me The Cache says. "It is just a report."

Logs are like mini-diary entries and can yield fun and interesting stories. They can also deliver information that helps you with your search. You can also think of logs as a kind of third-party validation of difficulty ratings. These are assigned arbitrarily by the cache owner, but visitors will often tell you the real difficulty level of the cache. If the logs refer to a "devilish hide," or to an inventive placement, that's a sign you'll have some work to do. Log writers often try to help future visitors by offering small clues, like "I never thought to look there," or "I've never seen a hide like this before." Sometimes they'll be quite direct: "Coordinates were off by 50 feet." Logs are your friends.

On the other hand, don't become discouraged if you spend an hour looking for what logs describe as "an easy find." We usually blame it on Muggles or wildlife when we can't find something that seems so obvious to other players. Make any excuse that makes you feel better and move on.

Don't underestimate the power of a good online log. When logging your own searches, try to say something about your activities for the day or the experience of finding that particular treasure. Cache owners love to read the logs and it's always nice to offer them a compliment. Show Me The Cache advises you think of something besides acronyms and write something funny or entertaining instead. SMTC sometimes even puts a footwear rating on his online log, stating what type of shoes he wishes he'd worn. It "tells them much more than a numerical rating," he says.

Pocket Queries, Bookmarks, and Routes

If you visit **Geocaching.com** for more than a few minutes, you'll run into a term called GPX. This is a file format used to store information about geocaches, and it's a good thing it exists. GPX files are a standard that every GPSr maker and most software programs use to exchange information. It's like a digital Esperanto. That's all you have to know, although there's more detail about it in the next sidebar.

How Do I Get GPX Files?

Paid (aka premium) members of **Geocaching.com** can download any geocache description in a GPX file, but the real power comes from downloading collections of descriptions and then uploading them into your GPSr or to any one of several third-party software programs that enable you to manipulate information. Once you load multiple files into a software program, you can filter, sort, and select them by whatever criteria you choose.

What the Heck Is GPX?

GPX stands for GPS Exchange Format. It's a successor to the much more limited LOC file format that was used in the early days of the game. LOC files are still understood by most GPS receivers and free software packages. They provide the most basic information about a cache, like its name, waypoint code, and coordinates. Beyond that, though, LOC doesn't tell you very much.

GPX files, on the other hand, can tell you just about everything. Bear with us while we get a little technical for a minute.

The GPX format uses a data description language called XML that's very popular on the Web. XML is similar to HTML, the language used to build websites. It can be used to "tag" information for reading by other programs. Tags are simply standard strings of text that programs know how to understand. For example, if we were to describe our home town as <city>Boston</city> in an XML document, any program that reads XML would understand that Boston is a city.

If you want to see what this looks like, try opening a GPX document in a text editor like Windows Notepad. You'll see that the information inside is quite readable, but everything is surrounded by signs like <, >, and /. What's great about XML, and what makes it such a powerful format, is that you can use it to describe *anything*.

Constructing a geocache description in GPX is like putting it into a database. All of the information in the document, such as location coordinates, name, description, difficulty, size, and the like is stored and tagged separately, which means that data can be mixed and matched however you like. That's why databases are cool. Once you break information down into its component parts, you can mix it up again in interesting ways.

Every piece of information **Geocaching.com** stores about a geocache is deconstructed into these basic elements and reassembled as a description page. GPX files basically give you the component parts and let you create your own views of the information.

GPX files are super flexible. They can accommodate any kind of information as long as it's marked with those <> tags. For example, if you wanted to say what phase the moon was in when you logged a find, you could do that with XML tags. Or, you could add the names of other cachers who were with you at the time. Several third-party software programs make it possible for your to modify GPX files for your own use (see Chapter 9).

Geocaching.com uses GPX as part of the bait to get you to pay the annual membership fee. Believe us when we say it's worth every dime. People with free memberships can only download cache information in the limited LOC format. If all you're going to do is an occasional excursion, or if you don't mind printing out descriptions to take with you into the field, that's probably good enough. But once geocaching becomes a regular part of your outdoor activities, you'll want to switch to GPX. As we see in the rest of this chapter, it opens lots of new doors to geocaching adventure.

Geocaching.com offers several options for downloading collections of GPX files, but the most popular is an option called "pocket queries." Pocket queries are essentially collections of geocaches organized by the criteria you define, whether it's by location, difficulty, the date when the cache was placed, or just a collection you build yourself as bookmarks. The easiest way to create a pocket query is to go to the "Build Pocket Queries" option on the "My Profile" page. The pocket queries page also gives you the option of creating pocket queries from other collections of caches you specify, such as bookmark lists or caches along a route. A query is simply a command for the database to extract records that meet your criteria and send them to you as a GPX file.

When you click "Build Pocket Queries" from the "My Profile" page, you will be bounced to a page that looks like this:

New Pocket Query return to list

Query Name

Joy of Geocaching

Days to Generate (Server time: Wednesday, February 18, 2009 4:43:27 PM)

☐ Sun ☐ Mon ☐ Tue ☐ Wed ☐ Thu ☐ Fri ☐ Sat

Choose how often your query should run:

As you scroll down this page, you can select options to create your own personal collection of geocaches. For example, you can choose small, traditional caches within five miles of a designated ZIP code that are in pet-friendly areas. Go back to the top and choose how often you want the query to run, anywhere from daily to just once. Don't forget to select a day for the query to run. If you don't check any boxes here, the query won't show up in your inbox. Click "Submit Information" at the bottom of the page to start the process.

At the time you designate, a query will run that delivers a set of geocaches in GPX format to your e-mail's inbox. You can download the zipped file and then upload it into any one of several software programs or compatible GPS units.

Pocket queries have some limitations. You can only work with the list of criteria that **Geocaching.com** provides you, and that's far from comprehensive. For example, you can't ask only for a list of caches that are north of your location or caches that haven't logged a DNF within the last four attempts. To do that, you need to create a more general query and then slice and dice the results with a desktop software program. You're also limited to a list of 500 results in a single query. This isn't a big deal unless you're mining an area that has a high density of caches, such as the 10-mile radius around Dallas-Fort Worth airport, which has 1,150 hides. If you want more than 500, you need to create a separate query and vary the criteria for each. For example, limit one query to traditional caches and another to multis and puzzles.

Results usually arrive in your inbox within a few minutes if you have checked the box for the day you're building the query, but it can take as long as a day or two if **Geocaching.com**'s servers are busy. You can save queries if you want to run them again later.

Fun With Queries—No, Really!

There are other ways to create pocket queries. For example, if you're browsing through **Geocaching.com** and see an interesting cache, you can save it to a bookmark list using the "Bookmark Listing" option on the right side of the page. Once you've accumulated a list of interesting caches in a bookmark list, you can create a pocket query from it using a button on the site.

There are two other ways to build pocket queries that have great utility. One is to use **Geocaching.com**'s Google Maps mashup. You can find this by going to "Hide & Seek a Cache" from the homepage, choosing any search parameters to come up with a list of caches, and then clicking on "with Google Maps." This takes you to the Google Maps screen that is familiar to many Web users, only this map is overlaid with images of nearby caches. Click on any of the icons to view basic information and, optionally, save them to a bookmark list. This is great if

you want to see in real detail what a route might look like, albeit a slow way to build a target list. Also, the Google Maps mashup isn't perfect. Its performance varies with the browser you use and its 500-cache limit can be frustrating if you're trying to scope out a large area. If you simply want to find geocaches in a defined geographic area, such as a five-mile radius from a certain point, it's faster to create a pocket query.

Another useful option is to create a list of geocaches along the route. By entering starting and ending coordinates or addresses into a Google Maps mashup on **Geocaching.com,** you can create a list of caches that lie within a defined distance of your route. For example, you can specify that you only want to see caches within 200 yards of the road you will be driving. This entry generates a pocket query that can be loaded into your GPSr. You can then drive from Los Angeles to Las Vegas and stop along the way to pick up caches that are within 200 yards of the road.

This screen is a bit hard to find, because it isn't displayed on the "Hide & Seek a Cache" page. Instead, you have to go into "My Profile" and look down the right-hand column for the "Create a Route" link in the "User Routes" category. Enter the precise starting and ending addresses for a route of up to 500 miles and tell the program how far from the route you're willing to stray to find a cache. Keep in mind that lots of people have created and uploaded their own routes, and you may be able to use some of these

routes yourself. You'll also probably want to share the routes you create in the interest of building a common resource.

Pocket queries generate GPX files, which are, as we talked about earlier in this chapter, delivered as e-mail attachments. When these files are downloaded they can be directly sent to a GPSr that supports them or fiddled with in a program like GSAK. In Chapter 9, we go into some of the powerful uses for these files. Another premium feature that dedicated geocachers like is **notifications**.

Notifications aren't pocket queries, but they operate in a similar way. You can tell **Geocaching.com** to keep an eye out for changes to its records and let you know when something meets the criteria you specify. You'll get an e-mail almost instantaneously. Notifications are a great way to find out when new caches have been placed in your area and are a favorite tool of "first-to-find" fans.

Play Like You Want to Play

So now your head is full of acronyms and you're maybe feeling a bit overwhelmed. Take a deep breath and realize that you don't need to worry about GPX and LOC and queries if you don't want to. The best advice that the expert geocachers we talked to gave us was repeated over and over and over again: Play your own way. Before you start to plan your first outing, take this advice to heart.

Dana had a wise poetry teacher in college who taught about writing a poem: "When you get to the end, stop." That is, don't drone on for the sake of writing a longer piece. The same advice applies to geocaching, wherever that end is.

Show Me The Cache puts it like this: "Quit caching when it is no longer fun. That may apply to spending too long on a particular hunt that just isn't going well. Or, it may apply to the end of a long day when you are just too tired to enjoy it. It can also mean it is time for a break from the whole scene. Burnout from something you love is a terrible price to pay for overindulgence."

Keep in mind that it's not all about the numbers. Show Me The Cache says:

> When friends point to some of my so-called "accomplishments" in geo-caching, I quickly slide into my "legend in my own mind" routine. Reaching 10,000 finds was an important goal of mine. In retrospect, cohosting the first GeoWoodstock in Louisville was important to me. Having attended all seven GeoWoodstocks is important to me. Having been the #1 finder in the world at one time is important to me. Having had my 4K Gold Ammo Box Award presented by both President Bushes and my 10K Gold Ammo Box Award presented by Jerry Garcia were certainly great honors (oops, never mind ... those were Photoshop creations). See what I mean?

A Puzzle Cache Revealed

The puzzler that prompted us to reach out to pghlooking is "White Noise" (GCRFZB). Rated a 4.5 difficulty, this cache's description page consists simply of a blank white space. Pghlooking kindly agreed to forgo any spoiler concerns and let us reveal the secret to this cache as a lesson to those new to puzzles. Look up the cache online, then read the solution below.

Clicking around the description area reveals that part of the white background is actually an image file in the JPG format. Save the image file and then use the "View Source" option on the browser menu to see the HTML code behind the page. Puzzle cachers love to hide clues in the code, which is invisible to the casual reader but is easily revealed with the "View Source" command that exists in every Web browser.

Buried in the text is a comment: "Surely I wouldn't hide this cache without using Camouflage." The clue is the capitalization of the word "camouflage." Google that term, and one of the results is a free software program that "allows you to hide files by scrambling them and then attaching them to the file of your choice."

Download Camouflage (it's free) and unscramble the image file with the software. This reveals two barcodes that contain the coordinates of the cache. You can either print and scan the barcodes with a reader or run them through barcode-reading software on the Internet. Once you're done, it's easy to find the target. You'd think this process would stump all but the most determined puzzle cachers, but an amazing 67 people have successfully unscrambled the puzzle and logged the find as of this writing

Pghlooking is only too happy to help. "I place caches to be found," he says. "That's the point of the game. If people call me, I always try to step them through it, though I make sure they can get the answer on their own."

Actually, my greatest honor was receiving my 1K Gold Ammo Box. At that time, there were only five other people with 1,000 finds and three of them drove to Louisville one snowy January morning to honor me. That still absolutely amazes me.

Show Me The Cache knows it's all about personal taste: "Realize that there are few hard-and-fast rules in geocaching, and different people choose to play the game in different ways. It all comes down to personal standards. Refusing to be drawn into a negative discussion about how some people play the game, a recently departed geocaching friend in Louisville said, 'Seems like there are a lot of different ways to play this game, but I'm just glad there is a place in geocaching for me.' It is hard to argue with that attitude and logic."

EMC of Northridge, CA, simply says: "Don't be a geosnob." Try all types of caching, and then do whatever you like. At the same time, try not to limit other people's fun or their methods of caching, either. Everyone caches differently and everyone enjoys different aspects of the game.

HTML Basics

It doesn't hurt to learn a little about the *lingua franca* of the Web. **Geocaching. com** descriptions accept most common HTML formatting commands and you really don't need to learn very many commands to make your descriptions fun and interesting. In fact, most basic formatting tasks can be accomplished using just the few following tags:

`<p align="right">` and `</p>`	Whatever goes next will be aligned to the right (or left or center). End the alignment with `</p>`.
`<img src=http://www.yoursite.com/ images/myimage.jpg>`	Grabs an image from that location and inserts it in the description. Remember that the image must already exist online somewhere. Free photo-sharing services are a good place to upload your own images.
`Height="250" align="left"`	When used immediately following the "img src" statement, displays the image 250 pixels high and aligns it to the left with text wrapping around.
`<a href=http://www.yoursite.com/ cache.htm>Here's the cache!</a>`	Creates a hyperlink from the text "Here's the cache!" to a page called **"cache.htm"** on **yoursite.com**.
`<font face="comic sans ms" color="green" size="4">`	Displays green text using the Comic Sans font at a large size. The larger the number, the bigger the font.
`<td>` and `<tr>`	Used to create tables, which are a nice way to display lists.

<hr>	Creates a horizontal line across the page.
<ul> followed by <li>	<ul> creates a bulleted list while <li> begins each bulleted item in the list. Be sure to end with the </ul> and </li> closing tags.
 	Starts a new line.

Remember that most tags need to be "closed" with a corresponding tag at the end of the section to be formatted. For example, a <ul> tag should be closed at the end of the bulleted list with a </ul> tag.

A simple way to experiment is to code your description in a simple text editor like Windows Notepad and then save the file with an HTML extension like "test.htm." If you open that file in your Web browser, you'll see exactly what the Web page will look like.

There are lots of great free HTML tutorials online. A popular one is at W3Schools (**www.w3schools.com/html/**).

WAYPOINTS
Geocaching Toolkit

Dragonflys and the Amazing Caching Vest. (It's really a fishing vest from LL Bean.)

We asked dozens of geocachers to recommend gear to bring on the outing, beside their trusty GPSr. Here's what they advised us, listed in order of importance from essential for your safety to merely convenient.

Cell phone—If you're geocaching alone, don't leave home without it. Many caches are located in remote places and you don't want to be down with a fractured leg waiting for someone to pass by. Cell phones also have rudimentary location features that rescuers can use to find you. Of course, if you're really out in the boonies, coverage could be sparse.

EMC of Northridge, CA, says, "Keep a lot of phone-a-friend phone numbers handy in your cell phone, so you can call someone who's found the cache or even call the owner of the cache when you can't find one." Her phone-a-friend bank is up to about 130 people.

Mrs. Captain Picard says, "I believe in phone-a-friend. I'd rather call someone whom I know has found the cache I'm looking for instead of looking for it in 100-degree heat!" Because she lives in central Texas, we can understand her point.

Whistle or horn—Again, for the solo cacher, a noisemaking device can alert others if you get into trouble. They can typically be heard from farther away than yelling can be.

Spare batteries—This is also essential for safety. You never want your GPSr to die while you're out in the field. These devices can devour battery power quickly, so always keep spare batteries. If you want to invest in rechargeables, we recommend

Nickel Metal Hydride (Ni-MH) or Lithium Ion (Li-Ion) batteries, which hold a charge longer. Mark Schmidt (Hosta Hillbillys) points out that Ni-MH and its predecessor nickel cadmium (Ni-CAD) batteries have a nasty way of losing juice while sitting in your caching bag. He recommends you use standard alkaline batteries, which hold their power for years, as your backup.

Show Me The Cache learned the hard way to always bring extra batteries for his GPSr. Early in his caching career, he and his wife were caching in a forest in Indiana. They were wrapping up a long day of hunting and they set up their tent and decided to go for "one more [find] before dark." His wife decided to wait out the last one of the day. SMTC was about 15 minutes and two or three ridgelines into the search when he found the cache, just about at the time when his batteries died. Of course, he had no extras. "All my best guesses at how to get back to my wife were wrong," he remembers. And he was too far away for her to hear his shouts. Just before total darkness set in, he stumbled upon his wife and safety. "Luckily she was too scared to be mad!" he says.

Gloves—You never know what you're going to encounter outdoors, and sharp rocks, stinging insects, and unrecognizable liquids are a constant concern. Of your five senses, touch is the one you want to use the least. At the very least, bring surgical gloves to keep your hands clean.

First aid kit—It's easy to cut yourself outdoors, but even urban caches can be hidden under sharp edges. Make sure the kit also includes snake bite medication.

Hiking boots—Believe us, sneakers don't cut it in the woods. If you do want to try them, it will probably only take you one time sliding on a pile of wet leaves to agree with us! Your journey is likely to take you over rough terrain or through the woods, where rocks, tree roots, and puddles are a constant hazard. There's nothing like stepping in a puddle early in your search and spending the rest of the day with wet feet. Hiking boots give you better footing and some protection from moisture. Even for the casual geocacher, good hiking boots are worth the investment. Most veteran cachers also keep an extra pair of boots and socks in their car, just in case.

Warm/wet weather gear—These are especially important if you're going to spend several hours outdoors. Know the local climate or consult **Weather.com** before you head out.

Hat—It protects you from the sun and helps keep you warm on cold days.

Sunblock—You can get a nasty sunburn even on a cloudy day. Block up with SPF 15 or above and reapply sunblock every two hours.

Mirror—A pocket or cosmetic mirror can be a great help when peering over railings or under benches. The less you fish around with your hands, the less chance you have of hurting yourself. Get a plastic model that won't shatter. With mirrors, we've found magnetic caches under ground-mounted mailboxes, nanos in pipes, and even containers in trees that would have taken a lot of finger-poking to discover. Of all the "nice to haves," our little pop-open mirror is the tool we use most.

Tweezers—The second most useful "nice to have" tool for us is a pair of tweezers. The first time you try to dislodge the log book from a bison tube by smacking it with your hand, you'll understand why a 97-cent pair of tweezers can come in handy.

Flashlights and/or head lamps—Even on a bright day, your search may involve looking into dark rock outcroppings or into hollow tree stumps. We always carry a small LED flashlight and keep a large D-cell unit in the car in case we need it. An environmentally friendly alternative is to use a flashlight that can be wound up or shaken to charge. Some units actually include emergency radios, LED lamps, and other niceties. Headlamps can be helpful even if you're not planning on going spelunking because they let you navigate in less-than-sunny territory while leaving both hands free.

Bug repellent—If caching in warm months or in the evening, you'll be glad you brought this. Deet is the most effective (and probably safest) chemical to use in the war against biting bugs.

Water—Long hikes can dangerously dehydrate you. Plus, if you're injured and need to wait for assistance, you don't want to go thirsty.

Walking stick—Useful for long hikes over unsteady ground. Candy Lind (Moosiegirl) uses an old ski pole, which is a great idea. You can also use the stick to snag caches hanging in trees or hidden in hard-to-reach places, not to mention poking in that suspicious-but-yucky pile of leaves.

Power transformer—If you're planning to spend the day geocaching and want to use PC-based software like Geocaching Swiss Army Knife to help you, invest in a transformer that lets you plug your laptop into a car's cigarette lighter. Cheap transformers can be had for as little as a couple of dollars, but we recommend you invest a little more to get one that won't quit on you.

Amazing Adventures

"I once swam to an island to find a cache. It was only 400 yards away and I held the GPSr in my mouth. About halfway across, a speedboat approached and the driver asked if I needed any help. Which I didn't! I found the cache and swam back."

—*Graeme McGufficke (OzGuff)*

Snacks—Power bars and granola are nourishing and portable.

Pen—You'll need a writing implement, since small caches rarely have them. Mrs. Captain Picard clips a pen to her GPSr, so she's never without one.

Camera—We've seen all kinds of wildlife out in the woods and some beautiful scenery on our excursions. Portable digital cameras costing less than $200 can make sure you never miss a photo op. We use a Panasonic Lumix DMC-TZ5K, but there are lots of options. Just remember that the vaunted megapixel rating is far less important than the quality of the lens.

Knife—You'll sometimes have to cut away vines or undergrowth to reach a cache or use the knife blade to pry open a sticky lid. A Swiss Army-style knife also gives you tweezers and a screwdriver, which may come in handy. Just a note if you're caching on a trip you flew to take—check your geocaching knife in your luggage! The security people will not take your word that you have good intentions.

ROT-13 decoder—ROT-13 is the simple letter-substitution cipher that **Geocaching.com** uses to encode hints. It's an offset method in which A = N, B = O, C = P, and so on. Owners are fond of encrypting clues in the field using ROT-13, so carry a piece of paper with the substitutions written on it.

Trash bags—We encourage you to adhere to the geocachers' motto of "cache in, trash out" (CITO). Make it a point to pick up a few items of refuse and leave the area cleaner than when you arrived. Doing this good work benefits everyone in the caching community and the community at large.

Plastic bags—Electronics don't take kindly to the rain, and if you get stuck in a downpour you'll want to stash your cell phone, GPSr, and any other delicate goodies in a plastic bag, preferably one that zips closed. Most GPSrs are waterproof, but testing that notion when it's raining and you're far from your car is probably not the best idea. It's also a good practice to carry a **compass** as a backup in case the worst happens and your GPSr dies in a rainstorm.

Cache repair kit—Pam Sheil (Whoo's Cool & Timbo) carries a small pack inside her backpack that includes a few log books, ziploc baggies and pens so she can repair caches she comes across. She advises, "A small towel or some napkins can also help dry off the items in a cache that have gotten wet." Wayne Lind (The Outlaw) of Austin, Texas, is known to pack these things, too, plus bison tubes, Tupperware, and other containers. He keeps the larger items in his car, so he's not schlepping around 50 pounds of gear.

Where Do I Keep All this Stuff?

Invest in a water-repellent backpack with lots of pockets. Always tuck your equipment away in the same pockets so you won't have to rummage around for it. If your funds permit it, wear a fishing vest. It's got lots of pockets that are ideal for the small items you have to carry and you can keep it stocked and hung in your closet between outings. Another option is a large fanny pack like the Trailmate Lumbar Pack pictured here. It has space for nearly everything mentioned above and fits conveniently around the waist. At about $40, it comes highly recommended by the folks at Cache Advance (**cache-advance.com**).

CACHER PROFILE
Peasinapod

Geocaching.com handle: Peasinapod
Name: Ray King
Claim to fame: Airline pilot who started caching at the top of Kilimanjaro at 19,000 feet
Location: Phoenix, Arizona
Caching since: August 28, 2001
Total finds: 15,368
Total hides: 66
Preferred GPSr: Garmin 60 CSx

Favorite Cache Types

He's grateful for every cache that's placed, "Because they give me something to do."

Special Equipment

"Never leave home without a pen, spare batteries, water, and a hat."

Great Caching Story

Peasinapod discovered geocaching from a magazine article. Shortly after that, he flew to Africa (and we mean *fly*; he's a pilot for U.S. Airways) and climbed Mount Kilimanjaro, GPSr in hand. That was his first official cache—at 19,000 feet.

Since then, Peasinapod has been hooked. He found out from a caching friend about a compilation cache called "Found 50 States, I'm Going to Disneyland!," so he set out to grab at least one cache in every state of the United States. His airline flies to about half the states and he went on trips with his wife for the other half, logging a few states per trip. The couple flew into Memphis and grabbed Mississippi, Arkansas, Alabama, Tennessee, and Kentucky in one day. They then flew into Rapid City, South Dakota, and did both Dakotas, Montana, and Wyoming in one day. When he had an overnight stay in Hartford, Connecticut, he rented a car and drove 440 miles to log caches in Massachusetts, Connecticut, Rhode Island, Maine, Vermont, and New Hampshire, all in one day. He grabbed Hawaii last—flying to Honolulu and back in one day. A year and a half after he started the quest, he e-mailed Team Geo-Rangers, who owns the Disneyland cache, and proved he had met the guidelines. Team Geo-Rangers e-mailed Peasinapod the correct coordinates (the ones on the cache page are a few hundred yards from the actual location of the cache) and he was second to find (STF) for that treasure. He could have been FTF, but he let his friend get that particular designation.

Most Memorable Find

One of Peasinapod's favorite caches is in Oregon. It's located in a park and involves counting hundreds of steps up a volcanic hill, then finding a benchmark at the top, doing some math and projecting bearings. There's a container full of a certain kind of tool that helps a player get to the final. The tool you're looking for is actually a fake nut on a bench in the park. If you take one of the nuts off, you'll find coordinates on it. Follow the coordinates to a fence with caps on the posts. One of the caps is loose, but peering down doesn't reveal any container. On the fence about 10 feet away is a piece of string. If you attach the nut you retrieved from the bench to the string and let the string fall down the hollow fence post, it grabs the magnetic container and—voila!—you have your cache! Most of the logs for this multi/puzzle cache mention how memorable it is and how creative navdog is for devising it.

Words of Wisdom

Whenever he gets near a cache, Peasinapod asks, "Where would I hide it?" He says, "Look for physically possible locations. When you still can't see anything out of place, expand your radius—your coordinates could be a little bit off. Review the description, hints, and past logs for any clues you can glean from the words other people use. Open your mind a little bit, but keep in mind the cache-listing details, the terrain and difficulty ratings, and also the size. If the listing says you're looking for a regular-sized container, that helps."

SECTION II

In the Field

CHAPTER FOUR
Finding a Geocache

Trey Bielefeld (TreyB), Paul Albert (HiDude_98), Julie Perrine (Mrs. Captain Picard), and Bill Angel (Habu!) prepare to tackle The Basilisk (GCPX5Q). *Trey Bielefeld*

Paul: "Do you hunt?"
TreyB: "I hunt geocaches."

Ready to hit the trail at last? Not quite yet, Bucko! A serious geocaching adventure requires forethought and equipment. We've already given you some advice from the experts on planning your route online. Now let's look at what to do before you venture out-of-doors.

Geocaching can be a multi-day trip or a quick diversion as you drive home from work. Many people squeeze geocaching into their lunch hours as an excuse to get outside. Our favorite story about rapid caching comes from Peasinapod, who, you'll recall, is a U.S. Airways pilot. Peasinapod's job enables him to cache all over the country, but our favorite story was about the time he logged a find during a 30-minute layover in Omaha. He ran off the plane, through the airport, and across the parking lot; he nabbed the cache and was back in the cockpit for an on-time takeoff.

Grabbing a nearby cache on your lunch hour doesn't require much forethought, but good planning is important for an extended outing. Think about how much time you can devote to the hunt, how much daylight you have, your tolerance for weather conditions, and your frustration threshold. There's nothing like searching for a cache for three hours, only to come up empty-handed (not that we know anything about that!). A good rule of thumb is to mix one challenger in with several easy finds. That'll make the day worthwhile, even if you don't log the big treasure. Geocaching Swiss Army Knife (GSAK) is a great tool for planning your outing (see chapter 9).

Regional Variations

There are clear differences in the types and hiding places of caches that owners place in different parts of the United States. For example, the Southwest has lots of parking lot caches because of the large number of sprawling shopping malls in urban areas. Containers tend to be smaller in that region because there's less vegetation in which to hide them.

Floridian InfiniteMPG notes that crevices inside palm tree trunks are such popular hiding places that cachers refer to them as a "typical Florida hide."

California has "lots of grab-and-gos and puzzles that end at a street lamp," says dgreno. When hiking through the California desert or elsewhere, look for containers placed under rocks or inside cactuses (just be careful of the needles!).

In the rocky, hilly Northeast, geocache density tends to be much lower. It's harder to run up big numbers there, but searchers are rewarded with long hikes through beautiful wooded areas and a preponderance of multi-caches. Owners are fond of placing containers in the stone walls that snake through the region and caches tend to be placed higher off the ground for accessibility during the winter.

Canadians are fond of burrowing containers into the dense branches of the region's many fir trees.

We've observed anecdotally that there are regional differences in geocache types and styles around the country, but we wanted to test our hypothesis. We ran pocket queries in four areas of the country: Phoenix, Chicago, Knoxville, and our hometown of Framingham, Massachusetts, which is 20 miles west of Boston. A search within ten miles of each city hall returned 689 caches in Phoenix, 432 in

Chicago, 332 in Knoxville and 340 in Framingham. It's clear that if you're looking to run up your numbers, Phoenix is a good place to go.

We then ran the results through GSAK and analyzed the cache types. We found some striking variations.

	Phoenix	Framingham, MA	Knoxville, TN	Chicago, IL
Traditional	86%	57%	92%	80%
Multi-cache	6%	22%	4%	9%
Puzzle	4%	24%	2%	9%
Small/micro	67%	40%	68%	84%
Large/Regular	19%	54%	23%	7%

Phoenix and Knoxville have similar characteristics, although Phoenix has twice the cache density. Chicago has a much larger population of micro caches, which isn't surprising given its dense urban environment. Our hometown is the outlier: Searchers are much more likely to encounter multi- and puzzle caches, which take longer to find. However, the reward is more likely to be a large container overflowing with goodies.

Dgreno notes that difficulty and terrain ratings vary by region, too. "Three-star terrain in Utah is what Mt. Everest would be in California," he says.

Given these facts, it's not surprising that the most prolific geocache finders tend to live in the southwestern United States, while the outward-bound extreme cachers cluster in northern and mountainous regions. Keep this analysis in mind when you decide how ambitious you want your own adventure to be.

Different World

Ether Bunny tells the story of a friend he met through geocaching who taught him a valuable lesson: Be grateful for the bounty you're given. We take for granted the fact that when we want to go looking for geocaches, we'll find some in our vicinity. Not so for bushratgh, who lives in Ghana and wants to be a geocacher.

Bushratgh has hidden six caches and found exactly one. In January 2007, he successfully sought the cache G.G. friendship (GCZH49, now disabled or "archived"). He was only the second person (of two altogether) to log this find. Of the caches bushratgh has hidden, only one has been found, and it took six years for someone to log the first-to-find. "Caching is apparently a lonely sport in Ghana," says Ether Bunny, in an understatement.

Be Prepared

The better you prepare for your journey, the better your experience will be. (See "Geocaching Toolkit" following Chapter 3).

Sweat the basics. "There is nothing more frustrating than to hike for a cache for hours, only to have your GPSr batteries die a few hundred feet from ground zero, or to find the cache and have no pen," says InfiniteMPG.

Veterans tell us that they often spend as much time in preparation as they do in the field. Checking difficulty ratings or scrutinizing puzzles will tell you if you're in for a 10-minute grab or an afternoon-long excursion. If the last three players have logged a DNF, that's a warning sign that the cache might be missing. Little checks like these make the difference between frustration and salvation.

Complex excursions like power caching runs and series may require a month or more of planning. And then there are extreme examples like the DeLorme Challenge, a contest that requires players to find or hide a cache from each page of the DeLorme atlas of their state. Players who complete the gauntlet must send the final coordinates to a designated owner, who e-mails the coordinates of the final container. There is a DeLorme Challenge in nearly every U.S. state and hundreds of people have completed the circuit, with some needing three years to do so.

Read the cache description to know what you're getting into. Many owners will give you an approximate time to complete the search, particularly if it involves multiple stages. We budget a half hour to find even the most basic woods cache, and we add 15 minutes for every stage of a multi.

Map the parking coordinates on Google Maps and measure the distance from the cache location. You can do this by clicking the Google Maps link just under the hint section in the cache description, then clicking the location of any parking coordinates and plugging the result into the "Get Directions" option on Google Maps. Google Maps will give you the distance between them. Or, you can just eyeball it.

If no parking coordinates are listed, you'll want to use a map before you set out on your journey. Driving as close to the coordinates as possible is often not a good strategy. There may be obstacles like cliffs or waterways in your path and simply finding a parking place can be a challenge. Always use posted parking coordinates when they're available. Owners usually go out of their way to make sure people can find their caches without having their cars towed.

Choose your time of day so you don't get stuck after dark in the deep woods. There's nothing like spending two hours getting to a final destination, only to discover that it's too dark to see anything.

Michael Jacobus takes appropriate precautions because he knows that, like it or not, geocaching can be dangerous. If you've ever seen *The Blair Witch Project*, you know how easy it is to get lost in the woods. "If we're going to be away for hours," he says, "we have a geocaching backpack with first aid equipment, water, snacks, map, compass, extra batteries, flashlights, a change of shoes and socks, and a fully charged cell phone. And we'll always let somebody know where we're going and when we should be back."

Check the weather forecast before you leave. If you get caught in a sudden thunderstorm with the wrong clothing, you may get soaked, sapping your body heat. Dress for wilderness geocaching as if you were camping out for the night. You never know when you might have to do exactly that.

Consider the terrain rating as expressed in the cache description. A rating of 3 or above may indicate a steep trail or lots of rocks or other hazards. Match this ranking to your skill and stamina for that excursion. You can double-check your work with Google Earth, which will give you a 3D-like view of the area. Or, you can purchase a topographic map for your GPSr or computer, like DeLorme's Topo USA.

Tips from the Experts

The most important thing to pack is knowledge. You should know what dangers are out there in the area you plan to hike. This may include harmful bushes and wild animals. In our area we have poison oak, as well as stinging nettles. These plants should be left alone. Be sure you know what they look like in all seasons. Poison oak looks shiny green in summer, yet sheds ALL its leaves in winter. Touching the leaves on the ground can cause a reaction as bad as touching the live plants.

Spend some time becoming familiar with the local fauna and animals. Many parks and recreation departments offer classes about these things.

Rattlesnakes are common in most states, but don't usually attack hikers. Over 80 percent of bites are caused by hikers trying to move them, touch them, or pick them up. Ticks are the most dangerous thing in our area. If they attach themselves, you may contract Lyme disease. Find out what type of ticks live in your area. Mountain lions and bears are rare and seem to move away when they encounter humans.

—*Stephen O'Gara (ventura_kids)*

Unwritten Rules

There are several nuances to geocaching that aren't evident to the novice, so let's go over a few of them here.

Logs—You must sign the log book in order to legitimately claim a cache. This may sound like a nuisance, since there is very little chance that anyone is going to check the paper log against the online equivalent. However, religious wars sometimes erupt in online forums over this issue. If someone is verifying the legitimacy of another cacher's claim and discovers that your online log doesn't have a corresponding paper equivalent, you could get hate mail. All you need to do to log a claim is write your **Geocaching.com** username and date in the book. Some people write considerably more than that, but it isn't necessary.

Many people also leave behind cards they've created that include photos, logos, and website addresses. This is a terrific idea and it's not expensive or difficult. You can buy perforated business card stock at the office supply store and download free Microsoft Word templates that make it simple to create your own cards. While you're at it, use the same approach to create miniature stickers that fit into micro caches.

Online, it's considered rude to log a find without entering some kind of comment. In fact, comments are what cache owners find most fulfilling. Your comment doesn't have to be long, but it should be unique. In other words, don't just repeat the same phrase for 50 different caches.

Trading swag—Many people delight in trading small items that are sometimes stashed in the container. Many experienced geocachers eschew this ritual, preferring to simply log a "TNLN" (took nothing, left nothing), but kids in particular enjoy the thrill of fishing for a bit of treasure. The kids of the ecorangers family are known to bring along tackle boxes to trade trinkets.

Geocaching.com: PnD
JoyOfGeocaching.com
Authors: *Joy of Geocaching*
Spring, 2010, Linden Press
Contact us to tell your best
geocaching story!
contact@joyofgeocaching.com

Paul & Dana
Found this cache on

You can print basic cards like this one on your home printer.

The rule of thumb is always to leave something more valuable than what you take (which, admittedly, can be a judgement call when you're weighing a little rubber ball versus a nifty keychain). If you plan on exchanging geo-swag, carry with you some small toys or useful household items. Key ring accessories are popular, since they fit into almost any container. A trip to the local dollar store can yield plenty of useful accessories at minimal cost. More valuable items such as trackables (travel bugs, geocoins, pathtags, geofish, etc.) are coveted items, since they elevate a cache's appeal. (More on trackables following this chapter.)

Did Not Find—You won't find every geocache you seek, and even the most experienced enthusiasts occasionally walk away disappointed. It might seem pointless to log a DNF, but it's actually very important. A DNF is a sign that a cache may be missing. If two or three DNFs turn up sequentially, there's a high likelihood that the cache is gone. Owners pay more attention to DNFs than they do to finds because of this possibility. Frequent DNFs may also indicate that the difficulty rating is too low.

Veteran owner InfiniteMPG looks at DNFs as important indicators of geocache health. "I keep an active spreadsheet of all my caches and whenever I get a DNF on one, I note it," he says. "If several DNF's appear on the same cache, especially if they are from experienced cachers, then I flag it and post a note that I will be checking on it soon."

So logging your DNFs is a courtesy to everyone. And don't be ashamed of them. It happens to everyone. We once spent an hour looking for a supposedly simple geocache in Puerto Rico only to walk away empty-handed. We were convinced the cache was missing, but just two days later it was logged as found by another visitor. Even worse, the finder described it as "easy." Grrrr.

Re-hiding—Always re-hide a cache the same way you found it. Small changes in cover or camouflage can elevate a difficulty 1 to a difficulty 3 in no time. Owners take pains to set their difficulty estimates as accurately as possible, so please honor their intentions. On the other hand, if a cache is plainly visible and carries a difficulty rating of three, it probably could benefit from some extra camouflage. Make sure to note any changes you've made in your log so that the next visitor is aware of them.

Broken or compromised caches—It's not unusual to find a geocache waterlogged, cracked, or otherwise damaged. Owners always appreciate it if you can save them a trip by repairing the container. It's nice to carry a small roll of duct tape for this purpose and we always throw in a couple of bison tubes and log sheets in case a micro has gone missing. If you can't repair the container, move it to a place where it will be protected from moisture and always note in your log that a repair is needed. There's a special label you can use for these comments on **Geocaching.com**.

Just Remember the Geocacher's Creed

Back in the early days of geocaching, a group of passionate trailblazers got together online to address growing concerns that the game could be banned in some areas because of abuses by a few people. They hashed out a set of voluntary principles for the community.

The seven principles stated below may look simple, but they were the product of months of debate and fine-tuning. They were created by consolidating existing information and behavior "into a concise format that serves both to guide geocachers and to instill a sense of trust in landowners and land managers." Learn more at **geocreed.info**. Here is the creed:

When placing or seeking geocaches, I will:

- *Not endanger myself or others*
- *Observe all laws and rules of the area*
- *Respect property rights and seek permission where appropriate*
- *Avoid causing disruptions or public alarm*
- *Minimize my and others' impact on the environment*
- *Be considerate of others*
- *Protect the integrity of the game pieces*

Into the Woods

There are some special considerations for seeking containers in woods. We'd like to share just a few tips we've gleaned along the way.

The first thing you should do upon leaving your car is **create a waypoint on your GPSr designating where you parked** so you can find your way home. Tami and Wade Mauland (ecorangers) stress the importance of getting into this habit, so that you can find home base after a few hours of hiking in circles around the woods. In a similar vein, they say, "You're not a crow," so don't pay attention to the distance on your GPSr from your car to the cache, which is marked in "as the crow flies" measurements. Often, what appears to be a two-mile hike on a GPSr turns out to be closer to six or eight miles because of the trail's meandering.

If you're caching alone, which we don't recommend in the deep woods, **leave a copy of the cache's information page,** with the coordinates highlighted, in your car in case someone has to find you later.

Enter at the recommended trailhead. Most cache owners aren't interested in endangering you or getting you stuck in dense undergrowth. They'll generally tell you where to enter the trail. Take their advice.

Stay on the trail. As we mentioned before, one of the most common mistakes novice cachers make is to plunge into thick undergrowth for the last 300 feet of their search. After all, the trail appears to be taking them in the wrong direction and 300 feet doesn't seem all that far. Trust us: It is. When you're out in the deep woods with thorns penetrating your flesh and branches slapping you in the face, 300 feet can seem like miles.

Most cache owners place their hides near marked trails for their own convenience as well as for the convenience of seekers. Keeping seekers on the trail is also more environmentally friendly. Trails tend to meander and double back upon themselves. If your GPSr indicates that the cache is at a 90-degree angle to your direction of travel, chances are the trail will make a big turn ahead. If you can find a trail map before entering the woods, all the better—you'll know where you're headed.

Mark Eisenbraun (Bigdaddy Mark) found this out the hard way. While caching in Columbiana County, Ohio, he and a friend decided to go after a cluster of five large caches in a nearby park. Here's what he told us:

> The GPSr was heading us down a steep but nicely maintained packed gravel trail. We headed in for about two hundred yards, when the GPSr started pointing us into the woods. We still had about five hundred feet to go when the trail turned behind this monstrous hill.
>
> We discussed if we should bushwhack to the cache or stay on the trail. I said the cache is only rated at a 1.5 difficulty, so I couldn't see going through the woods. So down the path we headed.
>
> At the bottom of the hill, the GPSr turned perpendicular to the path, reading less than two hundred feet. We left the trail and started climbing the hill. It was at such a steep angle that standing straight up I could touch the hill face with an outstretched arm. We dug in and kept climbing. The higher we got, the softer the ground became. With every step I got dirt over the top of my hiking boots.
>
> Huffing and puffing, I pulled myself up, using any sapling I could get my hands on. After what seemed a lot longer than it was, we got to where the cache was and quickly came up with the find. While I was standing with both hands on my knees trying to catch my breath, I looked off to the right. You guessed it: There was a nice flat path cut through the woods. Now, whenever we wonder which path to take, I always think of this cache.

What to Do when You Get Close

It's easy for novice cachers to believe that technology will lead them to their goal. But many veteran cachers we spoke to stop paying attention to their electronics when they're 30 or 40 feet away from their target. They count on their instincts to get them the rest of the way. Keep in mind that even the best GPSr units are accurate to within no more than ten feet. Do the math and that translates into a 400-square-foot area. Even if you're standing on the precise coordinates, your goal could be ten feet in any direction and probably more. That's why some veterans put away the GPSr units so early.

It's a good idea to check your GPSr accuracy when you get near your target. Each manufacturer's products have quirks. Magellan receivers are known to have what is called the "boomerang effect." They may be off by over 40 feet at first, and then improve their accuracy if allowed to rest a while. Garmin units also sometimes benefit from being pulled back for a minute and then consulted again. "If we don't spot the cache in a minute or two, we walk 40 feet away and walk back to zero," says Steve of ventura_kids. "Sometimes the position varies by over 20 feet. If you are searching for a nano, you may need to be quite accurate."

The infamous "unnatural pile of rocks." Look for sticks and stones that are a little out of place.

Even then, we've found that accuracy ratings can be, well, inaccurate. It may take a GPSr a minute or two to convey its confusion, so it's a good idea to check back repeatedly as you start your search. While your GPSr is contemplating your precise location, Mondou2 advises that you look long and hard before you touch anything in the area. Here's what to look for:

Think like the owner. If you owned the cache, where would you hide it? For difficulty 3 and below, the old staples are a good bet: tree trunks, rock piles, and hollow stumps. For difficulty 4 and above, the owner has probably come up with something more devious. Try looking overhead or search for heavily camouflaged items, like false rocks or containers suspended by wires.

Look for anything out of place. Survey the scene and ask yourself if anything appears out of place. Is there a pile of leaves that doesn't look like it came together naturally? Is the bark covering that tree stump the wrong color? Do those rocks look like they've been placed there by human hands? If the scene doesn't look natural, it probably isn't. Owners factor these small clues into their difficulty rankings. The placement of a large piece of tree bark can turn an easy find into a challenging one.

Seek out natural hiding places. Fallen trees are a favorite hiding place because their root balls and gnarly trunks present natural crevices. Don't give up too easily. Remember that many caches are covered with camouflage tape, which can make them all but invisible in a wooded setting.

Look up. Look down. Containers may be hung in trees or suspended from light poles. Look for items in the branches that don't look quite right. Is that pinecone an unnatural color? Have you burrowed all the way to the center of that pine tree to see if something is attached to the trunk? Keep an eye out for fishing line, which is difficult to see, especially in the low light of tree cover. If you're stumped, run your hand carefully around the area to see if you catch onto anything.

Camouflaged pill bottle.

Consider the obvious. In our experience, our instincts are usually right and the most likely hiding place turns out to be the correct one. Our mistake is usually giving up too early. We don't find the cache quickly, so we move elsewhere. If we had spent a little more time investigating the most obvious candidate, we would have saved ourselves time and earned that elusive smiley.

Triangulate. If your GPSr is flaking out (often a problem in the woods), there are two techniques you can use to zero in on your target. The first is the "Cloverleaf" approach, in which you walk toward the spot indicated while looking at the distance measurements as you go along. When the numbers start to go up, reverse course and then bear off at a 90° angle until the numbers start increasing again. By following this pattern, you'll eventually close in on the target even if you don't have a very good signal.

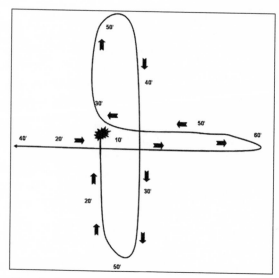

Cloverleaf your way to the cache.

Another tactic is to walk around the target area in a large circle and take bearings from three different places, a tactic known as triangulation. Note the direction of each bearing, and the point where the three lines intersect should be close to your target.

Traces of human activity. When InfiniteMPG is stumped, he'll back off and approach the hide area again, looking for reflective objects, threads, caps, bits of plastic bags and anything else that smacks of civilization. Some owners actually leave these breadcrumbs behind to let you know you're on the right track. Human footsteps are pretty helpful in the snow, too.

Clues from previous visitors. If the cache has been found more than 20 or 30 times, look for "geopaths," which are tracks left by geocachers when they leave the trail. This is particularly good advice in the winter or in thick brush, when geopaths can take you right to your destination. Look for broken branches or trampled leaves.

Previous visitors will also help you out by concealing their finds in ways that don't throw you off. It's considered good geocaching etiquette to cover a found cache with the same level of camouflage as the original owner intended. Most caching enthusiasts will try to leave something about the environment of a woods cache just a little bit "off" or out of its natural context for the benefit of future visitors. At first, it's difficult to detect these nuances, but you'll get the hang of it over time.

Keep an open mind. WE4NCS advises new players to let go of what they expect of a cache. He once hid a container and wrote in the description, "It's just another ammo can." What he failed to mention was that it was a toy GI Joe ammo can and measured about an inch across. Ecorangers are pretty proud of a cache they hid in the woods, which is described as a micro. ("There is no room for trade items.") It's actually a 17.5-gallon tub that is mocked up to resemble a giant micro.

Keep the size in mind. Cache owners can keep the size a mystery, so let your mind wander a bit outside the realm of possibility and consider some unlikely

scenarios. Looking for an ammo box when the container is actually a nano will almost ensure a DNF. Mondou2 says, "Don't have a specific container or hide or location in mind." He advises cachers to go to GZ and see what they see. We found a cache in a bush in the Austin, Texas, area for which we

This shinier leaf than those near it sure looks suspicious!

could have been searching for hours. The bush was on the outskirts of a parking lot and seemingly easy enough. But we searched for a few minutes until we saw one leaf in the bush look just slightly too shiny. It turns out the cache was the fake leaf and not at all a film canister or bison tube hanging from a branch, like we initially thought (see photo above).

Don't be afraid to call. If you spend a lot of time caching in your home area, as many people do, you'll get to know the active owners—those people who have placed a lot of caches. Don't be afraid to ask for their phone numbers and to call them if they've hidden the cache you're seeking or if they've found it previously. Enthusiastic geocachers are usually happy to drop what they're doing and help out someone who's stuck. After all, they've been there before.

Know when to quit. Giving up the search is one of the hardest things to do, but knowing your limits can make for a more fulfilling experience by moving you along to more promising targets. Everyone has a different threshold for giving up and logging a DNF. In most cases, those limits are situational. Players are more likely to spend a lot of time searching for a difficult or devious hide than they are for a quick grab.

At the risk of repeating ourselves, it pays to do your homework and to have a good idea of the cache's history. If no one has logged a DNF recently, then there's a pretty good chance the container is still there. But if the last two visitors were frustrated, you should probably cut your losses. It can also pay to have a stated time limit.

OzGuff has a simple guideline. He gives up the search "when [he's] no longer having fun."

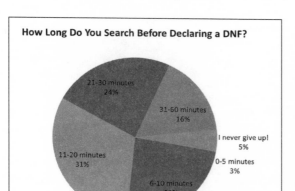

How Long Do You Search Before Declaring a DNF?

21-30 minutes
24%

31-60 minutes
16%

I never give up!
5%

0-5 minutes
3%

11-20 minutes
31%

6-10 minutes
21%

Our online survey revealed most people look for a geocache longer if they've prepared for the search more.

We put the question to our survey panel and found that many people allocate between ten and 30 minutes for a search, with a third of the respondents saying that "It depends on how much time I've invested." And then there were 5 percent who responded "I never give up!" They have our respect.

The Beauty of Woods Caching

The most challenging and unpredictable geocaches are usually those you find in the woods. They may involve hikes of several miles, in some cases, and finding even large containers can be challenging in dense underbrush or poor light. Add to that the fact that GPSr devices don't like thick woods. Signals may suddenly drop or become unreliable and signals bouncing off of rock walls can suddenly render them almost useless.

So why bother with woods caches at all? Because they're great exercise, a never-ending source of challenge, and a wonderful way to discover new places to hike and explore. We like urban geocaching, but bouncing between parking lots and street signs loses its novelty pretty quickly. Urban caches are great for running up your numbers, but woods caching is what makes the game special to us.

When he started geocaching in 2005, Paul had lived in the same area for nearly 20 years. Imagine his surprise to discover that nearly every search took him to a park, reservation, or nature preserve that he had never seen before, some less than a mile from his home. Now our mantra is: "We never knew this park was here!" That's what's great about geocaching: It's a chance to discover the little-known getaways that other people love and to make them your own.

Clever Hides

In geocaching lingo, an "evil hide" is a compliment. Cachers always appreciate an ingenious container or inventive placement, which can turn a simple difficulty 1 into a devious difficulty 4.

One of our favorites was in Texas. Imagine finding more than 200 film canisters velcroed to the underside of a stairway (below)! What words might come out of your mouth? We set to opening the containers and found that each held a different message telling us that it wasn't the cache. We had popped open about a dozen when we realized that no owner would be mean enough to force a player to go to that much trouble (we've since learned that there are *plenty* who are mean enough!). We theorized that the collection was a decoy meant to confuse us. And we were right. It turned out the treasure was about 20 feet away, hidden in something that was nothing like a film can.

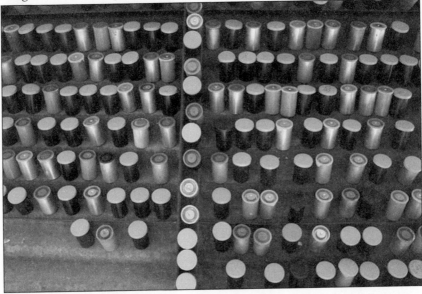

And there's one of the secrets of geocaching. **If it looks like the cache is in an impossibly difficult place, then it probably isn't in that place.** Veteran cache owners are skilled at throwing players off the track with startling locations and then placing the actual target in a mundane spot. It's one of the things that makes them so evil.

Clyde England offers a great example of this. The developer of the Geocaching Swiss Army Knife software was once searching for a container that had been described in the hint as magnetic. There were lots of metal objects in the search area and England examined all of them to no avail. After more than an hour of fruitless searching, he pulled out his cell phone and called the owner, who told him that the cache was indeed magnetic, but that fact had nothing to do with its location. England quickly found the container in a nearby tree. There was no metal in sight. The "magnetic" label was strictly meant to throw searchers off the trail!

Suspend Belief

Although the rules of the game dictate that geocaches can't be buried, that doesn't mean they can't be concealed in devious ways. Owners often stash them in holes in the ground or suspend them in trees. As long as the cache isn't covered with soil, anything is fair game.

The most common hiding spots for woods caches are piles of rocks, branches, or leaves. Urban caches are usually attached magnetically to the underside of signs and utility boxes or hidden under the plastic skirts at the base of light poles. However, containers can also be suspended or camouflaged in interesting ways.

Fishing line is a favorite tool. Small caches are often hung from this nearly invisible thread and lowered down into hollow fence posts or storm drains. It turns out that fishing line is almost impossible to see if you aren't looking for it. We once searched for a half hour for a cache that was hidden this way. Several times we had our hands right on the fishing line but didn't feel it.

Hooks and wires can be used to suspend caches at eye level or above. These 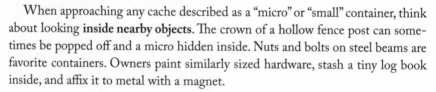 materials are especially popular with owners in cold locations who want to keep their hides available during snow-covered months. If there's an "available in winter" icon (left) on the description page, you may find the cache elevated in some way.

When approaching any cache described as a "micro" or "small" container, think about looking **inside nearby objects**. The crown of a hollow fence post can sometimes be popped off and a micro hidden inside. Nuts and bolts on steel beams are favorite containers. Owners paint similarly sized hardware, stash a tiny log book inside, and affix it to metal with a magnet.

A hook or wire may be used to attach a small camouflaged container to a tree branch, like a Christmas tree ornament. Always look upward, and **always replace and secure suspended caches as you found them.**

One of our favorite hides used fishing line attached to an old basketball backboard that had been overgrown by woods. The line was tied to a container suspended from the top of the backboard. When the line was detached from a holding clip, it allowed us to lower the container from its hiding place, 15 feet above.

Unusual containers are the most difficult to find and give the greatest delight to their owners. It's not unusual for dedicated owners to spend hours crafting a container out of wood, rock, or bone. Sites like **CachingBox.com** sell pre-fabricated

From the top, a prefabricated rock cache looks like any other stone.

But flip it over and twist...

containers disguised as pinecones, rocks, and even snakes. CachingBox founder MacKenzie Martin of Scottsdale, Arizona, says his bison tube cache attached to the back of a rubber rattlesnake is a popular seller. People also request custom caches that resemble scorpions, lizards, rabbits, and other woodland or desert creatures.

Martin is always open to fashioning a cache out of unusual materials, but he has his limits. "I keep getting requests for the horse manure cache," he says. "I've even seen a couple of people selling them, but I wouldn't even know how to start making one. We've also had requests for road-kill caches. That's kind of disgusting." We agree, MacKenzie! Read more about off-beat containers in Chapter 5.

Sssssso realistic. This faux snake disguises a geocache glued to its underside.

"What the Heck Are You Doing?"

Early in your geocaching experience, you'll run into the awkward situation of noticing bystanders staring at you with expressions that range from puzzled to hostile. You really can't blame them: Why would an otherwise grown-up man or woman spend 20 minutes poking around under rocks in an urban park in the middle of the day or wriggling around on the sidewalk under a newspaper box?

Tales from the Trail: The Spider Cache Chronicles

We didn't know whether to categorize this story as scary or funny. We guess it depends on your attitude toward arachnids.

I once found a geocache under a lamppost skirt. As I lifted the skirt I saw nothing. Knowing that sometimes the cache is magnetic, I leaned down and looked up under the skirt. Just as I peeked up into the skirt, a giant wiggling spider fell on my face! Panic set in as I dropped the skirt and backed up. The spider fell to the ground and began chasing me as I moved backwards! It seemed like forever before I realized that I was backing downhill, and the spider was just rolling along with me. I moved to the side and watched it roll down the hill. After gaining my composure, and waiting for Sandy to quit laughing, we walked over to the spider. We quickly realized it was made of rubber, which made it wiggle, and the geocache was cut into the rubber body. Ever since then I love lamppost caches!

—ventura_kids

Muggles will stop and look at you while you're peering into dark places and rustling in the bushes, but few will bother to ask for an explanation. However, some will ask. It's nice to answer. When they're wearing blue uniforms, it's downright essential.

We've asked scores of geocachers how they deal with Muggles, and each has his or her own tactics and favorite stories. In general, the best approach is to tell people what you're actually doing—"We are engaged in a treasure hunt using global positioning systems"—or the terser option—"We are participating in an Internet treasure hunt." Most Muggles will be sufficiently baffled by this response and will move on. For the few that express interest in learning more, show them your GPSr and explain to them how you're trying to pinpoint the treasure. You can even invite them to join in the hunt.

If you're trying to look nonchalant, do something normal. Some cachers use their GPSr units as impromptu cell phones. Others whip out trash bags and start picking up garbage.

Some veteran geocaches have come up with original approaches to deflecting Muggles or avoiding questions in the first place.

Peasinapod invests in a bright orange reflective vest that gives him a built-in aura of responsibility. "If you're wearing an orange safety vest and carrying a clipboard, you can do practically anything you want," he says. We love this idea. It's like an invisibility cloak to Muggles. People wearing brightly colored vests and hard hats become almost transparent to the general public and can do unusual things without attracting attention. Several geocachers told us they've tried this approach in busy public areas.

Trey Bielefeld (TreyB) of Round Rock, Texas, carries a geocaching brochure with him to hand out to inquisitive bystanders. This satisfies most people and a few get interested enough to want to join in the game.

Thrifty-chick uses a simple yet effective tactic: "When I attract attention, I pull out my cell phone and sit down and pretend to talk on it. People usually turn away and mind their own business. I never really dial anyone; it just helps to look as though you're not up to anything."

Ken Alexander (Granpa Alex) of Sanford, North Carolina, uses the opportunity to recruit new geocachers. "I share the game with them and invite them to help me hunt as I sell them on the fun it brings," he says. "I have never had an experience that did not turn out well."

Ecorangers geocache with their two kids. One time they took a football out of the car to distract Muggles and Wade played catch with their son while Tami and their daughter nabbed the find. The family also advises, "Don't yell 'Found it!' if you're near Muggles. It'll raise their interest. Shout out like an owl instead: 'Whooty-hoo!'"

Show Me The Cache usually doesn't lie to Muggles, but he doesn't tell the whole story, either. He says, "When Muggles are unavoidable, I either speak in an imaginary foreign tongue, slide into role playing, or ignore them. If I really feel the need to answer to them, I explain that I am in their area checking on satellite reception. And I really am. Everyone seems to appreciate that. I love it when the truth is the best answer."

EMC of Northridge, CA, says, "Don't answer 'What are you doing?' by saying 'geocaching.' You'll end up spending 20 minutes there." (Spoken like a true power cacher!) EMC just replies, "I'm on an Internet treasure hunt."

People generally don't want all the details; they just want to know "that you're not a complete whackjob," says dgreno. His closing line to Muggles is usually: "I'm crazy, but I'm not dangerous." Some people get so interested they make him wish he could open his coat and sell them a GPSr, but most people just want to feel like they've ensured their own safety.

Avez Vous Une Cache?

We honeymooned in France for two weeks in 2007. The first week we stayed in Paris; the second week we took a driving tour of Burgundy, through towns so small that we were amazed they even showed up on our GPSr. One afternoon we were caching and crossed a small bridge, which couldn't have been more than 25 feet across. There's a cache under the bridge. So we parked about 50 feet away and walked back to it. We found a woman sitting on a fold-up chair (think one of the cheap kinds you have on your back porch) on the bank of the stream, guarding the bridge and eyeing us suspiciously. You could almost hear her thinking (in French), "They don't look like terrorists, but what are they doing?" We decided to walk right by her and ignore her curiosity.

We went down a little walkway at the water's edge, went underneath and around the other side of the bridge, and then found the cache up in a little crevice. Dana, being the more flexible one, climbed up and retrieved the cache container. We signed the log book and went out the way we came in. (It was either that or swim.) But now the woman was waiting for us. She was standing up, shooting questions at us in French.

Now, Dana speaks about five words of French ("Anglais, s'il vous plaît" are four of them), so she was a lost cause. Paul got us around pretty well in France, but what was the French word for "treasure hunt"? We had the phrase book on us at the time, so he's leafing through the pages, spouting words like "clue" and "prize." She finally understood we weren't a threat and let us go on our way. Moral: When in a foreign country, know how to say "Internet treasure hunt" in the appropriate language.

Geocaching at Night

We have enough problems finding geocaches during the day, so we don't understand why anyone would want to complicate the matter under the cover of darkness. Nevertheless, some geocachers have told us that there is nothing like nighttime for a good group experience. More power to them.

All we can say is: **Be Careful!** Our own experience with night caching has been mostly frustrating. Darkness accentuates the difficulty of finding an item that is already concealed, and even brightly lit urban locales can be treacherous after dark, depending on the neighborhood and the local residents. Also nighttime noises can freak you out: Paul once placed a cache after dark in a wooded area where the crash of large woodland creatures (probably deer) plummeting through the forest sent him clamoring back to his car.

We recommend against geocaching alone after dark. If you do, make sure that someone at home knows where you are, when you are due back, and how to reach you. Always carry a high-powered flashlight and a cell phone. And be prepared to get out of an area if you sense any danger—real or implied. This applies to urban as well as woods caches. Some neighborhoods that look just fine by day become downright petrifying after dark. Do yourself a favor and wait until daybreak. If you must city-cache at night, call the local police station to get an opinion on safety in the area.

Geocaching at night is at least three times as challenging as geocaching during the day, so plan accordingly. It's best to stick to relatively simple and large targets. Stay close to the road so that you can call for help if you get in trouble. That said, roadside caches are best avoided after dark, when poor visibility and impaired drivers are threats. We also recommend you avoid multi-caches, which often have small stages bearing only written coordinates, which are hard to see after dark.

Have we scared you off yet? Night caching can actually be fun if conducted in an area where there is a good lighting and other people are around. Sports complexes, highway rest areas, city sidewalks, and shopping malls are good spots. Consult resources like Google Earth to get a sense of where you'll be hunting.

Geocaching in Winter

We love living in the northeastern United States, but we're all too aware of the difficulties of geocaching in a cold climate. In addition to frostbitten fingers and toes, winter geocaching presents its own unique set of challenges, particularly when there's snow on the ground. We don't want to warn you off the sport in mid-winter, but it pays to know what you're up against.

Geocaching in snow probably adds two difficulty stars to the ratings posted on **Geocaching.com**. This is because cache owners in the Northeast are fond of hiding their treasures in the thousands of stone fences that ring the area. Once upon a time, these wooded areas were grasslands where cows grazed. The cows have long ago been replaced by saplings, but the stone fences that farmers created from the rocks they turned up in the fields will last for hundreds of years.

The fences present great opportunities for hides, but in winter they tend to get covered with snow. If more than a foot of snow is on the ground, many of the caches that would be simple finds in warmer months become almost invisible. Check the description carefully to see if the owner has taken this into account.

Veteran owners will usually tell you if winter caching presents any special problems. On the other hand, footsteps of seekers who have preceded you since the latest storm can lead you directly to a cache.

Snow isn't as much of a problem for urban caches, or for micros and nanos, which are more likely to be hung in spots above the snow line. When in doubt, opt for caches that the owners report are in these smaller containers.

Needless to say, dressing appropriately is a must. Heavy gloves, thermal boots, wool or fleece socks, a hat, and layers of clothing are a foregone conclusion. Use Google Earth to determine if you're going to have a long walk ahead of you. We recommend keeping a supply of those chemical hand and foot warmers with you in case you start to feel numb. And, don't forget the water bottles and sunscreen you would normally pack in the summer—they're just as vital in colder seasons.

WAYPOINTS
Bugs, Coins, and Other Trackables

Travel bugs can be attached to almost any object that would fit into a "regular" container.

It wasn't long after geocaching was born—July 2001, to be exact—that the idea of tracking the movement of items placed in geocaching containers came about. Like most caching-related phenomena, travel bugs have morphed over the years to become a specialty in themselves.

Early in your geocaching experience, you'll notice that many containers house small items affixed to dog tags with serial numbers etched into them. These are travel bugs, and their sole purpose is to be moved from cache to cache in a quest to reach a particular destination or just to travel as far as their virtual legs will carry them.

With great power comes great responsibility, and if you take on the duty of picking up a travel bug, you have the obligation of delivering it to another location. If it has a goal, try to move the bug closer to it. Owners watch the progress of their travel bugs carefully, so it is incumbent upon you to note in your log that you have one in your possession.

Log It

Logging a trackable item on **Geocaching.com** is as simple as clicking on the name of the travel bug (TB) on the geocache description page from which the item was retrieved. You can also search for the tracking code in the "Trackable Items" section of the website. Then note that you found the item by typing in the unique code on the dog tag. Once you find a trackable, you're responsible for delivering it to the next location. **Geocaching.com** keeps track of who has each bug.

Many TBs have no particular rules. Owners simply want to move them as far as possible. Some bugs, however, come with specific requests, such as being photographed atop mountains or in birdbaths. If you pick up such an item, you should comply with the request. Otherwise, leave it for somebody who will.

Owners usually want their trackable items to move as quickly as possible, so if you're not planning to travel soon, it's best to leave the trackable for somebody else. If you know you have a trip coming up that will include geocaching, then collect several travel bugs before you leave so you'll be able to move them along. Owners appreciate it when visitors move their travel bugs long distances.

There is an unwritten rule that visitors who pick up trackable items should place them within a couple of weeks. This isn't always observed (and we've been offenders of this on occasion, too), but it's courteous to the owner to keep the item constantly in motion. If you can't place a bug soon, e-mail the owner to let him or her know that the bug has been waylaid.

Travel bugs also have a tendency to become lost because sometimes visitors fail to log them. If you find a bug that isn't included in the trackables listed for a given container, simply look up the unique serial number, go to the trackable's page, and log an entry that you found it. This will reestablish possession and ensure that tracking can resume.

If you aren't soon going to move a TB nearer to its goal or will not travel soon, you can tell the bug's owner that you "discovered" it at an event or in a cache. **Geocaching.com** keeps track of how many TBs you move and discover.

There is no end to the innovation that dedicated geocachers bring to trackables. Some are linked to contests in which geocachers must log certain caches and carry trackables between them. Others have long personal histories tied to their owners or are backed by fanciful myths concocted by the originator.

Starting a Trackable

Launching a travel bug is easy. You buy a dog tag with a unique serial number at **Geocaching.com** for about $5. You get one tag to keep and one to send on its way. **You need to activate a tag before releasing it into the wild.** Otherwise, Geocaching.com has no way of tracking it and the item will be immediately lost to you. Fortunately, anyone can activate a code, so if you mess up and release a trackable without activating it, the first person to find it can start the process. Instructions on the site are straightforward enough.

Tags may be circulated by themselves, but usually they're attached to a "hitch-hiker," which is a term that refers to a character related to a story or identity attached to the trackable. Small, inexpensive toys and stocking stuffers are favorites; expensive hitchhikers tend to disappear quickly. Frequently, hitchhikers are stashed in plastic bags along with instructions for continuing the journey. These bags can get ragged pretty quickly, so do the owners a favor and re-bag items when possible.

When you register a tag, you also get a tracking page on **Geocaching.com** that's similar to a description page for a geocache. There you can enhance the mystique of your item by creating a story or objective behind it. Check out the trackables section, and you'll see that people have concocted some pretty amazing tales. This page also tracks the progress of an item on its journey. People can post travel notes and comments about the trackable separately from their notes about a geocache. In effect, a trackable is just a geocache that moves.

Best-Traveled Trackable

There is no official record of the travel bug that has moved the farthest, but a pretty good candidate would have to be Worldtraveler (TB27B), a bug that was released in Tennessee in October 2001 and that had moved over 634,000 miles by October 2009. Worldtraveler is a "personal travel bug," which means that the owner, who also goes by the name of Worldtraveler, keeps the travel bug with him and files a log entry every time he visits a new geocache. Anyone who meets him can log the bug as discovered. If that person asks, "Are you Worldtraveler?", he renews their premium membership for one year at his own expense.

Geocoins

Geocoins are a type of trackable that have spawned a craze in themselves. People create geocoins to commemorate all kinds of things—weddings, conventions, milestones, and places, just to name a few. Coins come in all shapes and sizes. These days, owners experiment with custom die cuts, elaborate color schemes, and special plating. Not only are geocoins tracked as they move from cache to cache, but they are also collected and traded like baseball cards. The Groundspeak forums bustle with messages from people seeking particular commemoratives or looking to swap coins of their own. There are hundreds of geocoins listed on eBay, with prices ranging up to $50 or even higher for rare editions. Many collectors have amassed inventories of thousands of coins, which they trade at events or online.

Most geocoins come engraved with a unique serial number provided by **Geocaching.com** or another tracking service (see Resources List, Appendix B).

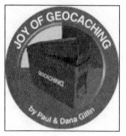

Like travel bugs, geocoin codes correspond to a unique Web page that tells something about the coin's origins and travels. The same rules that apply to travel bugs also apply to geocoins. Move them along quickly and update their status by logging pickups and drop-offs on the cache log pages.

Not all geocoins are meant to be tracked. Many are created specifically for distribution or sale to collectors and their codes are never activated. It's perfectly all right to keep coins you find in a geocache, but if the tracking number is live, you should correspond with the owner first. Some owners prohibit the collecting of activated coins, while others will ask for a fee to have their trackable taken out of circulation. Many owners distribute coins for commemorative or promotional purposes and are happy to let discoverers add them to their personal collections at no charge. They usually expect you to tell a good story on the log page, though.

Design for our *Joy of Geocaching* coin.

Make Your Own Geocoin

If you want to create a coin, dozens of manufacturers will be happy to oblige. Groundspeak maintains a list of approved suppliers and rules for creating approved geocoins at **tinyurl.com/mlfye9**. Be aware that the price listed on the manufacturers' websites, which usually ranges from $2–$4 per coin in small lots, can be deceptive. Those prices are for the most basic coins. If you want to add colors, finishes, raised surfaces, side etching, or a second side, the price goes up. Also, **Geocaching. com** charges $1.50 for each tracking code. By the time you're done, expect to pay $6–$8 per coin.

Most coin manufacturers will throw in the design service at little or no charge with a minimum order size. If you're not a designer, don't fret. You can build designs from website templates or commission designs from independent Web entrepreneurs. The cost of these services is plummeting as design work migrates overseas. Custom logo designs that used to cost $700–$1,000 from U.S. designers are now routinely turned out for $50 to $100 by operations in India.

Be careful not to use the Groundspeak logo, **Geocaching.com**, the Signal the Frog mascot, or any other registered trademark without playing by the rules. Groundspeak does permit some of its trademarks to be used without license fees, but there are strict guidelines in place. See the website address referenced above for specifics.

You should expect to see at least one round of proofs before your coin is committed to permanence. Check the colors, size, embossing, and particularly the spelling. Some dealers will let you pay extra for a sample of the real article. It's expensive, but if you're going to be minting 1,000 of these, it's probably worth the cost. You can't correct these things once they're out in the field.

Once your geocoins arrive, you'll probably want to save a few for your own collection, sell or trade some others, and cast some into the wild. If you want to track carefully the path your coins take, then activate them at the appropriate site before release. The coin manufacturer should provide you with a set of activation codes. You'll need two codes to activate each coin: The tracking number is stamped on the back of the coin and is visible to whomever holds the coin; the activation code is known only to the coin owner and is provided by the company that mints the coins. If you're going to send unactivated coins into the field, be aware that people need to contact you in order to activate them.

Like most aspects of geocaching, there aren't many hard rules. Geocoins make good gifts for geocachers and non-geocachers alike. They're also a great way to commemorate a special occasion in a distinctive manner. A blog called The Cachebug (**cachebug.blogspot.com**) does a good job of tracking the latest news about this topic.

Pathtags and Others

Some cachers who can't quite rationalize the thought of spending $1,000 or more on geocoins are turning to less expensive variations. **Pathtags** are miniature coins produced by some of the same organizations that make geocoins, but pathtags have no relation to Groundspeak. This is both a plus and a minus.

On the positive side, pathtags are much less expensive than Groundspeak-registered geocoins. They're also much smaller—about the size of a U.S. quarter. Pathtags have holes in them to make it easy for owners to display them on a pegboard or collect them on a keychain. Starter kits can be purchased for under $100. The downside of having no Groundspeak affiliation, of course, is that pathtags can't be tracked on **Geocaching.com.** But that's not a big issue, because pathtags are not technically trackables.

Each coin is etched with a serial number that corresponds to a unique owner, but unlike geocoins, pathtags are not meant to be moved from place to place. They are simply calling cards that owners leave for others who may "cross their path." Hence the name.

When you find a pathtag, you're asked to log the pickup at **Pathtags.com.** It's great if you can tell a little story about how you came upon the treasure, since that's the reason people release pathtags in the first place. Once you log your find, the tag is yours to keep or return to the wild. It's up to you, and you won't be yelled at either way. There are ways to track pathtags in the field, and you can find more information at **Pathtags.com.**

The use of **Digital Fish** was started by some avid geocachers in the San Francisco area who created little glass fish to use as signature items instead of coins or travel bugs. People who find them can log them on **Geofish.net.** While this is basically just another type of vanity trackage, it's an example of how geocachers can be innovative outside of the Groundspeak arena.

CHAPTER FIVE
Hiding a Geocache

Deermark feels tiny in Arches National Park as he seeks GCJG49. *Scott Wilcoxson (kepnfit)*

After you've spent a few months searching for other people's geocaches, you'll probably be tempted to place one of your own. This can be great fun. When you own a cache, you're in control. You make up your own mysteries and then watch how other people fare against them. "A clever cache is memorable if it's at the coordinates and you just can't seem to find it," says Steve of ventura_kids. "No bush hides, no digging in dirt, no sorting of rocks, just simple clever hides." And it's always a thrill to get your first FTF message, usually from someone who's delighted at the honor.

Sprinkler head cache.

Show Me The Cache says you should wait until you've seen some really interesting caches before you attempt to hide one yourself. "If all you have seen are a few lame caches, guess what you are likely to hide?" he asks.

Gary & Vicky think you should only place caches you'd like to find yourself, whether it's an interesting journey to get to the final, a remarkable destination, or a container that puts a smile on your face when you achieve the goal.

But placing a cache isn't necessarily simple, and there are responsibilities that go with being the "owner." For one thing, you are responsible for ongoing maintenance, which may mean trekking out in the middle of winter to replace a missing logbook or fix a pill bottle whose cap has cracked. For that reason, many owners maintain only a few geocaches.

Maintaining a cache can take dedication. InfiniteMPG remembers seeing a log for his Nowhere In Sight cache (GCT75R) that reported that one stage had melted from a brush fire. "I quickly adjusted my schedule and the next day spent four and a half hours mountain biking out to replace the stage," he says. "You might think it's a great idea to place a cache at the end of the 10-mile hike, but remember that if there's a problem, you have to return there to maintain it."

Those who count their hides in the hundreds usually rely on their contacts to help out with the maintenance work. As we noted in the "Waypoints: Geocaching Toolkit" section discussed previously, experienced geocachers usually carry an assortment of replacement items to repair caches that have been compromised. If your own network isn't very robust, you'll probably be on your own.

Another factor that owners must contend with is **Geocaching.com**'s review policy. The organization maintains a network of volunteers who screen every cache submitted for listing, and their styles are as different as their fingerprints. Our first five placements were all rejected by our screener due to problems that we didn't anticipate.

Gotchas

Geocaching.com provides a detailed list of rules about cache-hiding on its website, and it's a good idea to become familiar with these rules before making your first hide. In particular, here are some things to watch for:

Proximity—As a rule of thumb, your cache must be at least one-tenth of a mile from another cache. This may seem straightforward, but the rule also applies to intermediate stages in a multi-cache if they involve containers of any kind. In one case, we were twice rejected because our placement overlapped stages in a seven-part multi placed in the same area. We thought we were in the clear, but we hadn't bothered to complete and log every stage of the overlapping puzzle. In that case, we finally did what many cachers do when frustrated: We contacted the owner. He provided us with the coordinates of every stage and we were able to re-hide our ammo box outside of his domain.

In general, proximity shouldn't be a problem, but high-density areas require special vigilance. Load up your GPSr with a pocket query for the immediate vicinity that includes found and temporarily disabled caches, and be sure you are at least one-tenth of a mile from anything else that might be a problem. Note that in some densely populated areas, screeners will make exceptions to the proximity rule.

Prohibited areas—As noted earlier, the National Park Service prohibits the placement of caches on its properties, so don't even try. You can place caches that don't involve a container, such as waymarks (formerly called virtual caches; see the Waypoints section on "Geocaching Variations" following Chapter 2). Some state park services may have restrictions, but most seem more enthusiastic than apprehensive about the game. Still, it doesn't hurt to check. Other prohibited locations are government buildings, military installations, airports, dams, active railroad beds, and highway bridges.

High-security areas or those that may be targets of terrorist attack are the squishiest locations. For example, **Geocaching.com** prohibits the placement of caches within 150 feet of railroad tracks. If this number seems arbitrary, it is, but that's the rule. If your placement is even close to an area where security is an issue, you have a chance of being rejected. Very often this decision is at the discretion of the reviewer. If you have a good relationship with that person, you may be able to argue yourself into his or her good graces. However, our experience is that you shouldn't count on it.

Private property—Under no circumstances should you place a cache on another's property without obtaining permission. This usually isn't a problem, as many small business owners are delighted to have an excuse to bring visitors to their stores. But you may encounter another reaction if you're looking to place one in someone's foresty backyard. When in doubt, ask. If you don't get permission, you stand the chance of subjecting other players to embarrassment when an angry property owner asks just what the heck they're rooting for in the azaleas. And, if you do have permission, be sure to note that fact in the description so there's no confusion about whether players are welcome.

This doo-hickey may look like a geocache to players, but it looks much more suspicious to the authorities. *Ben Gracewood*

Suspicious Locations—Every couple of months, the press reports on another example of law-enforcement personnel being called upon to "defuse" a device that turns out to be a geocache. This is always a black eye for the game, and **Geocaching. com** is emphatic about avoiding containers and placements that may arouse suspicion. The photo at left is of a cache in Auckland, New Zealand, that mobilized local police. These incidents don't endear local authorities to geocachers and you should avoid any actions that may tempt fate.

Personal Injury—Geocaching.com disclaims responsibility for any injuries suffered by a cacher in pursuit of a goal, but that shouldn't ease your conscience if your hide causes harm to another. We learned the hard way that if people can't find your cache, they will sometimes go to extremes in the search. A pill bottle hide

Amazing Adventures

WE4NCS has endured a snake-infested swamp near the Peedee River for a smiley. It was March, so it was cool enough to keep the snakes calm and sleepy. WE4NCS, along with Dave Coffman (nittany dave) and Matt Busch (wimseyguy), were walking on ground that started quaking with each footstep, which, they discovered, was floating on the water of the swamp. All of a sudden, all three "old men" (WE4NCS' words, not ours!) were up to their hips in swamp water with lazy snakes all around. Because there was no direct route to the cache, which was about 300 feet in front of them, they had to take a circuitous route. Halfway through the swamp, with their hip waders filled with water, they saw a place in the swamp that smacked of alligator. They were sure they had just missed the prehistoric creature. So they snagged the cache and hightailed it out of the swamp as fast as the trio could muster, which was pretty slowly given that the muck of the swamp floor was as thick as glue. The irony of caches like this is that these smileys count just as much as a simple lamp post cache (LPC).

we had rated a modest 2/2 (difficulty 2/terrain 2 is a standard measure of cache accessibility) turned out to be a lot trickier than we had expected. One cacher ventured over a nearby fence and put his foot in a hole, severely twisting his ankle. We quickly amended the description to make it clear where visitors *shouldn't* go. That's why you should inspect the area for a good 50 feet around your hide and warn players of any hazards. Owners usually go out of their way to cite information about safety and special equipment.

That said, people who go after a cache rated 4/4 or above know that there is some risk involved. In Chapter 6, we discuss some of the physical challenges of these very difficult finds. Every extreme cacher we talked to understood that there were risks inherent in their pursuits.

Commercial/Promotional Language—Geocaching.com maintains a strict policy against promoting commercial interests of any kind on its site or in its forums. Of course, if you want to pay an advertising fee, the rules are different. The volunteers who approve cache placements can be sticklers for this rule. We had one rejected because we said some nice words about a nearby nonprofit animal shelter. To avoid delays like this, don't promote any organization, no matter how worthy.

Joy of Ownership

There are three basic components to hiding a cache: choosing a container, choosing a location, and creating a good description. We'll look at the first two here. Descriptions are discussed in Chapter 3 ("Understanding Descriptions").

Typical geocache containers (left to right): ammo box (regular), nut jar (regular), pill bottle (small), bouillon cube jar (small), candy sleeve (micro), and bison tube (micro).

Choosing a Container

Call us old-fashioned, but we love the traditional ammo cans and large plastic boxes. There's so much you can put in them and it's such a challenge to hide an object that size so it can last for years without being discovered. That said, the clear trend in geocaching over the last couple of years has been toward "micro" and "nano" containers. They're easy to hide and don't require much preparation.

When choosing a container, the watchwords are **durable, waterproof**, and **concealable**. Larger containers are more appropriate for woods settings, while micros and nanos fit better in urban locations. When re-purposing a container such as a pill bottle, be sure it's sturdy enough to last for several years in the field, or be prepared to replace it. Loose caps, broken seams, and thin materials may cause problems after a year or two. Also, be careful about poking holes in containers in order to affix screws or hooks. The smallest opening can let in water and destroy log books. Seal any openings tightly with a hot glue gun.

Tips from the Experts

Baggies always rip. Better to get a good container than attempt to protect the log book with a plastic bag.

A great container is a birdfeeder with birdseed glued to the inside walls of the feeder. When a cacher looks at it, it looks full of birdseed, but really it's full of a log book.

—*Mrs. Captain Picard*

The durable, water-tight bison tube is a popular container.

For large or "regular" containers, the venerable ammunition box can't be beat. Sizes range from dictionary-sized to containers big enough to hold a small child (which we definitely don't recommend). They're camouflaged, watertight, and last for decades. Ammo cans are available at Army/Navy stores and many online outlets. Another popular option is the popular line of food storage containers made by Lock & Lock Co. They're watertight (most have rubber gasket seals around the edges),

Ammo can in its natural habitat.

Nano caches can be no larger than a pencil eraser.

durable, and come in many sizes. They're also a lot cheaper than ammo boxes. Our advice: Invest a couple of bucks in a brand-name container instead of using the freebies supplied by the supermarket. They'll last a lot longer, and that means fewer maintenance headaches for you.

Pill and vitamin bottles make excellent and economical **small containers**, but chances are you'll want to cover them with camouflage duct tape, which is available at sporting goods outlets. Five dollars will buy you more tape than you can use in a decade. Duct tape will also strengthen the container. Military decontamination (decon) kits also make great small cache containers. They're two to five inches long, cost less than $5, and lock tight against the elements.

The most popular **micro caches** are film canisters, which are becoming harder to find as people move to digital photography, and "bison tubes," which are small metal containers originally designed to hold pills. Bison tubes are named after their largest manufacturer, Bison Designs. Bison tubes are popular because they're watertight and can be hung by the attached ring or stuck to metal with a small magnet. They also come in many colors. You can buy them for about $1 each on eBay or through online geocaching specialty stores. Micros generally hold no more than a logbook, although some can accommodate small items of swag.

Nano containers are actually kind of cool. They can be no larger than the tip of a pencil eraser and contain very small log sheets that barely accommodate a set of initials. You can put nanos almost anywhere because there are so hard to see. They are particularly popular as urban containers.

The rusty bolt looks innocuous enough...

Until the top is unscrewed. *(Photos by Jan Kaláb)*

Micro and nano containers have flourished in recent years with the growth of urban caching and because, frankly, they're easy to hide. They can also turn a simple hide into an evil one. Don't criticize owners for stashing micro and nano containers in vast wooded areas. They do it to make the hunt that much more difficult.

There's no consensus on what is the largest geocache container ever placed. We asked around and the best candidate we found was from OzGuff, who is a bit of a local legend for the volume and creativity of his hides.

For his 300th hide, OzGuff placed a multi-stage puzzle that led to a 24-foot square storage container covered by a camouflage tarp and placed about 150 feet from the trail. "It was basically a thank-you to the caching community," he remembers. "I stocked it with premium stuff: a George Foreman grill, an AM/FM radio, and things like that. It was thanks for two fun years." This cache has been archived, but you can find the description. The multi puzzle is called Cache, Cacher, Cache! (GCQC5A).

Offbeat Containers

Just about anything durable and hollow can be a geocache container, but true aficionados delight in inventing their own original and deceptive vessels. There is actually a small cottage industry of enthusiasts who invent and sell containers disguised as logs, rocks, leaves, and even woodland animals. And some just prefer to apply their own devilish creativity. We spotlight a few favorites below.

- OzGuff created a string of caches he calls the "atypical" series because the containers are each a little offbeat. There's a Barbie doll with the log book hidden inside her torso, a garage door remote control, a soccer ball, a travel toothbrush container, and a mailbox, among other things. "Most folks get a laugh when they find the atypical containers," he says.
- InfiniteMPG has "cored out bones, put micro containers inside, and used Quikrete to mold the cap of the micro container nested into the bone. Some people have taken pictures of a person frustrated after looking for one of my hides for 15 minutes when they're sitting right on it."
- TreyB says the best cache container he ever saw was a film canister hidden in a button on a pedestrian crossing sign in Chicago. "It took me 15 minutes to find it," says TreyB, who rarely needs 15 minutes to find *anything*.
- Wheeler Dealers converted their garage into a workshop so they can make unique containers more easily. And that workshop gets used! Wheeler Dealers have more than 1,100 hides under their belts. They told us, "If there's a hole somewhere, we'll fill it with a geocache." Some of their favorite hides are fake chains and locks, buttons retrofitted into holes in artwork, and false rocks finished with stucco. They make sure to bring paint when they hide a cache so they can match the color tone exactly to the surroundings.

The only hard and fast rules governing geocache containers is that they can't be buried. They can be *all but* buried, but they must still be retrievable without digging. This leaves quite a bit of room for invention. And, avid geocachers have come up with some remarkable ideas for hiding those tiny log sheets.

CachingBox.com founder MacKenzie Martin has an inventory featuring ten custom containers, including a pinecone, switch plate, rock, sprinkler head, and the unique rattlesnake cache. The pinecone container is "the most labor-intensive, but also the most popular," he says. "People pick up one or two with pretty much every order."

Martin likes to find ordinary objects in the woods and attach bison tubes to them in creative places. In addition to purchasing his normal inventory, geocachers have requested custom orders like scorpions and lizards. He advises buyers to harmonize the container with the environment.

"The best approach is to go to the location where you're going to hide the cache and look around," Martin advises. "If it's an urban area, you can find metallic wall plates at the hardware store. If you're around grass, you can do a sprinkler cache. Make sure it fits in with the surroundings."

If you decide to build your own container, think durable and waterproof. "Glue is important," he says. "It's going to get hot and glue can melt. Water-based super glues work the best. If you're going to use paint, be sure it's water-resistant. If you're going to put a bison tube into something, use a drill. Bison tubes fit well into drill holes and are less likely to fall out."

For true aficionados, the Holy Grail is creating a cache that is so well concealed that visitors can actually touch the container without knowing it. Stressmaster, who has more than 200 hides on his tally, is a master of caching disguise. One of his favorite tactics is laying the cache near ground level. InfiniteMPG contributed photos of some of his favorite camouflage jobs, which are shown in the next few pages.

And to satisfy his more evil side, Stressmaster has used fake fur material wrapped around a tube and placed inside a hollow tree. When you reach into the tree, the first thing you feel is fur. Can you say "sadistic"?

InfiniteMPG is a bit of a legend around Bradenton, Florida, for his dastardly disguises. "I've had a few cases of people spending four hours looking for a cache they had in their hand and didn't know it," he says. Geocaches hidden in hollowed-out tree branches have actually been carried by players for hours who didn't know that the target they were seeking was in their hands the whole time.

Inventive containers are actually a lot harder to create than you may think. In order to blend in with their surroundings, they need to look like part of the scenery. There is little you can buy at the hardware store that meets the criteria. A rubber snake picked up at the toy store is going to look like, well, a toy snake. In contrast, MacKenzie Martin's rattler is sculpted by a native American craftsman to look like the real thing. If your container looks contrived, you'll get humiliated in the log comments. And who wants to deal with that kind of abuse?

On the other hand, blending a little bit of real-life nature into the container can create a great hide. Stressmaster revels in Gorilla Glue, an epoxy-based adhesive that will "glue just about anything to anything. You can glue rocks to metal," he says. "I've covered an ammo can with lava rocks and placed it in a lava rock garden and it disappears," he says. "I'll coat the side of the ammo can with Gorilla Glue, immerse it in material like lava rocks and let it stick. I've had people stand on my ammo cans and not know it. They had just settled into the rock. It was findable, but you couldn't see it."

A Selection of InfiniteMPG's Favorites

We found that after hiding just a few geocaches, we developed almost a sixth sense about locations. When passing by a stone wall or a hollow tree stump, we look at each other and nod, "Great spot." Pill bottles (and really anything sturdy and watertight) are no longer discarded at our house; they're quickly covered with camouflage tape in preparation for their eventual deployment in combat.

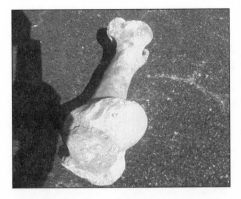

The bone cache.

Tree stump cache.

Cinder block cache.

Switch plate cache.

Photos by Scott Veix (InfiniteMPG)

Owning a geocache has its own unique rewards. Each discovery has a story, and players are sometimes effusive in their comments and compliments. It's rewarding to get the occasional "great cache!" or "evil hide!" and even a TFTC ("Thanks for the cache") is appreciated. Finders can sometimes be quite creative, too. We had one cache we dubbed "24," although it had nothing to do with the popular television show. Nevertheless, one of the first finders wrote a log in the form of a journal entry from the popular thriller. "If I didn't get feedback on the caches, I'd probably stop hiding them," says InfiniteMPG, who has nearly 300 hides to his credit. "Owners put a lot of effort into hiding and maintaining caches. It's nice to know it was worth it."

Hiders and seekers actually have a sort of unspoken lingo that communicates appreciation and approval. The more ingenious the hide, the longer and more detailed the log entries are likely to be. It's actually considered a bit of an insult to leave a short log entry for a cache that was brilliantly hidden.

By the same token, a description that misleads players into thinking a cache is easier to find than it really is, or that subjects them to physical danger, will be rewarded with blunt feedback. Geocachers are a pretty civil group in general, but they have ways of making their displeasure known. If your hide is generating immediate disapproval, fix it.

Basic hides are easy, but the most delightful ones lead players to new and exciting locations or are accompanied by good stories. Owners often use a geocache as a way to lead people to a place that has sentimental value or historical significance to the area. We go out of our way to look for these treasures, because they help us understand our own community better or learn more about the history of the place we are visiting.

Most Extreme Geocache?

Nobody keeps formal records of the most difficult geocache in the world to find, but many people would probably agree that it is Rainbow Hydrothermal Vents (GCG822). The goal is a small plastic sea horse with a travel bug placed beside a hydrothermal vent about 7,000 feet below the ocean. The owner explains that expeditions regularly visit this area, but that only a few dozen people each year have the opportunity to get that far. "I presume one will be a geocacher like me... sooner or later!" writes owner Lord British, who has placed one geocache and found one geocache in the past seven years.

We'll admit a bias for large cache containers. They are more difficult to hide, but more rewarding if you can come up with a crafty solution. They also reward finders with a place to deposit trackables and interesting trinkets. There are even geocaches designated as "travel bug hotels" that function as stopping points for trackable items making their way around the globe.

Logbooks

Next to the container, a logbook is the most important element of a geocache. As we noted earlier, a cache is considered logged when the finder signs the logbook; noting the find on **Geocaching.com** is optional. Choosing a hardy and appropriate logbook and protecting it are a bit more involved than you might think. The book needs to be an appropriate size for the container and include as much free space as possible so that you won't have to make frequent visits to replace it. It also needs to be protected from the elements. Water can quickly leak into an improperly sealed container and destroy the paper.

Logbooks come in different sizes, depending on the container. For ammo boxes and Lock & Locks containers, a small spiral notebook is ideal. Be sure to seal the book in a plastic zippered bag for extra protection and include a few spare bags for others to use when the first one invariably becomes too ragged. Even better, seal the logbook inside a small plastic container that won't quickly become victim to pen points and other sharp objects.

Micro and nano caches require scrolled logbooks. These can be as simple as a few strips of paper stapled together, but it's always nice to use one of the many templates that cachers have shared on the Web. **Geocaching.com** has a small collection on its "Hide & Seek a Cache" page, but the resource we like best is Geocacher University (**geocacher-u.com/content/blogsection/8/54/**). The site's free downloads section features logbook templates for everything from nanos to waterproof match holders. There's even a two-page printable brochure that explains geocaching. Stashing one of these in your container can save your cache from a Muggling. There are even videos that show you how to cut and fold your own logbook from a sheet of plain paper.

If you're willing to spend a few extra pennies for protection, consider Rite in the Rain or National Geographic Adventure Paper. Rite in the Rain is water-resistant paper, although not fully waterproof. You can buy small spiral notebooks made with this material for about three dollars each. Adventure Paper is fully waterproof and can be purchased for about 80 cents per sheet. Both are easy to find in online stores.

Log books that become soaked must be attended to by the owner or a designate. Avid cachers will often carry spare logbooks with them to save the owner a trip to replace a full or soggy log. Sometimes you can get away with simply posting a log entry asking future visitors to bring a replacement with them. But you can't always count on this. A bit of protection up front can save you a long hike after the next rainstorm.

This container looks like an ordinary light bulb—until you unscrew the bottom.

Choosing a Location

Pick a place that gives you the opportunity to show off your knowledge of the area. Tell stories and reveal little-known details about the location. Puzzle caches may challenge seekers to gather bits of information from multiple spots—dates on a plaque, letters in a name, numbers in an address—to piece together the final coordinates. The more you can relate these puzzles to local lore, the more you'll delight your visitors.

Hiding spots should provide ample protection from the elements as well as from the eyes of passersby. As a cache owner, you are responsible for the preservation and integrity of your hide. If a cache disappears, it's your obligation to replace or disable it. For this reason, few owners place caches very far from home.

Always choose locations that are safe and warn players if there are potential dangers nearby. **Geocaching.com** prominently disclaims any responsibility for injuries to players, but you don't want to live with the guilt that your hiding spot causes someone to break a leg.

Be aware of local conditions. We live in New England, which is covered by snow several months of the year. For that reason, we avoid hiding caches on the ground if we can. Areas that are covered by ice during the winter may also present hazards, so think before you place. In warmer climates, consider the effects of boiling sun, harmful plants, and local wildlife.

Consider the reward you want to get from the experience. A devilishly difficult hide probably won't be found very often, but you'll enjoy the logs of the people who persist. An easy find may generate a lot of logs, but they won't be very exciting to read. Most veteran owners mix up a combination of simple and difficult hides to keep themselves interested and players on their toes.

WAYPOINTS
Memorable Hides

The most common hiding spots are under a rock, inside a tree or hollowed-out stump, and magnetically attached to the back of a sign. Parking lights in lots across America are festooned with film canisters hidden under the plastic skirts at the base of light poles. These routine locations are good for running up your numbers, but they don't challenge you very much. Most people won't congratulate you for putting them through two hours of mindbending frustration, but then again geocachers aren't like most people. Some of the greatest enjoyment we got out of researching this book was asking expert cachers to share their stories of "great hides." These were caches that put them through mental and physical gymnastics, but rewarded them with ingenious placement, camouflage, or containers. Here are some of the best stories they told us.

Which of these Doesn't Belong?

Steve of ventura_kids explains one of his favorites.

> The owner (Agoura Charger) was known for some devious hides. We had already searched the area and found nothing. Obviously we were not looking in the right spot. My daughter, Theresa, concluded that if the cache was exactly at the coordinates, it must be directly over our heads. We split up and started scouring the tree canopy above. Theresa spotted a great big pinecone in the oak branches above. "A pinecone in an *oak* tree? I found it, I found it!" she cried.
>
> And so she did. She was happy until I explained that we need to actually sign the logsheet and that it was 40 feet above us! After a bit of searching the area, we found the other end of the string two trees away and lowered the cache for signing.

Go Get It—We Dare Ya!

Sometimes you don't even need to hide the target. We learned of one high-difficulty cache that is actually a large ammo box painted bright orange and placed atop a pillar on an island in the middle of a rushing river. The cache is visible from a half-mile away, but the trick is getting to it!

InfiniteMPG is proud of another large container that he disguised so well that he was able to hide it in plain sight. "It's a full-sized Lock & Lock right in the view of 10,000 people," he says, with no small amount of pride. The key is to camouflage the container so it blends in with its environment, like a mailbox cache set amid a cluster of mailboxes.

Wrong Number

Mrs. Captain Picard's favorite find was in the Northwest. There are a few clues in the description of the cache, including the address of the final location and a toll-free phone number to call if you need help. The coordinates bring you to the front of a factory. On the porch is an old-fashioned pay telephone with an "Out of Order" sign on it. If you dial the "Help" number on that telephone, you'd expect something wonderful to happen (cache found?), but all you get when you pick up the handset to dial is a recording: "This phone is out of service. For further help, dial this number ...." Obviously, you're barking up the wrong tree. But every cacher knows persistence is the key to success. If you dial the toll-free help number during the out-of-service message, you hear a series of beeps. Mrs. Captain Picard had to dial three times to get the cadence just right, but she was rewarded when the bottom of the phone popped out, revealing the cache container.

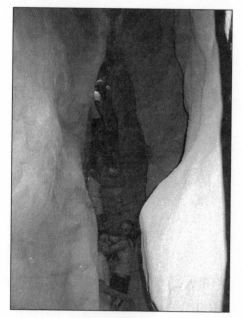

Scaling the Basilisk. *The DAKGirls (via geocaching.com)*

Rock Star

The Basilisk in California (GCPX5Q) requires a 13-mile trek over unpaved road to even reach the beginning point. But then it gets even trickier. "The Basilisk enjoys feasting on most varieties of humans, including geocachers," says the description page. The Basilisk is inspired by a creature from the Harry Potter series, and the description features "Hints From Harry on How to Slay this Basilisk." The terrain is rated at 5, but even that understates the difficulty. The Basilisk "challenged me to overcome my fears and push myself past the edge of my known capabilities," wrote Mrs. Captain Picard in the log. You start at the bottom of a very narrow slot passageway inside Sandstone Canyon and crawl up impossibly steep walls. The logs reveal that many people use ropes to scale the walls. Others shimmy up, seemingly defying physics. While some quit halfway to the top, an amazing 46 out of the first 50 logs show a successful find.

Choose Wisely

Another favorite cache of Mrs. Captain Picard's is one she placed herself. It's called "Kirk vs. Picard" (GC18433), where a cacher can vote for their favorite Enterprise captain. The two voting boxes were originally not that far away from each other. The Picard box had a slit in the top for incoming voting slips. The Kirk box, however, was covered in chains and locks, with no way to slide a piece of paper in for a vote. "Do you honestly think a cacher called 'Mrs. Captain Picard' would let you vote for Kirk?" Mrs. Captain Picard asks. The chained box was repeatedly stolen, so the second iteration of the cache (in a more remote park) cites the Kirk box at the South Pole. The Mrs. promises she'll tally those votes when she makes it down there the next time.

Just Plain Gross

WE4NCS is known for evil hides, not the least of which is a 5/5 called "Holy Wastewater! (She it?)" in which he warns cachers against, well, against everything you can warn people who go for 5/5s: infection, disease, treacherous conditions, water-borne viruses, raw sewage, you name it. "If you suffer from any form of heart disease, dizziness, or vertigo, discretion is advised," the description declares. "The nearby Lake Crabtree is full of PCBs, which are hazardous. Don't even think about going near it. There is toxic waste and sewage being discharged from the nearby wastewater treatment plant. Be sure your health and life insurance are up-to-date.... If you are afraid of alligators, bacteria, microbes, bad odors, methane gas, staph infections,

Some people were troubled by this photo of a visitor to Holy Wastewater! HexTheKiwi (via geocaching.com)

mosquitoes carrying West Nile virus, viruses in general, flesh-eating bacteria, or cannot swim, then you should avoid this cache."

Almost every log for Holy Wastewater! is disgustingly graphic. CacheCredit wrote: "I am not sure what makes up the bottom of this 'toilet,' but whatever it is, the container was glued in place by this *merde*. I finally managed to work my fingers in the goo and under the cache enough to pull it free. Once I got the cache into view, my eyes and nose were treated to sensations that I am sure will be burned into my memory for the rest of my life." Fraygirls remarked, "This was without a doubt the worst cache that we have ever attempted to find." CarolinaCardsFan noted, "Nothing could have prepared me for this cache.... I knew it wouldn't be pleasant. But ick! This was awful!"

WE4NCS loves this hide, and he's not alone. A geocacher from the United Kingdom came to North Carolina *just* to find this cache. A swift-water rescuer from Ohio warned WE4NCS in no uncertain terms that this hide was unsafe and should be removed. So either WE4NCS is putting all seekers of this find in danger of triggering another bubonic plague, or else there's a trick he's playing on us. The cache was Muggled in early 2009 and has been replaced by "Holy Wastewater II," which is in the same vein as the first terrible hide. Go look for this one in North Carolina—if you dare!

Fill'er Up!

Mike Robinson (bluedevils23) tells of another ingenious bit of geocache engineering:

> In the Lake of the Ozarks area of Missouri, I found one of my favorite caches. The owner asked that you bring a gallon of water with you. When we arrived at the coordinates, we found a four-foot section of PVC pipe attached to the back of a telephone pole. When we poured the gallon of water into the top of the PVC pipe, a small cache about the size of a medicine bottle floated up to the top. The pipe had small drain holes drilled in the bottom so that the next hunter would have to fill it again. I loved this one.

Strikingly Obvious

Not all of WE4NCS' caches are difficult. He owns a 1/1.5 on a guardrail that has signs blanketing the immediate vicinity shouting "CACHE IS HERE!" with big arrows pointing at it. In the description, he wrote: "It makes even those many guardrail and streetlight pole caches look hard, and it redefines the park-and-grab cache. If you cannot find this one, it is because you haven't been here yet." The hint is: "The only hint you need here is be able to read English!"

Engineering Genius

EMC of Northridge, CA, has a favorite find in California: a multi in which the final container is on the other side of a fence from a trailer park. There's a bolt that looks just a little bit out of place, and when she pulled on it, up popped a spatula with the cache attached to it. She also heard music that was queued up just for the find. In the trailer park, there's a small radio band that comes into play earlier in the multi. At designated coordinates, EMC tuned her radio to a certain station to hear a strange weather report, complete with the coordinates for the next stage of the cache.

Does that Log Look Familiar to You, Too?

Show Me The Cache's favorite hide is now archived, but it was a multi called Deja Vu (GCBAA5). This multi brought you to a log, at the end of which were identical coordinates to another stage, which was a nearby water tower. The coordinates hidden at the water tower directed you via a different trail to the original hollow log. The path was confusing enough that people often didn't know they had just walked in a loop. "It was my honor to witness two of the world's leading cachers struggle with this one," he says. It has since been archived because of maintenance problems, but the logs are still on the site for your entertainment.

CACHER PROFILE
InfiniteMPG

Photo by Cathy O'Brien

Geocaching.com handle: InfiniteMPG
Name: Scott Veix
Claim to fame: Noted for his devious hides. At nearly 1:3, his hide:find ratio is one of the highest of any active geocacher.
Location: Bradenton, Florida
Caching since: March 6, 2005
Total finds: 908
Total hides: 290
Preferred GPSr: Garmin 60 CSx

Favorite Cache Types

"I enjoy caches of any type in any type of location as long as there's a high degree of uniqueness or creativity in the hide technique, location, or listing. Variety is the spice of geocaching!"

Special Equipment

In addition to his GPSr, he carries a Palm Tungsten TX loaded with pocket query info and extra batteries. "I have a passion for photography, so I often have a camera in tow, too, even when kayaking and caching. And my cell phone for emergencies and for the weather radar, which is pretty important in Florida."

Great Caching Stories

"In doing some genealogy searching for my mother, I found a long-lost cousin living in Christchurch, New Zealand. We began talking about family and my kids, Mitch and Nikki. He e-mailed me stating his wife was pregnant, and then after their son was born, it turned out he also named his son Mitch. So I made a travel bug of my son's little 'Mitch' bike name tag and sent it off to find its way to my cousin's son in New Zealand. Within two months, the bug traveled 9,323 miles from a travel bug motel cache in Tampa and was hand-delivered to my cousin's son in Christchurch. That got me hooked on geocaching big time."

Photo by Cathy O'Brien

"My girlfriend, Cathy, and I were geocaching near Tampa and looking for a geocache that was on the other side of a river from us. I found a downed tree that spanned the river, dropped my gear, and scampered across. I found the cache and, while signing the log, heard something nearby that I assumed to be a family of wild hogs. I quickly zoomed back across the tree, weaving between the branches, only to see at the last moment that Cathy had grabbed my camera and snapped a picture. A little while later the local reviewer asked if I would let them use that picture for their official 2007 Florida Geocaching Association geocoin." (above)

Most Memorable Find

"Nowhere In Sight (GCT75R). Cathy and I stumbled across Gilley Creek Track using the *Southwest Florida Water Management District Recreation Guide*. Gilley Creek Track is a 5,700-acre preserve with many miles of trails and no geocaches. I decided to place a long multi there. It took 11 miles of hiking. I was new to the game and I forgot my water and did just about everything wrong, but managed to put out a tricky 5/4.5 challenge. It caught on with other local cachers and we started the 'Nowhere' caches at Gilley, which have grown to around 50 hides now."

Words of Wisdom

"Be observant for something that's a little out of place. Look for threads, bottle caps, and pieces of plastic.

"Respect the hider. It's discouraging when people make disparaging comments in the listing. Owners work hard so somebody can have fun. It's also considerate to put more than just a 'TFTC' in a log. It's rewarding when somebody makes an effort to write a thoughtful comment.

"If you're new to the game, be careful about logging a DNF. I had two DNFs one day that said the cache was 'definitely missing.' I put off my lunchtime plans only to find it hidden exactly where it should be. Then I noticed that one of the cachers who logged the DNF had only one find and the other had only two. They probably should have gained a little experience before making that judgment."

CHAPTER SIX
Caching to the Limits

Extreme geocacher DJ Trievel seeks a 5/5 geocache. *Dutch Sanders (Linuxxpert)*

We encountered two kinds of extreme geocachers when researching this book, and they couldn't be more different. In fact, they don't like being lumped together in the same category because their approach to the game is diametrically opposed. Nevertheless, we couldn't resist spotlighting these people in the same chapter because both groups push the game to its logical limits. It's just that one of them uses a car.

Extreme geocachers place and hunt for targets that require extreme skill, physical fitness, and a tolerance for occasional terror. Power cachers cope with sleeplessness, anxiety, and mental exhaustion in their attempts to log the maximum number of finds in 24 hours. We hope you enjoy meeting them. Let's start with the crazy ones.

Extreme Cachers

When Wouter "Dutch" Sanders was growing up in Europe, he was fond of windsurfing, hiking in the Alps, and engaging in any "crazy stuff" he could find. Moving to the United States (specifically Macungie, Pennsylvania) and getting married settled him down a bit, but the spirit of adventure was still there.

Linuxxpert (so-named because of some early computer work he had done) discovered geocaching in 2007. Like many novices, Sanders started with the standard parking-lot and suburban finds, but he quickly grew bored. He noticed that some geocaches carried much higher difficulty/terrain ratings, including a few that were classified as 5/5—the very pinnacle of geocaching challenge.

Caches rated 5/5 are rare. If you were to draw a circle with a radius of 500 miles around Knoxville, Tennessee—a 785,000-square-mile area that reaches roughly from Baltimore to Jacksonville, Florida—you would find only 236 5/5 classifications out of the tens of thousands of caches in that range. A hide with a difficulty rating of 5 is "a serious mental/physical challenge that requires specialized knowledge, skills, or equipment," according to the **Cacheopedia.com** website. A terrain rating of 5 means the cache "requires specialized equipment (for example, scuba gear, rock-climbing gear, a boat, or a four-wheel-drive vehicle) and the skill to use it, or is otherwise extremely difficult." In other words, you'd better be in excellent shape to attempt a 5/5 geocache. Or, you'd better be a little nuts.

Linuxxpert is both. Among his 368 finds are 21 rated 5/5 and dozens more rated higher than 3.5 difficulty or terrain. He's also placed four 5/5s and several others rated at the upper end of difficulty.

Linuxxpert's geocaching adventures may involve ropes, ladders, mining helmets, and life rafts. He frequently places himself in situations that others would consider dangerous, even life-threatening. But for this extreme geocacher, part of the fun is conquering his fears. "I love to see people pushed to the limits," he says.

He practices what he preaches. Linuxxpert has rappelled off cliffs over 100 feet high and dangled from railroad trestles spanning major rivers. He has spent over ten hours to find a single geocache and has tracked down some multi-stage puzzles that had 11 stages. "Some of the stages you can find in five minutes, some take two hours," Sanders says. "That's one of the thrills of the game."

His hides are as daunting as his finds. For one recent placement (GC1G86E), his tongue-in-cheek warning stated:

> Do NOT attempt this cache if you are not in good physical shape, or if you are afraid of heights. Climbing gear WILL be needed, and you may get your feet wet. WEAR A HELMET WHILE CLIMBING THIS PILLAR AND/OR WHILE STANDING NEAR THE BASE! There is a lot of loose concrete debris that will fall down. Watch out that you do not knock the container off the pillar with your gear. It will kill you when hit, or more important, it will damage the container.

Rare Breed

Jef Spencer (SNSpencer) is another thrill seeker. In the fall of 2007, he teamed up with a companion and headed out to grab and replace a 5/5 underwater container near Lake Tahoe that had been reported to be leaking water (GCG62F). He tells the story:

> We grabbed a few caches on our way up the mountain, then rented a kayak to go 700 feet out on the lake and do what we came to do. That's when the day became an adventure. By the time we arrived at the boat launch, the wind had picked up and the water was getting rough. We headed out anyway, and found the cache on our first try about 12 feet below the surface. But a gust of wind suddenly blew us away. Within seconds, the GPSr showed we were 130 feet away.
>
> We circled back, found the cache, and were blown away again. This cycle was repeated over and over. We finally decided that on the next pass I would dive into the water with the new container, dive down, unhook the old, hook on the new, and swim back to the kayak.
>
> I rolled off the kayak with the new container in hand and swam down, but I couldn't find the carabiner holding the old container on the anchor's rope. So I had to pull the whole rope back to the surface. That wasn't so hard, but the coffee can filled with cement that served as the anchor made it a real challenge! Kicking as hard as I could to stay afloat in the surf, I struggled to switch the containers, but the anchor was too much for me. I had to let the rope go.
>
> Defeated, I swam back to the now-overturned kayak, where Dichroic was floating in the water. We took a short rest, holding onto the kayak, while I put on my life vest. We righted the kayak and paddled back to shore. Waiting for us there was a park ranger who'd been called by

someone who thought we were drowning. We were okay, but the worst thing is that we were defeated! Mark my words: We will be back!

Life on the Edge

"Feeling like I'm going to die is exhilarating," says George Merenich, a Dorrance, Pennsylvania-based extreme geocacher who goes by the handle of keoki_eme. "If it doesn't involve a hike that means risking at least a little of my life, then I don't want to do it."

Keoki_eme and Linuxxpert enjoy a friendly competition in their region. Each says the other is nuts and both go to great lengths to prove his rival correct. They place caches intended to be so difficult that the other can't find them. So far, neither has the upper hand, although keoki_eme takes particular pride in having subjected Linuxxpert to ten and a half hours of hell to retrieve The Gauntlet (GC1NEPJ).

As keoki_eme tells it, "The Gauntlet is at least eight stages with an extreme elevation change. It's a killer hike for about a mile-and-a-half; you're almost going straight up. Every stage is tough. At least three stages require rope. I conned my brother to help me place it and I don't think he'll ever go back in the woods again."

The cache description begins with a four-minute YouTube video that advises the player to bring at least 150 feet of rope and plenty of water. "Start your journey EARLY," it recommends. "This ain't no walk in the park."

Indeed it isn't. The experience of completing The Gauntlet is best summed up by this edited log entry from Clancy's Crew, which found the final in March 2009:

> Although we had all rappelled down structures, done some free climbing, and climbed many radio towers, some bridge girders, and a telephone pole with spikes, the whole ascending technique was new to us.... My trip down the cliff didn't take long, although the lack of a wall to push off the last 15–20 feet was disconcerting. The highlight of the trip for me: After nine hours, I ascended a structure at one of the last stages, grabbed the cache, and ended up hanging in mid-air while removing the ascending gear. You have to trust the safety gear and harness, because it took two hands to remove the carabineer, pulley, and other equipment, with nothing to hold on to, and snow, ice and rocks below.

Now we know what you're thinking, but don't worry—the cache wasn't damaged.

Keoki_eme and Linuxxpert are sometimes joined by Maureen McArdelle, who got hooked on extreme geocaching when it taught her how to rock climb. Like

A member of Team Getz ponders life from 40 feet up. Note the smiley. *Dean Roth*

other extreme geocachers we interviewed, the challenge of pushing herself to the limit is an important motivator. Extreme geocaching "has made me feel more empowered," she says. "There is nothing I can't do. You place it, I can get it. You create that puzzle and I will solve it. It has given me more confidence in myself."

Being female has raised the stakes, since so few extreme cachers are women. She enjoys the odd blend of camaraderie and competition that's typical of extreme sports enthusiasts. Players use good-natured insults to urge each other on. Her male compansions "are always teasing me about what color bandana I am going to wear, what color my toenails are going to be painted," she said. But the taunts help her along. "I honestly don't think I would have gone over the top on any of [Linuxxpert's] pillar caches (GC1F925 and GC1G86E) without Dutch standing there telling me I am such 'a girl' if I couldn't do it," she says. And she adds, with some pride, "I climb barefoot and I think it amazes them."

Hiding What They Find

With 5/5 geocaches being so challenging and rare, the people who find them are also like the people who hide them. Linuxxpert recalls his favorite hide, Conquer Your Fears (GC17VAR):

> There's a big industrial park on the Lehigh River and this cache is hidden near an old iron furnace. There's a[n abandoned] train trestle that crosses the Lehigh River and one of the containers is underneath the bridge. You have to crawl out to the middle of the river on the rail trestle and then climb down. The hint says to "look for what all geocachers desire" which is a smiley. I painted a smiley on the bridge.
>
> In another stage, you have to crawl down into a hole that used to be an old iron furnace. And in the last stage, you have to crawl into the ceiling of another tunnel and make your way around a 90-degree bend.

Keoki_eme remembers another Linuxxpert challenge called "Too Difficult, Too Dangerous And Just Too Crazy!" (GC1812Z):

> The first stage is on a[n abandoned] railroad trestle 30 feet above the river, but you have to climb a support tower another 20 feet above the trestle. The second stage is a 40-foot-high concrete pillar in the middle of the woods that you have to climb without a ladder. The third stage takes you down a long tunnel for several hundred feet, and the next stage is hidden in an old signal light.
>
> The final is another trestle that's missing most of its railroad ties. You have to balance yourself across the beams and walk to the middle of the river. There's a magnetic ammo can that you can get to by crawling across the trestle.

Extreme-difficulty geocachers don't play by the same rules as everyone else. One thing they agree upon is that after subjecting searchers to an hours-long physical ordeal, they won't finish them off with a devious hide. "I make it a physical challenge to get there but there's no way you're going to miss the cache when you arrive," says keoki_eme.

They're also quick to call owners for advice on how to attack a challenge, and the owners are pretty reasonable about helping out. Everyone knows this is a potentially deadly pursuit, and they don't want to make a determined player's job more difficult than it has to be.

And even the extremists will admit that some finds are barely worth the effort. Asked if he remembers a time when he thought he was going to die, keoki_eme remembers one adventure on the Hawaiian island of Kauai with Tunnel #1 (GC146Q9) and The Other Way To Hanalei (GCHH2F):

> It was the most grueling hike I've ever had. It was two-and-a-half miles on a mud trail as narrow as six inches from start to the finish. Then there was a mile-long tunnel with only a little dot of light at the other end and six inches of water all the way. It took us 45 minutes to get through the tunnel. Then we had to walk back the whole way again. My wife, Amy, was exhausted. I remember thinking, "If she goes down, there's no way we're getting out of here." I'm not sure I would do it again, but I'm damned glad I did it.

Power Caching: Joy in Numbers

Ed Manley, the man we met at the very beginning of this book, who had planned to end his life before he found geocaching, prepared for GeoWoodstock IV for months. The annual gathering of thousands of enthusiastic geocachers had been a fixture on his calendar for years, but this year's event was different. In 2006, GeoWoodstock would take place in Dallas, one of the caching capitals of the world.

Holding GW IV in Dallas was like staging a wine lover's convention in Burgundy. The Dallas-Fort Worth area is infested with geocaches. In one six-square-mile area of Dallas alone, there are more than 80. Within about a 10-mile radius of Dallas-Fort Worth Airport, there are an incredible 940 caches.

So this was the geocaching Olympics, and Manley (TheAlabamaRambler) wasn't going to pass up an opportunity to break the world record of caches found in a 24-hour period: an incredible 246 found by a team in Jacksonville, Florida, in October 2004. Manley thought it was possible to log 300 finds in one day, a figure that would have seemed absurd just a few years earlier because of the relative sparseness of hides.

The planning took more than two months. TheAlabamaRambler and seven other enthusiasts—three Americans and four Germans—had met and become friendly in geocaching forums over the last couple of years. They reached a consensus that Dallas was the chance to break the world record and, operating as a loosely confederated team, they had scoured the list of cache candidates to identify the optimal route.

They boiled it down to 500 cache possibilities, but that was just the beginning. Each cache owner needed to be contacted individually and had to agree to participate in the record attempt. Not all owners approve of team caching, you see, and the record attempt would be made by a group of eight men who, in the interest of time, would sign the logbook only once. Owners had to be cool with that.

Fortunately, the owners thought the thrill of being part of a record attempt was enough incentive to bend the rules. Everyone agreed. Meanwhile, a few of the members began playing with Microsoft Streets and Trips software to create an optimal route. Time was of the essence. Team members calculated that they could spend no more than three minutes looking for any one cache.

The 12-person Chevrolet van would have a driver, a scribe, and a group of designated hunters. When the location was reached, members would jump out of the van and search for the cache in a choreographed arrangement. While a few were searching, others would be in their van feverishly preparing for the next find.

The team gathered on Friday evening, laptops in hand, to go through a practice run. They hadn't gone very far when it became clear that they had a problem. The process of digging the logbook out of each cache was going to slow them down to the point that the 300-find goal would be impossible. So they devised a workaround: Instead of signing the logbook, they would use a felt-tip pen to mark the outside of each found container. They believed that mark would be sufficient proof that they had found the cache and, after all, the purpose of the logbook was mainly to establish proof of the find.

On Saturday morning, the team hit the road in the van for what would become one of the most memorable days of TheAlabamaRambler's life. "We laughed the whole time," he says. "The Germans didn't speak English, and we didn't speak German. You can imagine the scene!"

Twenty-four caffeine-fueled hours later, the team staggered back to their hotel. They were bleary and exhausted, but they had found 312 caches out of 352 attempts, obliterating the previous record. In the end, they would agree to record only 295 of those finds, the result of a dispute that arose when the team split up to retrieve a trove of 17 caches clustered together. In fact, a debate raged on Groundspeak forums for nearly three weeks after the team's feat was recorded, with members debating nuances of the caching rules.

The record wouldn't stand for long. In late August 2009, a team of three geocachers—f0t0m0m, ventura_kids, and EMC of Northridge, CA—logged 413 finds in 24 hours (see sidebar next page).

Geocachers, it appears, are sticklers for the rules. Several forum members took issue with the Dallas team's decision to sign the caches on the outside rather than opening the log books and signing each one individually. Some members argued that record-setting attempts in themselves debased the spirit of geocaching by reducing the game to a mere numbers competition.

One for the Record Books

Power cachers are always pushing the limits of the game, and as we were in the final stages of writing this book, we received word of a new record claim by a team that included two people we quote extensively elsewhere: Steve O'Gara (ventura_kids) and Elin Carlson (EMC of Northridge, CA). They joined with Jim Hoffman (f0t0m0m) on August 29, 2009, in a midnight-to-midnight run that netted 413 caches in one day.

The trip involved extensive planning using GSAK, Google Earth, and Geocaching.com. Ventura_kids created nine possible routes, consuming an estimated 45 hours of preparation. The team figured they needed to log a find every three minutes and 22 seconds to hit the record. Searching time was limited to one minute once they stopped the car and considering that, it's remarkable the team logged only 23 DNFs for the journey.

Their odyssey started near Denver airport with five "warm-up" caches just before the midnight kickoff. The team logged its 100th find at 5:30 A.M. By then, they had already battled swarms of grasshoppers who thought their car was a nifty place to hang out in the darkness of night. All day long, our heroes suffered through heat and dehydration in the process of traveling 471 miles.

"There were no bathrooms," ventura_kids told us. "Anytime somebody needed to go, I'd say, 'Cache is on the left, bathroom is on the right.'"

Everyone had a role. Ventura_kids has a near photographic memory for routes, so he did the driving. EMC posted constant updates on Facebook and Twitter. F0t0m0m was in charge of music (and decided on country music just to annoy EMC, who sings mostly classical music and opera for a living).

"We discarded the multi-stage caches and worked every puzzle we could," ventura_kids said. "We got rid of the ones that even looked like a problem. I had a map with approach drawings on the left and departure drawings on the right. As we approached a cache, the others would pour out of the car, with Jim saying, 'I've got the left!' and Elin saying, 'I've got the right!' I'd turn around and be ready to depart when they got back."

Fatigue nearly robbed the cachers of their record, as the hours passed. "You don't realize how tired and emotional you're going to be," ventura_kids said. He told jokes to lighten up the crew, even when he was feeling the stress of the day. EMC sang for her friends. Everyone was energized by the prospect of setting a new record, and in the end, they were rewarded with a new world record to their name. Will their feat stand for long? No doubt there are others plotting right now to make sure it doesn't. (In fact, as we went to press, word came in that a team in Sweden had logged over 500 caches in 24 hours!)

Despite the controversy, the so-called "power caching" phenomenon has gathered steam. In a community in which the number of caches a member has found can bestow a kind of celebrity status, enthusiasts are increasingly challenging themselves to amass impressive totals.

What Is Power Caching?

Power caching is an extreme version of the game that can push participants to and past exhaustion. An outing typically consists of a frantic run through an area of dense placements with the goal of finding each container in just a few minutes. The activity usually involves teams of people, but even individuals have been known to log well over 100 finds in a single day.

In the process of researching this book, we were treated to a power cache excursion by a team of two Austin, Texas-area veterans—The Outlaw, who organized the day, and TreyB. (See "Power Caching Journal" following this chapter.) We logged 102 finds for the day, but we had several advantages, including the fact that The Outlaw had found nearly all of the targets previously and had hidden a third of them. The adventure took an exhausting 15 hours and instilled in us profound respect for the enthusiasts who power cache on a regular basis. These people are just as nuts as the extreme cachers.

There is little elegance about power caching. Difficult or cryptic hides are usually avoided in the interest of time. Participants seek to maximize the number of easy-to-find caches and to optimize their route so that a minimum amount of time is spent in the car. A one-day power caching excursion may be preceded by two months of planning. Veterans say the activity is physically draining and can be monotonous, since it focuses on the least-challenging caches to find. Do it for variety, they recommend, but only in moderation.

Still, the act of running up numbers can be exhilarating. Among the more than 20,000 finds that EMC of Northridge, CA has rung up were 300 on July 4, 2007, with Andy and Jen Perkins (Team Perks) and Bill Varney (Cachepal) in a manic run in Porterville, California.

Ventura_kids (Steve and Sandy) usually power cache with Jim Hoffman (f0t0m0m). Steve drives to the cache in his trademark Jeep. He's the driver because he has an incredible photographic memory and knows the routes to and all the details of all the caches he's ever sought. (This is a truly impressive and savantish feat when you consider Steve's found over 18,000 geocaches.)

Once they get to the location, Steve starts counting down from 40. By the time he gets to 10, f0t0m0m or Sandy has usually found the cache. F0t0m0m hands the cache to Sandy, who retrieves the log as she and f0t0m0m rendezvous with

Steve. They each attach log stickers, rehide the cache, and jump in the car for their next destination.

Meanwhile, Steve has started the Jeep up again and is ready to head to the next location. Sandy is the second one in the car and Steve keeps an eye on his dashboard for a signal that the right rear door has closed, indicating f0t0m0m is back in the car. When he sees that dashboard indicator, he goes. He doesn't turn around to check, as that would mean wasted time. Of course, this means that sometimes they leave without f0t0m0m being in the car. Usually Sandy notices this and yells at Steve to stop.

As for the day's timing, Sandy keeps the time for the group's trip, and she's as severe as a drill sergeant: The rule is if they don't get 10 caches each hour in the morning, then the team doesn't get to have lunch. "We created the seven-minute limit to ensure we never waste too much time," Steve says. "We start our little timers [originally an actual timer; now it's just Steve counting backwards] as we exit the Jeep, and if the cache hasn't been found when the alarm goes off, we leave."

WE4NCS agrees it's necessary to have a plan when power caching. A 61-year-old who goes on regular power caching trips with Roger Dillard (rldill, age 55) and Granpa Alex (age 63), WE4NCS loads power caching trips from GSAK (once he's filtered them for ease and cluster locations) to Microsoft Streets and Trips. Then he plugs in his portable USB GPSr and tracks the car's progress on his laptop, in addition to tracking the progress on their GPS units.

Using this method, the team can alter their plan while on the go and get the most caching bang for their time. They've been known to cache for 40 hours at once without stopping to sleep. What possesses 60-year-old men to do this? "It's better than sitting in front of the television!" WE4NCS says. The team plays so often together that they've created a name for themselves—Team CHS (Cache-Hunting Studs).

Why Would Anyone Want to Power Cache?

Doesn't that mad dash betray the Zen of the game? It's true that the goal of traditional caching and power caching do not mesh. Traditional caching is usually about a good walk, fresh air, discovering a new park or trail, the thrill of the hunt for that one elusive hiding spot, the details you write in your log, and that one smiley that means so much because of the experience.

Power caching is about getting there and moving on. It's a numbers game in which your eyes only leave the GPSr long enough to fix on Ground Zero. It is hours of heart-pounding, focused intensity. "When you're power caching, you can't be bothered whether the sun is shining," says dgreno. "Just make sure you carry big flashlights and plenty of extra batteries." This explains his penchant for 36-hour continuous power runs.

Power cachers often have a goal, such as 100 finds in 8 hours or 500 in a week. They pay the price: Ankles and hamstrings throb the next morning from climbing into and out of the car and dashing between targets. Logging finds can be a chore when you can't really think of anything special to say about your 78th cache after 11 hours. And that one smiley that means so much in traditional geocaching is only a means to an end in power caching—that final count for the day.

Mrs. Captain Picard's Power Caching Rules

How to find lots of caches in a day:

- Go in a group. Four works well because you can fit four in a car. Then you have a driver, a navigator (who can sit in the car and figure out the next route when the seekers are looking for the cache), and two people to jump out and find and log each cache.
- Have a plan. Know which caches you're going to and in what order.
- Weed out long multis and puzzles for which you don't have the solutions. A long multi in power caching is anything over two stages.
- Have people load each GPSr the same way, so when someone calls out the name of the cache, everyone can find it that way in their GPSr.
- Weed out time-consuming hikes by looking at the terrain rating. Not all high-terrain caches are hikes, though!
- Use a route optimizer, like in Microsoft Streets and Trips, to optimize your driving route.
- Have one person in charge of the list, reading the notes ahead of arrival.
- Have a dedicated driver whose only job is to park well and be the first one back to the car so it will be unlocked and ready to go again.
- Set a time limit and keep an eye on the clock to keep pace with your goal for the day. Why waste time looking when there's another cache on your list waiting to be found? No one likes a DNF, but then no one likes looking for an hour for a cache that isn't there, especially when you don't have time to burn.
- Have a cooler in the car so you don't waste time at the convenience store.

But power caching is actually more than numbers. It's about setting and pursuing goals and pushing yourself to the limit. It's about competition with others, personal records, and new targets to shoot for. Ask a power caching veteran to tell you about her personal records and she'll usually rattle off a string of numbers, dates, and locations, frequently recalling memorable finds along the way.

Power Caching the USA

When elite geocachers conspire, weirdness ensues.

It took a team of three geo-fanatics—dgreno, Alamogul, and Roger Seaman (retiredprof)—to dream up the most remarkable geocaching story we heard during our months of research and scores of interviews. The team, which has more than 68,000 finds between them, geocached across all 50 U.S. states in just 10 days.

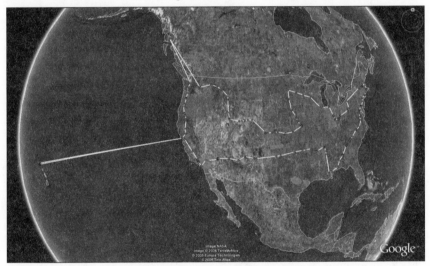

Fifty states in 10 days: The cachers' circuit.

Their odyssey covered 12,000 miles, not including the two plane flights needed to log Alaska and Hawaii. It was a masterpiece of planning and execution.

The goal was to qualify for and grab the "Found 50 States, I'm Going to Disneyland!" cache (GCRFNN), which they nabbed in world record time. In fact, like DiMaggio's 56-game hitting streak, their record is likely to stand for a long time.

The adventure began in San Francisco, where the team rented a new car with less than 200 miles on the odometer. They drove north to Seattle, logging Oregon along the way. Their flight to Alaska was longer than their stay there: just three hours on Alaskan soil.

The plan was to take the northern route east and the southern route west. There would be no sightseeing or lounging by the pool for these men on a mission. Dgreno had been planning for two months.

The goal wasn't big numbers. In fact, the players set out to log only two finds per state in order to make sure that at least one was recognized. As it happened, they finished with 350.

Among the time-saving shortcuts they employed:

- Staying on interstate highways to maximize speed.
- Renting rooms at the cheapest hotels with Internet access every other day to shower,—"so we could stand to be in the same car with each other," according to dgreno.
- Equipping the rental car with power converters and plenty of batteries to keep computers and GPSr units humming 24/7 without stop.
- Alerting cachers along the route of their arrival so that events could be planned—and logged—as they passed through.

Somewhere in New Mexico near the end of the trip, Alamogul slammed his laptop shut with a pen still lying on the keyboard. The screen was destroyed. He called a friend in California to say that the trio would reach Albuquerque two hours later. Could the friend please find some local cachers to lend them time on their computer?

They shortly got a note from a family of Albuquerque enthusiasts who said they'd be happy to meet the team. Dgreno, Alamogul, and retiredprof pulled up at 6 A.M. to find a hot breakfast and a warm computer waiting. They downloaded the missing data, ate, bid adieu to the family, found a cache on the front lawn of the house, and hit the road again.

The Alamogul laptop tragedy aside, the trip went surprisingly smoothly. Returning to California ten days after they started, the team boarded a plane for Hawaii, cached for a few hours and flew back to complete the run. Disneyland, here we come!

Oh, we forgot to mention one big cost-saving tip: renting a car. The bill for the 12,000-mile journey was just $250 (plus gas, of course), thanks to unlimited-miles pricing. The only unfortunate part: The team discovered only on the final day that they had had access to satellite radio all along.

WAYPOINTS
Power Caching Journal

Austin, Texas
Friday, Nov. 28, 2008

Weary warriors (left to right): Paul, Dana, TreyB, and The Outlaw at the end of their 102-cache odyssey. *Candy Lind (moosiegirl)*

Over Thanksgiving weekend, 2008, we set out to experience a power caching adventure firsthand. We had met Wayne Lind (The Outlaw) and Trey Bielefeld (TreyB) through our initial interviews. Each had well over 10,000 finds at the time and they kindly invited us to Austin, Texas, to take part in a chase intended to snag 100 caches in a day.

Impressed? Don't be. Some hard-core cachers we talked to for this book have logged more than 130 finds a day *with no assistance whatsoever*. Right before we handed this book in to our publishers, we heard from EMC of Northridge, CA about a 413-cache run by a team just east of Denver, Colorado (see sidebar in Chapter 6). We're telling you, these people are nuts. And for a day, we were two crazy geocachers, too. But even with The Outlaw and TreyB custom-designing the course with dozens of caches they had already found, we were barely able to stagger toward our goal after 15 hours of searching. Had The Outlaw and TreyB not helped us, we probably would have logged no more than 30 or 40 finds.

It turns out that power caching is taxing, not only in the execution but in the preparation. The following is our diary from that grueling, challenging, rewarding, exciting, funny, unforgettable day:

7:02 We meet in the parking lot of a shopping mall near Austin and log our
A.M.   first find. The Outlaw remarks, "Walking is the enemy of power caching." We are driving even ⅒-mile increments because it's faster. TreyB is behind the wheel the whole day and he knows his way around every parking lot and one-way street in the greater Austin area.

7:11 The Outlaw explains that the social rules of group caching dictate that if you find a cache first, you walk away and let everyone else take turns finding it. Normal social rules don't apply to a power run, where quantity is everything. First finder immediately alerts everyone else.

7:15 We find a match holder under a rock in a parking lot island.

The Outlaw and TreyB are talking about a series of local geocaches in which the posted coordinates are labeled as bogus, but the descriptions appear to provide no help whatsoever. It turns out the clues are there, but they're hidden on the page. One appears if you highlight the area with your mouse, because it's written in white font on a white background. Another is embedded as a comment in the HTML.

7:26 We log our first DNF with My Latitude Attitude, a tongue-in-cheek screed about the evils of longitude that offers only the latitude coordinate and challenges you to figure out the rest. The Outlaw did, and he tells us how. It didn't matter; we couldn't find it. Rats. Moving on ...

7:33 Dana finds a pillbox in a bush. We're at a McDonald's, so we grab breakfast.

The Outlaw is telling more stories. In one memorable find, he was required to find serial numbers on hand dryers in both the men's and ladies' rooms at a state-line welcome center. The men's room was no problem, but he had to seek help from an employee to get the other number. She listened carefully to his request and then cried out, "Are you one of those geonuts?!" Turns out she practically had the number memorized.

7:49 D finds a film can in a tree after only 15 seconds.

7:51 We log our second DNF. The cache is down for maintenance.

8:01 It's raining. We decide to hoof the .15 miles to this micro, but agree it's about the most time we can afford to lose. TreyB bags a film can hanging from a tree in a jiffy. We lose three minutes coming back while we scrape the thick Texas mud off our shoes.

8:11 Another longish walk through a pretty park. D finds the decon immediately. Decons are boxes the military uses to hold a decontamination kit.

8:19 This cache is missing, but we still get to log it as found. That's because The Outlaw has found this one before and knows where it should be. He figured out from recent logs that it was probably gone and arranged with the owner for a replacement.

The Outlaw has brought along a half dozen containers and logbooks on the trip, just in case some caches are missing. The protocol is to call the owner before setting a replacement, although cachers who know each other very well can often skip that step.

8:22 D is on a roll. She nails this one, a camouflaged bison tube in a tree, in about 10 seconds.

8:25 Paul quickly finds a camo'd water bottle in a hollow tree stump.

8:33 We're at a beautiful sculpture in a park in a ritzy section of Austin. There's a film canister here somewhere. P's baffled, but D finds in about two minutes.

8:43 Here's a virtual and a micro in the same place. The virt is easy enough: Just write down some words from a sign to send to the owner. The micro is tougher. TreyB knows right where to look, though. He has the uncanny geosense of a veteran cacher.

8:52 PnD had tried to find this one after dark the previous night, but it turns out the cache had been moved temporarily and they were looking in the wrong place. The Outlaw and TreyB know where to go, but that doesn't help. The cache isn't there. The Outlaw fishes a replacement bison tube and logbook out of his bag and hides it.

There are geocaching jokes, as The Outlaw relates:

A man meets a woman in a bar. They talk. One thing leads to another and they end up spending the afternoon in bed. What's the guy going to tell his wife? On the way home, he gets out of the car, rolls around in the dirt, and scratches himself all over with greenbriers. Arriving home, he's a mess.

"Where have you been?!" his wife demands.

"I can't lie, dear," the man says. "I met a woman in a bar and we spent all afternoon making love."

"Don't give me that!" she screams. "You've been geocaching again!"

9:03   Quick grab of a bison tube in a tree. This is the first of a five-part series. Each part contains a clue to a bonus puzzle at the end. You need all five parts to solve the puzzle.

9:10   Another one is missing! The Outlaw calls the owner in Indiana to get permission to replace.

9:26   We walk about 150 feet to a grove of cedar trees. The hint says "eye level," but we can't find it for several minutes until The Outlaw spies the bison tube attached to a tree.

9:35   We skirt a swimming pool in a complex of nice homes to find a series of live oak trees. The hint says you won't find the cache in the trees. That's technically true, but our goal turns out to be a magnetic key holder attached to the underside of a light fixture affixed to a tree. A little sneaky. We wouldn't have found it quickly without help from The Outlaw.

9:38   We cross a wide park to pluck a micro from a tree about 400 feet from the car. This is the second stage of the five-part series, so we grab the second set of clues for the bonus final. The Outlaw CITOs a gatorade bottle.

9:42   We walk across a wide athletic field to the next goal, a plastic jar at the bottom of a metal tube near a light post. On a true power cache run, we wouldn't waste time like this. Someone would stay in the car and meet the cachers at their destination. Oh, well! TreyB makes the find.

9:48   We walk 220 feet to the edge of a hill that slopes away sharply. There's lots of limestone on the ground, but TreyB quickly nabs the bison tube hanging in a tree.

P has got a calculator in his head. We're at 23 searches and 21 finds a little under three hours. The Outlaw says we're on a good pace for 100 for the day. P's not so sure.

10:15   Another DNF! This one is all the more frustrating because it's part of the five-cache series. Without the coordinates, we can't go for the bonus. Everyone looks for this longer than we should. The Outlaw has found it before, but says the container has been changed and his experience is useless. We finally give up.

10:25   We need a lift and get it with a small camo'd nut jar that TreyB quickly grabs. This is one of the few caches we've found that isn't a micro. The Outlaw explains that power caching runs nearly all involve micros and nanos because the quest for quantity demands that players look in urban locations. Since shopping malls don't lend themselves to ammo box hides, most of the targets are small. The rest of the day's experience bears this out.

After three and a half hours, we've found 22 out of 25 caches sought. At this rate, we'll never hit our goal. The Outlaw says some high-density areas are coming up that will yield big numbers in a short time. We take a bio break and then head toward a new run beginning almost seven miles away.

In the car, we talk about good ideas to throw off Muggles, or bystanders who look on, often suspiciously, as geocachers go about their searches. TreyB comes up with a good one: Carry a tape measure and pretend you're measuring a fence as if to replace it. Since so many geocaches are located near fences, it's a perfect cover story.

10:40 The trick to this puzzle is to read the description carefully. The coordinates are actually written out and hidden in the text. TreyB says you can find them by pasting the description into Word, filtering out the spaces between the words and then searching for numbers.

10:45 We walk 250 feet down a path and find our first ammo can of the day. It's an easy find under a tree.

11:00 Wayne thought he had entered the corrected coordinates from this puzzle solution, but they aren't in our GPSr; it directs us to a location 420 feet away. We have to fall back on what The Outlaw calls FPS (Friend Positioning System). He basically tells us where to look and TreyB makes the quick grab. We're at 28 searches, net 25 finds. At this pace, we'll need to cache until almost midnight to hit 100. That isn't an option, as we have an event cache to attend at 7:00, which TreyB, The Outlaw, and his wife, Moosiegirl, have arranged for our visit to Texas.

11:10 Are we beginning to cut corners? PnD look for a couple of minutes before TreyB jumps out of the car and strides toward a tree. "Have a look at that rock," he says. Underneath is a film canister.

11:16 The solution to this puzzle is related to the interval between musical notes. It isn't a hard one to figure out if you read music. Fortunately, Moosiegirl does.

11:18 Another container gone missing. Wayne pulls out his third film canister of the day as a replacement.

11:19 To solve this one, you only have to know the correct order of the reindeer on Santa's sleigh, which D does.

11:21 A quick skirt-lifter that the group lets P handle solo.

A "skirt-lifter" is The Outlaw's term for light-pole caches (LPCs), which are micros hidden under the plastic shirts that protect the base of many parking lot light poles. We'll do a ton of them today. They're fast and predictable, but, as we'll soon see, they can also be a clever diversion.

11:24   The coordinates are a little off on this one, so The Outlaw offers guidance. D finds the camo'd metal light switch cover within a minute. It's the same color as the box to which it's attached, making it particularly challenging. Micro caches are frequently painted to blend in with their surroundings.

11:30   There are several caches close by, but we instead drive a couple of miles to our next goal. The Outlaw and TreyB explain the reason: Instead of bouncing from side to side of a divided highway, it's faster to knock down a series of caches heading in one direction, then turn around and find another series coming back.

11:36   TreyB hasn't logged this one yet, so he takes the lead. It's a film canister underneath what The Outlaw calls a URP (unnatural rock pile). Geocaches are frequently hidden under rocks, which owners arrange to just barely conceal the container. Experienced finders learn to look for rocks that appear to be out of place. As a hyper-experienced finder, TreyB has no trouble with this one.

11:49   The clue is the cache name in reverse. We end up pounding the object upside down to dislodge a match holder. It's a quick find once you know the naming trick.

11:50   We're at 35 finds with three DNFs after nearly five hours, which is way off the pace we need. The Outlaw improvises. We're going to go off the plan and pick up a few caches that weren't on our itinerary in order to catch up a bit. We'll use what The Outlaw calls TOPS (The Outlaw Positioning System). Basically, he's going to lead us to within a few feet of our goal and then let us search.

         Our first target is a match holder suspended from a fishing line hung inside a hollow stone pillar. P finds this because, at 6'3", he's the only player tall enough to see over the top.

12:02   We log our second unscheduled find and head back on course.
P.M.

12:07   What would we do without our experienced guides? PnD both look down a hollow metal pipe and move on. TreyB looks in the same pipe and sees a fishing line wrapped around a metal rod. Suspended from it is a camo'd match holder.

12:13   D finds a black-on-black key holder stuck to a utility pole.

12:18   "Grab a fork," says the hint to this one. The cache is inside a tri-forked tree with a few rocks in unnatural places.

12:30   We log our fourth DNF of the day. It will be our next-to-last, a fact that will contribute to our being able to reach the 100-find goal.

12:41   Another example of the value of experienced cachers is they have cell phones stocked with the cell phone numbers of friends who can quickly help. The film canister is actually 100 feet away from the coordinates, but Wayne knows this cache owner was a little careless with puzzle solutions at times. He had called in advance to get the correct location, saving us from a certain DNF.

12:50   Looks like a sure skirt-lifter but there's nothing there. Then D spots a key holder about 12 feet off the ground. She climbs up on the light pole pad and stretches to make the grab.

12:55   We stop for lunch at a fast-food place and plot the afternoon's strategy. We have barely 40 finds after six hours and less than five hours of sunlight left. P says there's no way they'll get to 100, but The Outlaw says we're going to step it up in the afternoon. "We'll get to the mid-90s for sure," he says.

1:28   We begin the hunt again after refueling. This one is a micro hidden in the tip of a fence post in a shopping mall.

1:34   A rare traditional ammo box lies about 75 feet into the woods across from a golf course. As PnD enter the woods, they hear a rustle and two small deer dash up the hill in front of them. The deer watch curiously as P grabs the find and drops off a travel bug.

1:43   Another quick traditional in the woods. P finds it quickly. D admires the beautiful log book. "You don't often find fine paper like this in a geocache!" It's the crafter in her.

1:50   We begin a run of 11 in the Quick Sax series. There's nothing fancy about these. They're all easy park-and-grabs intended to help people trying to build their numbers. We start the run with 46 finds to our credit after nearly seven hours. Our only hope of getting to 100 is to knock these off very quickly.

2:31   We complete the Quick Sax series, saving time by sending P out solo to grab the micros and quickly place a sticker in the log book. D hands him each sticker in advance and logs the time of find. We average less than 4 minutes per find during this sequence.

    In the middle, we stop for our only find inside a place of business. The container is a beauty: a rock with a film cannister embedded in the base (see next page).

2:35   A quick park-and-grab brings us to 58 with four hours to go. We need to average one every six minutes from here on.

2:41   It's all about speed now. The Outlaw points out a bison tube directly above P's head while P searches fruitlessly. This marks the start of the "No more messing around" portion of our day.

2:42 The Outlaw's improvising again. We're going to swing by a couple of unscheduled caches he knows of and then start a big series of more than 30 to the north. We log a quick skirt-lifter. Our second quick grab, a hanging bison tube, is missing, though. It's apparently the victim of tree-trimming. It will be our last DNF of the day.

2:55 We head north for a nine-mile drive culminating in a series of thematic caches placed at the side of a country highway. Our ability to knock these off quickly will make or break our 100-find goal. We have an unnatural advantage: Most of these caches were placed by The Outlaw himself in honor of his friend's birthday but he was too rushed to take detailed notes when he hid them. So our hunt has a dual purpose: It will run up our numbers quickly and also enable The Outlaw to document his hides in detail.

The Outlaw is meticulous about record-keeping. He takes detailed notes on every find and hide on the theory that they could come in handy if a fellow geocacher calls him needing help. Although he doesn't remember the precise location of each and every one, we can count on him to keep us close.

Dana's knees are sore from swinging into and out of the back seat all day. She decides to stay in the car and take dictation on details about each cache from The Outlaw. TreyB and Paul will do most of the searching.

3:18 We begin our mad dash as TreyB snags a film canister.

3:41   TreyB has logged the first four finds. The fifth cache is missing, apparently the victim of a crack in a wall. The Outlaw replaces it. We log a find because we knew it was there.

3:51   TreyB logs his eighth find in a row. The boy is on a run!

3:55   P redeems himself with a blue bison tube.

3:57   TreyB grabs the next two.

4:08   P and TreyB scramble up a gravely hill to grab a red bison tube.

4:10   "What size is this one?" P asks, as he looks around. "It's a decon container," says TreyB, as he reaches for the find. The boy is too good.

4:32   Our two hunters trade finds before they're stumped by a particularly evil hide. There are lots of interesting hiding places on the ground, which is what makes the placement high up in a tree so tricky. That's the point, The Outlaw explains.

4:46   P finds a nano on a fencepost, putting us at 81 for the day. The sun is getting low in the sky.

4:53   Someone's moved the nano way down from its original location, ten feet off the ground. The Outlaw isn't pleased. Height is a key variable in cache placement, and the repositioning makes the find too easy. P leaps and manages to replace the container out of reach.

4:58   The Outlaw and TreyB have cached so much together that at times they seem to read each other's minds. The Outlaw says this cache is on the ground. P can't see a thing, but TreyB immediately dives into a pile of leaves and recovers the decon container. How did he know?

5:12   TreyB spots a magnetic nano ten feet up a pole. P leaps and whacks it 20 feet away with a stick of wood. Fortunately, TreyB watches the trajectory and recovers the tiny container. We figure out a way to return it to its original spot, using objects we find on the ground. Geocachers are resourceful that way.

5:19   The sun is sinking below the hilltops as we log number 86 for the day, a small decon.

5:33   We've been caching for more than ten hours, but the group is at peak performance. Paul and TreyB reel off a string of seven finds in 14 minutes to complete the series in 2 hours, 15 minutes. We've averaged one find every five minutes during that time and stand at 93 caches as darkness settles in.

        We head toward the PnD Meet & Greet! event cache that our hosts have graciously arranged. On the way, we strategize about our tactics for getting to 100 for the day. We'll swing by four locations that The Outlaw knows on the way to the event. All are quick grabs. We'll log the event as number 98 on the day. Afterwards, we'll clean up a couple of quick finds on the way back to PnD's car.

7:00   Caching after dark is always a challenge. We find a wonderful container carved out of a brick of limestone. D snags a traditional behind a large rock to the side of the highway. We cruise into Rudy's Country Store and Bar-B-Q to meet with a few local cachers who have come for our Meet & Greet.

Rudy's is about as Texan a restaurant as you can get: melt-in-your-mouth brisket, ribs, chicken, and sausage accompanied by some fine barbecue sides and served up with Texas hospitality. For two people, the bill was less than one of our entrees at a swank eatery the night before.

We meet some great cachers at Rudy's, although PnD are so exhausted they can hardly speak. Among our dinner companions are the Deafdillos, a local couple who has amassed more than 5,000 finds despite being totally deaf. We know we'll want to learn more about these remarkable people!

8:45   We bid farewell to TreyB, our driver on today's journey of more than 200 miles. He's a great guy and someone we won't want to lose touch with. The Outlaw and Moosiegirl set their coordinates for the car we left at the meeting point some 14 hours ago. We resolve to pick up four quick park-and-grabs on the way just to be sure we log 100 for the day. Now's not the time for formalities. The Outlaw all but places the caches in our hands as he guides us to a small container, two micros and a virtual.

9:00   We night-cache our way to a decon hidden near a car wash.

9:10   Easy virtual, as we take in Austin's famous Round Rock. We don't even have to leave the car to get the answer to the question, which we must submit to the owner in order to get credit.

9:15   We think this is number 101, although there's some discrepancy at this point about the exact count. We log it, just to be sure.

9:17   And one more, just for more insurance. We're quite positive we're over 100 now. It turns out this was number 102.

9:55   We arrive at the hotel more than 15 hours after we had left that morning. We're wired, tired, satisfied, and thinking ahead to the task of logging all those finds. But maybe we'll wait until tomorrow.

CACHER PROFILE
The Outlaw

Geocaching.com handle: The Outlaw
Name: Wayne Lind
Claim to fame: Teaches day-long courses in how to use Geocaching Swiss Army Knife (GSAK).
Location: Austin, Texas
Caching since: March 10, 2002
Total finds: 13,342
Total hides: 133
Preferred GPSr: Garmin 60 CSx

Favorite Cache Types

Anything that involves kayaks, bicycles, and long hikes. He also loves the occasional power cache outing.

Unique Approach

The Outlaw is to geocaching what Bill James is to baseball: a tool-lover who brings an engineer's discipline to the game. He frequently teaches full-day tutorials about how to use GSAK and he's a master at integrating Garmin's MapSource mapping software with field notes.

The Outlaw sees one of his roles as being a resource to other geocachers. As he walks a trail, he marks trail heads, paths, bridges, hazards, uncharted roads, and an assortment of other notable features with his GPSr. When he returns home, he exports the track file to Mapsource for future use and to share with others. The next time he visits that location he has a trail map that's more detailed than anything provided by the local park service. He also takes detailed notes that he can retrieve for stumped cachers who phone.

He carries a bag full of film canisters, bison tubes, and log books in his car to fix compromised caches in the field. If a cache shows two recent DNFs, indicating that it may no longer exist, he'll call the owner and offer to replace it.

Great Geocaching Story

The Outlaw tells of looking for a cache that involved climbing down a sheer rock cliff. The cache was hidden in the roots of a tree protruding from the rock. Once he reached the ledge, he realized he couldn't climb back the way he came. Then he spied another ledge to the side that he had to reach. Climbing toward the ledge, he brushed his head against a spider's nest. "Suddenly, there were hundreds of daddy long-legs spiders crawling all over me," he remembers. He had no choice but to crawl back up the cliff with spider swarm in tow.

Words of Wisdom

"Be careful of stone walls. Many were built by farmers or slaves more than 100 years ago and are legally protected from being disturbed. You should never move rocks [in a wall] to hide a cache," he says. "And you shouldn't place a cache in a location that would encourage others to move the rocks while looking for it.

"Get to know cache owners in your area. Owner styles are almost as distinctive as fingerprints. Many owners prefer certain cache types, hiding places, and containers. Knowing that an owner has an affinity for hiding caches in trees can help when you're on the trail."

SECTION III

Taming Technology

CHAPTER SEVEN
Navigation Basics

In order to get the most from geocaching, it's helpful to understand how human beings have learned to map the world around them. This chapter provides some basics. We don't go into a lot of detail about the science of navigation here. There are many good resources on that, including the **Geocaching.com** website and the book *Geocaching for Dummies*. Use this chapter as a practical guide and check those resources to satisfy your inner geek.

You don't need to master navigation with compasses and paper maps in order to be a successful geocacher. GPS technology has evolved to the point that traditional aids are rarely needed. However, understanding a few basics will help make sense of the sometimes confusing geo-jargon you'll encounter.

In the Beginning

If you remember your junior high school geography class pretty well, you can skip this section, but for the forgetful, here's what you need to know.

Most navigation systems work by triangulation. Ancient mariners figured out 5,000 years ago that if you could determine the angle of a celestial object relative to a known point on the globe, basic geometry would tell you with pretty good accuracy where you were. This principle has served humans well for a long time and remains the foundation of navigation systems to this day.

Once people figured out how to measure long distances with accuracy—and disposed of the pesky debate about whether the Earth is round or flat—they set about mapping the world. They came up with a system of parallel lines running east to west and converging lines running north to south. Each line represents 1° of the 360° that make up a circle.

There are 90 parallel degree lines that circle the globe from the Equator to the poles, or 180° of total latitude. There are also 180 converging longitudinal lines that run north-south and emanate from the big mama of all longitudes: the Prime Meridian, which runs through Greenwich, England. Because it's pretty unspecific to divide the whole world up into just 360 individual degrees, each degree is composed of 21,600 smaller units: There are 60 minutes (displayed as ') and each minute is divided into 360 seconds (displayed as "). Using all these points together, we're able to pinpoint any location on the Earth to about ten feet. That's pretty precise, and it's a big reason that GPS navigation is so effective.

Changes in Latitude, Changes in Attitude

Latitude is the angular distance in degrees between a given location and the equator. Latitude coordinates range from 0° at the Equator to 90° at the North and South poles. The North Pole is at 90° north and the South Pole is at 90° south. New York City is at approximately 40° north, while Buenos Aires is at approximately 34° south. All latitude lines are equidistant from each other.

Longitude refers to the angular distance in degrees between a given location and the Prime Meridian, which runs through Greenwich, England, just north of London. Longitude is also expressed in degrees, with the Greenwich meridian at 0° and longitudinal lines running east and west to 180° at the International Dateline on the other side of the planet. New York City is at approximately 74° west, while Beijing is at approximately 116° east.

If the Earth was flat and you divided it into 360 degrees, then each one degree of latitude or longitude would measure just over 69 miles, or 111 km. While the distance between latitudinal degrees remains constant, that isn't the case with longitude. Spheres present some tricky mapping and navigation challenges because flat maps and globes don't behave the same way.

A gridwork of lines works best when the lines are equidistant and don't converge (that is, when they're parallel). The problem with globes is that lines running north to south have to converge at the poles. That means that a 10° distance between two longitudinal lines at the equator is much greater than the same distance 45° to the north. In fact, it's twice as long. That's because the earth is basically round and the distance between those lines narrows as you go north, eventually meeting at the poles. For this reason, we can't rely upon simple coordinates to determine distance.

Man using sextant. *Wikimedia Commons photo*

Early navigators and cartographers used primitive instruments like sextants to figure out geographic coordinates. With the advent of geostationary satellites, our ability to pinpoint location became very sophisticated. The U.S. Department of Defense began using global positioning systems in 1973. A decade later, the Reagan administration opened the satellite network to civilian use, but the quality and cost of available receivers limited GPS use largely to industrial applications. In 1990, the U.S. government actually made GPS *more* difficult to use by imposing Selective Availability. That program introduced artificial error into GPS signals in order to prevent enemies from using the satellite network to their full advantage. People could technically get access to the GPS network, but with accuracy limited to about 300 feet, it wasn't good for much.

It wasn't until 2000 that the GPS network was opened for full civilian use, giving anyone on the planet the opportunity to take advantage of the 30 geostationary satellites circling the globe. (The number of available satellites that provide GPS navigation services has varied over time, depending on how many are functional and in orbit at any given time.) On May 3, 2000, just one day after the Clinton administration unlocked the network, the first geocache was placed.

Geocaching.com was launched in September of that year, with a list of about 75 known caches in the world. The numbers grew rapidly from there. By January 2003, there were 41,000 caches in 160 countries. Two years later, there were 140,000 caches worldwide and, as of February 2010, that number is rapidly approaching one million.

The Satellite Advantage

A global positioning system works by the same basic triangulation principles that guided prehistoric mariners, but satellites can provide a better fix on position than the Sun because they are a lot closer to the Earth. Triangulation from objects delivering very precise electronic signals is also much more accurate than celestial navigation.

The 30 or so GPS satellites have accurate clocks on board that timestamp the signals they transmit. GPS receivers can look at those time signatures and compare them to each other. Receivers look for subtle differences in the timestamps to calculate how far away each satellite is. By triangulating the satellite's position in the sky with the knowledge gained from reading the timestamps, receivers can calculate with a high degree of accuracy their exact location.

Actually, a better term would be "quadrangulation." Most GPS receivers can get a reasonably good fix on their location with signals from only three satellites, but the best results come with four or more signals. With this information, most receivers can pinpoint their location to within about 15 meters (about 50 feet), which is close enough to find a geocache. Accuracy is further improved through the use of WAAS (wide-area augmentation system), a network of ground reference stations that cleans up signal interference and improves accuracy to less than three meters (10 feet) about 95 percent of the time. Most modern GPS receivers can use WAAS out of the box, although the system does consume additional battery power and may not be worth the trade-off in all cases.

Signal quality was further improved in 2005 when newly launched satellites began using a civilian code signal called L2C, which allows for better error checking capabilities. You don't need to know anything more about that, though.

Most current high-end GPS units use an embedded chip set manufactured by SiRF Technology. At this writing, the SiRFstarIII was the latest model in production. SiRF basically makes receivers more accurate by processing more channels at once and by locking on to satellite signals faster. However, no chipset or receiver will give you pinpoint accuracy. In fact, one of the secrets of using a GPSr is not to become too dependent on it.

Even in ideal conditions, receivers are generally accurate only to within about 15 feet, and even then they're not entirely reliable. Your GPSr may pretend to know where you are but then it will suddenly jump to a spot 40 feet away. This is frustrating, but veteran geocachers accept it with a shrug. In fact, most experienced geocachers put away their GPSr units about 40 feet before they reach their destinations and start looking for hiding places. As you practice, you'll learn to trust your instincts, too.

Back to the Future: Using a Compass

It helps to understand a little bit about compass navigation. Compasses are one of the oldest navigational devices; the earliest uses have been traced back to twelfth-century China. All handheld GPSr units include a compass, but in most cases the GPS compass isn't very good for navigation. That's because most GPSr devices estimate compass directions from satellite signals rather than magnetic poles. Some older GPSr units also require the receiver to be moving at approximately 4 mph to obtain an accurate compass reading. This equates to a brisk walk and is not really practical if you're standing in the middle of the woods trying to figure out where to go.

Modern GPSr devices increasingly come with integrated magnetic compasses. This can be a very useful feature, but it also adds to cost. A good handheld navigational compass can be had for about $10, making it a cost-effective alternative.

We won't go into a lot of detail about compass navigation here. Both the *Complete Idiot's Guide to Geocaching* and *Geocaching for Dummies* offer good tutorials on compass navigation. There are also many online lessons in places such as **Compassdude.com** and **Wikihow.com** that provide extensive background on how compasses work, how to use them with maps, and how to adjust for variations between magnetic north and true north (this difference is called "declination"). Unless you are an advanced geocacher or a serious outdoors enthusiast, you don't need to know the details. For most casual urban/suburban geocaching, it's enough just to understand the basics.

Go North, Young Geocacher

A compass basically shows you which way is magnetic north. It also displays the three other cardinal points (west, south, and east) and has a rotating ring around the outside, sometimes called the housing, which has 360 degree marks. There are also usually some straight lines painted on the clear inner housing of the compass. These are called orienting lines and they are used to align the coordinates on the compass with true north so that you can get an accurate reading.

To figure out which way you want to go, place the compass on a map in approximately the same place you're currently located. Line up the compass arrow with the lines on the map that point north. Rotate the housing so that the number zero corresponds to north. Place a straight edge between the center of the compass pointer and your destination. Your straight edge will pass over one of the numbers on the housing. This number is your bearing.

Once you know your bearing, you can set off in that direction using your compass as a guide. Remember that the needle of a compass always points toward magnetic north. Don't be misled into following the needle. The number that's important to you is the bearing. As long as you carry your compass correctly (level, and somewhere between waist and chest height) and the magnetic fields around you aren't disturbed by large metal objects or magnets, you can reliably follow the same bearing by keeping the number zero on the compass housing aligned with the magnetic arrow.

Some people like to point the orienting arrows in the direction of travel. That's fine, as long as the relationship between the compass pointer and the orienting lines remains the same. To return, simply follow a bearing that is 180° in the opposite direction (this is called a back bearing).

Why Are We Telling You This?

It's possible to geocache using only a compass (instead of a GPSr), but you probably wouldn't want to do so. Unless you get excited by the challenge of navigation, chances are you'll need to know very little beyond the basics described above. It is important, though, to understand the fundamentals of navigation, because GPS coordinates are expressed in degrees and minutes, which is the global language of navigation. The compass can also come in handy for situations in which the GPS signal is inaccurate or unreliable. Also, many GPSr devices offer the option of navigating by compass to your destination. You might find this preferable to tracking yourself on a map.

Here's how we've used a compass to help us in our search. Let's say we are searching for a cache that's located at the following coordinates:

N 41° 40.514 W 073° 53.969

Our GPS successfully guides us to the general vicinity, but the dense trees overhead cause us to lose our signal just short of our goal. Our last reliable reading put us at:

N 41° 40.529 W 073° 53.919

In other words, we're about 15" north (529 minus 514) and about 50" east of our goal. That's too far away to just start thrashing around in the woods, but if we take out our compass, we can estimate the distance to our destination.

We know from experience that at our current latitude and longitude, three paces equals about one navigational second. So pulling out our compass, we find magnetic north and rotate the orienting arrow to match the compass needle. We then turn due west and walk off 150 paces. Then we turn due south and walk 45 paces. This may not put us square on our goal, but we're a lot closer than where we started.

Many Ways to Say It

GPS coordinates are displayed as intersections of longitude and latitude called **waypoints.** Any location on earth can be plotted on a map according to its waypoint. The first set of numbers in a waypoint refers to the location's angular distance from the equator on a north/south trajectory (latitude). The second set of numbers refers to the location's angular distance from the Prime Meridian on an east/west trajectory (longitude).

Both sets of coordinates are typically displayed as either positive or negative numbers or are preceded by a letter corresponding to their north/south and east/west positions. Coordinates that lie north and east of the equator and Prime Meridian get positive numbers, while those south and west get negative numbers. So the following two numbers refer to the same waypoint:

N 25° 07.450' W 80° 17.800

25 07.450 -080 17.800

All this would be easy if everyone referred to coordinates the same way, but alas, that's not the case. There are three popular standards for expressing GPS coordinates in the popular WGS84 datum format (if you must know, WSG84 stands for World Geodetic System 1984): decimal, DDD MM.MMM, and DDD MM SS.SSS. The same waypoint can thus be expressed three different ways. For example, all three of these designations refer to the same location:

Three Ways to Note the Same Waypoint

Decimal	45.23143 -122.7558
DDD MM.MMM	N 45° 13.886 W 122° 45.348
DDD MM SS.SSS	N 45° 13' 53.1588" W 122° 45' 20.8800"

If this confuses you, don't be alarmed. The differences are actually easy to understand once you break the code. Note that if you multiply the numbers immediately to the right of the decimal points in either of the top two examples by 60, you get a result that's very close to the number to the *left* of the decimal point in the example immediately below it. Rather than trying to unravel this, we'll quote this excellent explanation at **DiveSpots.com**:

> Using the latitude N 25 07.450 as an example, we can represent this same location as N 25° 07' 27", or simply 25.124167. They all refer to the same location. This is the most common source of confusion. I get e-mails saying things like, "Your site lists the Christ of the Abyss as 25 07 450", but this book I have has it as 25 07 27." See the problem? Don't ignore the decimal point! If it's there, then the seconds are represented as a fraction of the minutes. If it's not there, then the third value is the number of seconds. Let's break it down:
>
> N 25 07.450 is read as 25 degrees and 7.450 minutes north of the Equator. To convert this to the second form, simply take the fraction, .450, and multiply it by the number of seconds in a minute, .450 × 60 = 27. Thus, 07.450 minutes is the same as 07 minutes and 27 seconds, or simply 07' 27".

The third format, 25.124167, is just the degrees as a pure decimal number. Take the fraction, .124167, and multiply it by the number of minutes in a degree. Thus, .124167 × 60 = 7.450 minutes.

You might ask why the people who make up these things invented three different ways to represent the same information? It's because each of the designations has different value. For example, the pure decimal expression is more useful for calculating distance between two points than either of the other two expressions.

If you're not confused enough, there are more than three standards for expressing geographic coordinates. In most cases, WGS84 is the only one you need to know. There's an older standard called NAD27 that still turns up on some maps. There's also an alternative to WGS84 called Universal Transverse Mercator (UTM) that a lot of people like better.

Understanding UTM

UTM uses kilometers and meters instead of degrees, minutes, and seconds. It also divides the world into 60 equal sections of 6° each. Each of these grids is then subdivided into kilometers, meaning that the numerical designations in a UTM coordinate are actually distances rather than degrees. The advantage of this is that there is no need to adjust for the distant variances caused by the curvature of the earth. There are also no positive or negative designations to cause confusion, and square grids allow for more precise measurement than curved parallels.

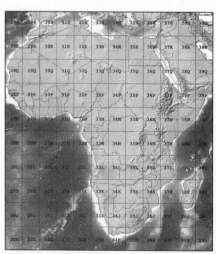

Some avid geocachers say that UTM is a better way to navigate and that it's easier to use once you understand it. It's easy for you to make up your own mind. **Geocaching.com** can convert any coordinates into UTM and, as long as you choose the corresponding setting on your GPS, you should have no problem switching between them. Most modern GPSr devices don't care. They'll display coordinates in any format you choose and help you find the cache either way.

Continent of Africa on a UTM map.
Wikimedia Commons illustration

However, it is important to understand what format your GPSr uses. When Paul was new to geocaching, he tried downloading waypoints from **Geocaching. com** into a freeware mapping utility and then into his GPSr. The waypoint designations on the website always changed when loaded into the device. After tiring of correcting each coordinate by hand, he figured out that by simply changing the mode on the GPSr, he could bring the world back into sync. Life has been much better since then.

You don't need to be a cartographer or geographer to have fun geocaching, but you do need to understand how to make sense of this slightly ovular marble called Planet Earth. Once you have these basics in place, it's time to head out the door.

Uncertain Future

The nation's network of geostationary satellites, which is maintained by the U.S. Air Force, won't last forever. New satellites must be regularly deployed to replace aging technology. As we were going to press, disturbing stories were emerging about the future reliability of the satellite network. "It is uncertain whether the Air Force will be able to acquire new satellites in time to maintain current GPS service without interruption," warned an April 2009 report by the U.S. General Accounting Office (GAO). "If not, some military operations and some civilian users could be adversely affected." It seems that the Air Force is running seriously over budget, and some satellite launches may be delayed or scrubbed as a result. The GAO report said the loss of satellites could affect the accuracy of GPSr devices, although it didn't quantify the magnitude of the impact.

Don't despair yet. Alarmist reports like this are often intended to inspire action. Geo-positioning is now so critical to the nation's economy that the government will be motivated to find the money to keep the network stable or to beef up alternatives, such as the ground-based, long-range radio navigation (Loran) system operated by the Coast Guard. A similar European network called Galileo is expected to go into operation by 2013.

WAYPOINTS
Curious Cops

Few geocaching experiences are more awkward than trying to explain to a police officer why you're crawling around in the bushes or skulking behind a fast-food restaurant after dark. Geocaching always looks suspicious to Muggles, and in these days of amber and red alerts, you don't want to mess with the law.

Police officers are increasingly familiar with geocaching, but that doesn't mean they like it. That's particularly true for cops who have had the experience of going on a wild goose chase to "defuse" a device that turned out to be a spray-painted Lock & Lock container. To these public servants, geocachers are weird at best and trouble-makers at worst. Don't ever lie to or argue with them. You don't know what their experiences have been or how much tolerance they have to learn about a "global Internet treasure hunt." Have a quick (and honest) explanation in mind and, if you see the officer's eyes begin to narrow, be ready to quickly and politely abandon your search.

With those caveats in mind, we have to admit that some of the funniest geo-stories we heard involved the long arm of the law. Here are a few favorites.

Don't Throw Stones

"We approached the cache site in the Riverside University parking lot," remembers Steve O'Gara of ventura_kids. It was just after the 9/11 attack, and there was a police officer at every public building and school. There was a cop in that lot, parked about 200 feet from the cache site. Since there's nothing illegal about geocaching, ventura_kids decided to go ahead and find the cache.

The officer was standing outside his car, reading his Bible. The cachers continued past him and parked just ten feet from the cache. They spotted an obvious clue: a softball-sized rock near the edge of the parking lot with a clear fishing line tied around it. Quick find, right? The cop had put his Bible aside and was staring at these suspicious characters. As Steve picked up the rock, he realized the fishing line was strung through the top of a nearby parking sign and served to lower a bison tube hidden inside the sign. As Steve lifted the rock just above his shoulder to allow Sandy to open the tube, he realized he made quite a puzzling sight.

"So I'm standing there with a softball-sized rock in my hand, just above my shoulder, facing the police car 200 feet away," he says. Oops. The officer approached, unsnapped his service revolver and said, "Are we about to have a problem here?" The situation was quickly deteriorating. Steve remembered what he had learned as a kid: Show respect to officers of the law. He yelled, "No, sir! This girl told me to hold this rock just like this." To his relief, the officer started laughing. "When in doubt, blame the girl!" he said. Steve and Sandy spent the next ten minutes explaining geocaching to him.

Masochists or Troublemakers?

The Deafdillos can't hear cars approaching and so they must stay constantly on their toes. "It was completely dark on the country road," Richard recalls. As if finding a micro in a cedar tree isn't hard enough, they tried for it at night, using headlights and flashlights. Deafdillos are just that good. Natalie headed back to the car, while Richard was signing the log sheet. Suddenly, a patrol car appeared with full headlights and sirens. Natalie was already in the car with Bella, the couple's Boston Terrier geohound. Richard stood on the edge of the road, pointing at his ears and making "decline" signs like a football referee. The deputy walked toward him while his partner checked out the cachemobile. Moving slowly, Richard showed them a Muggle card about geocaching. The young deputy asked to see the log sheet that was in his left hand. He scanned it, handed it back, and quickly turned around and departed. The worst part is that Richard couldn't locate the cache again to hide it; Natalie had to come back and find it again.

Mr. Cache Goes to Jail (Almost)

On a solo trip to an isolated part of Kentucky, Show Me The Cache (SMTC) found himself without a place to stay when his targeted campsite was full. A campground employee suggested a spot near the river. It looked a little creepy, but SMTC didn't have a lot of options.

Sometime after midnight, he was harshly awakened by three high-intensity flashlights streaming through the van windows. SMTC tried to reassure the officers that he had permission to be there, but they would have none of it. "You're a nice fellow, but the last nice fellow who stayed here was from Virginia and he got his throat slit in the middle of the night," said one. That's when one officer piped up, "You're going to jail!"

"I'm sure the expression on my face was of total alarm," SMTC told us. But the cop quickly reassured him. "No, no! There's a little picnic area right behind the jail and you're welcome to stay there." Our hero jumped at the offer, glad to not face a morning of Cheerios in a stainless steel bowl. Little did he know, the cops had *My Cousin Vinny*'d him: Ten minutes after falling asleep, he was awakened by a rushing train 30 feet away. "It's amazing how loud those whistles are in the middle of the night," he relates.

Welcome to Independence

Aurelia Taylor (Meriadoc2003), Dave Meyers (Dave w/o id), and Dorothy Grueber (Dove78) were in Independence, Ohio, the evening after an event put on by Tom and Anna Mary Bowers (SerenityNow). The trio decided to go for a few more caches before calling it a night. (It's amazing how many stories start off that way!) The two targets were woods caches, which they nabbed just as the fireflies were coming out. All of a sudden, the trio heard a commotion in the woods and voices yell something. Meriadoc2003 recalls, "Considering the area, I thought for sure we'd stumbled into someone's drug territory and we might end up as headlines or statistics."

Suddenly, three flashlights popped on and the team could see the glint of badges. "FREEZE! Put your hands in the air!" the officers yelled. The geocachers actually relaxed a bit, as they knew they were going to be okay. Now the only worry was if there was poison ivy on the ground where they would be asked to lie down.

It turned out the officers were familiar with geocaching, so they lightened up pretty quickly. The cops explained that the local neighborhood watch had called them when they saw three figures enter the woods near twilight, thinking them to be drug dealers or murderers. The officers even suggested a safer entry point to the woods, which the team added to the cache's page as updated coordinates. As the cops holstered their weapons, one officer laughed. "Welcome to Independence!" he said.

Is that a Gun or Are You Just Happy to See Me?

Shortly after 9/11, ventura_kids were caching at an old Coca-Cola plant in California. They were exploring a defunct train car on a dead-end track that led into the plant. Steve was rummaging around the train car when he saw police cars on the nearest road. One officer got out and started walking up the dirt road toward them.

The Kids did what they've learned always to do in such a situation: explain themselves. As they went to meet the cop, another police car came screaming up in front of them. A policewoman jumped out, brandishing her weapon and, her hands shaking, yelled, "Put your hands where we can see them!"

Fortunately, the more experienced officer who was walking toward them admonished the female officer, who was evidently new on the job, and told her to put her gun away. Ventura_kids now makes it a point to proactively explain to nearby police officers what they're doing. Downloadable explanatory pamphlets from Geocaching University (**Geocacher-u.com**) help.

Why Alamogul Never Lies to Cops—Anymore

Alamogul learned the hard way that honesty is the best policy with officers of the law. About two years after 9/11, he and bthomas were caching near a construction site when they were stopped by a curious cop. "We're just taking pictures of this cemetery," bthomas said to the officer, who then asked to see the camera. It was full of photos of bridges considered high-risk areas for terrorism. After several uncomfortable minutes with the officer, the cachers sheepishly walked away, having learned a good lesson. "Always tell them the truth about the game and no trouble will befall you," says Alamogul.

CHAPTER EIGHT
Choosing a GPSr

G PSr buyers have never had more options to choose from, a reality that's both a blessing and a curse. **Amazon.com** lists more than 400 handheld GPSr options, ranging in price from $70 to nearly $1,000 (or up to $3,000 for high-end marine units). You can buy GPSr units that have integrated cell phones and MP3 players, as well as devices that connect to each other wirelessly and deliver traffic updates. For many standard geocaching applications, these features are overkill. In fact, our research showed that the Garmin GPSMAP 60CSx device, which costs less than $300, is the most popular receiver among prolific geocachers.

All handheld GPSr units do a pretty good job of telling you your coordinates, but beyond that, features and functions vary widely. We strongly recommend you invest in a unit that is specifically designed for outdoor use. Most manufacturers make portable GPSr devices for auto navigation. These attach easily to a dashboard or windshield mount and provide good-quality roadmaps and voice navigation. However, they're usually not up to the unique demands of geocaching.

Limitations of GPS

GPSr devices are pretty phenomenal in the right conditions, but they aren't perfect. The world's best handheld unit may leave you stranded and confused in the middle of New York City, as we found out the hard way. Here are some shortcomings of GPS technology that you should know about.

There's no such thing as pinpoint accuracy. No GPSr will identify your location to within less than about a 10-foot radius. The U.S. government doesn't allow it. This inaccuracy factor inherently makes geocaching a guessing game. Because the GPSr devices used by both you and the person who hides a cache have a margin of error, even the most precise coordinates may only take you to within 20 feet of your goal. That's why intuition and observation are such important caching skills.

GPS receivers work better when stationary. Receivers use a technique called "averaging" to constantly poll satellites and refine their position over time. Movement decreases accuracy, so when you near your destination, stop for a minute to get a better reading. However, certain structural limitations may prevent your GPSr from ever giving you an accurate signal. Read on.

GPS receivers don't work indoors. There's no way to get around this. The devices need a line-of-sight to satellites. You can sometimes get a reading indoors by placing the receiver next to a window, but that's touch-and-go. Fortunately, most geocaches are placed outdoors.

GPS receivers are subject to interference by tall buildings and trees. Yes, trees, even though lots of caches are hidden in densely wooded areas and on tree-lined city streets. When satellites on the horizon are obscured by buildings or dense overgrowth, signals may be lost entirely. This is especially true in cities. You can be standing in an open square and get no better than 50-foot accuracy because of surrounding buildings. Out in the wild, rock walls can cause "signal bounce," which makes coordinates jump around crazily. The only solution to this problem is to move to an area with a reliable signal, point yourself in the direction of your destination, and count off steps until you're in the right vicinity.

GPSr devices can't calculate altitude very well. Even the most accurate systems generally won't give you a reliable altitude reading to within less than 100 feet. Fortunately, this isn't a problem for most geocaching situations. In some cases, though, topography does factor into the clues and a handheld altimeter is a good accessory to have with you.

What about GPSr units intended for road use? For one thing, they are not made for use in outdoor environments. Geocachers find themselves in all kinds of weather conditions, and we've dropped our GPSr devices onto wet ground and even into water more times than we care to remember. The rugged quality of units built for the outdoors protects their internals from breaking when dropped (to a point), but drop an auto navigation GPSr on a rock and chances are you can kiss at least some of its functionality good-bye. Secondly, auto navigation features like road-maps and driving directions won't do you much good when you're hiking through the woods. Thirdly, auto navigation units aren't designed to be as precise as handheld units and their visual display accuracy may be no better than a 60- or 80-foot radius—fine for driving, but not for geocaching. The dashboard-mounted units also can be awkward to hold or attach to a belt.

What about PDAs and Cell Phones? Another option is to outfit a personal digital assistant (PDA) or cell phone with GPSr capability through specialized hardware and software. This option has become more appealing since manufacturers like Apple and Motorola have started embedding GPSr functions into their products. We haven't tested the iPhone 3G hands-on, but reviewers have said it isn't precise enough to be used for geocaching. Our new Motorola Droid is nearly as accurate as a dedicated GPSr. However, in our interviews with veteran cachers, we didn't find a single one who used a PDA or telephone as a principal GPSr. This may change over time, but for now the specialized navigational devices meant for the outdoors rule this market.

What to Look for

Let's look at some common features of handheld receivers that you should consider, even if you decide you don't need all of them.

Barometric Altimeter—The satellite-based altimeter offered in most GPSr devices can give you at best a reasonable approximation of your altitude, but it's not their strong point. Some units have a built-in secondary barometric altimeter, which uses barometric pressure instead of satellite triangulation to estimate altitude. That's nice to have, but you probably won't need it unless you plan to search for some very challenging caches.

Antenna jack—An outboard antenna can come in handy in densely wooded or urban areas. With prices starting at under $20, an antenna is a low-cost way to boost reception quality, but it's also another accessory to carry.

Turn-by-turn directions—Units with auto navigation can guide you to a point with voice guidance. Few handheld units do this very well. You can invest in software that turns your handheld into a decent auto navigation system, but screen size can be a limitation. If you need extensive auto guidance, it's best to buy a unit designed specifically for that purpose.

Alarm—Some units can warn you when you're approaching a waypoint. We can't imagine why you'd want this for geocaching, because you're presumably scrutinizing your destination anyway. What we'd really like to see is an alarm that reminds you to look up so you aren't smacked in the head with a branch.

Camera—Magellan's new Triton series includes a 2-megapixel camera in the handheld unit. Because geocachers love to exchange photos of their adventures, a camera as part of a GPSr can be a helpful tool. However, internal cameras can't duplicate the quality of a photo taken with even a basic digital camera. Lens quality is far more important than a megapixel rating. Consider buying a good, small digital camera to record your outings.

Flashlight—Some units include LED flashlights, which can be handy when you're poking around in caves and wooded areas. LED isn't a replacement for a conventional flashlight, but it's nice to have in a pinch and not too taxing on the battery.

Basemap—There are two kinds of maps involved in a GPSr purchase. Basemaps live on the PC and store information sent to and from the GPSr. Navigation maps live on the handheld device and guide you around. Some GPSr devices can download maps from the PC, but not all of them can do so. Most PC basemaps can be updated with information from the GPSr, such as the track a person took while walking a trail through the woods. Also, many basemaps can be overlaid with information like geocache locations and waypoints downloaded from online services.

Garmin's MapSource is the most widely used basemap. It's easy to read, although its features are pretty basic. Magellan's AccuTerra basemap is an excellent choice for outdoor enthusiasts. We also like DeLorme's Topo USA series for its rich detail; the problem is that the graphics chew up PC performance.

Desktop mapping software has become less important over the last couple of years, as services like Google Maps have evolved to provide superior utility. Still, the desktop software is often the only means to reliably transfer routes and maps to the GPSr. Some vendors also make updates to the maps available as free downloads. Keep an eye on **Geocaching.com** for further developments. As developers take advantage of Google Maps' openness, the service's utility as a geocaching tool will improve.

Be sure the mapping software you use can import GPX files, which contain all the relevant details about a cache. Incredibly, we found that some products marketed to geocachers didn't support this basic function. You might also want to see if map updates can be obtained via a subscription. You can also invest in Topgrafix's GeoBuddy software, which downloads maps as you need them. At $50 at the time of this writing, it's a good value.

Some basemaps come pre-installed on the GPSr. You want to be very comfortable with the map you choose, since you'll be looking at it a lot. That's why it's important to test-drive any GPSr you're considering buying.

Lines should be of sufficient thickness to distinguish between roads and waterways. Colors should be vivid or user-definable. Take some time to test different candidates and choose one that feels right to you. In our experience, most retailers will let you take a GPSr outside for as long as a day or two if you leave a driver's license or credit card.

Resolution should be good enough to clearly delineate wooded from urban areas and you should be able to display points of interest that can serve as a reference. You actually don't want too much detail on a basemap, since too many waypoints can be distracting. A good map should let you clearly identify your target and give you an idea of the surrounding terrain. Most auto navigation systems don't give you that level of precision, which is another reason they make poor geocaching devices.

Be sure the handheld unit you buy comes with an installed map that covers at least a several-hundred-mile radius around your home location. If you're going to be geocaching internationally, check the vendor website for available international maps. These usually come on plug-in SIM cards, which can cost up to $100 each. However, they're a lot simpler to use than scribbling waypoints on Google Maps printouts.

Tracking—Look for a unit that can store a breadcrumb trail of your path as you search. Not only is this useful when you're trying to retrace your steps to find your car, but viewing your route can help you avoid duplicating effort when you're hunting around at the cache site.

Most GPSr units let you download and save tracks to a basemap on your computer. You can annotate these or simply store them for later upload if you plan to revisit the area. The Outlaw annotates tracks while he's in the field, noting trails, waterways, and other fine details that may not be documented in the basemap. When he revisits an area, he knows precisely where the trails and hazards are. Few basemaps provide detailed trail information, so the ability to annotate is a plus.

Battery—Most handheld GPSr devices deliver 10–12 hours of service on a set of two alkaline batteries. Rechargeable receivers, while common in auto-mounted units, are rare in rugged handheld devices. We recommend you buy a unit powered by rechargeable lithium-ion batteries. The newer models last almost as long as the alkaline stalwarts. A solar battery charger is an option that can save you aggravation on long hikes.

How to Buy

We'll admit a bias to online shopping for small electronics. You almost always find a better price. The big advantage of retail stores is customer service, so if you're a little technophobic, that's the place to go.

When buying online, comparison shopping sites like **MySimon.com**, **DealFinder.com** and **Google Product Search** will do the grunt work for you. Pay attention to seller ratings and avoid the one- and two-star candidates. Also be wary of unreasonably low prices. These deals often mask damaged units or high shipping fees that make up the difference. Factory refurbished units are often just as good as new ones, but they may not have the same warranty coverage.

We've bought and sold hundreds of items on eBay over the years without incident. EBay's "Buy It Now" feature can quickly find the lowest price from its database of online retailers. If you choose to bid on an auction item, use one of the many "sniper" services that will bid a price up to your pre-set limit in the waning seconds of an auction. We use **AuctionSniper.com**, but **Gixen.com**, **EZSniper.com**, **BidNapper.com**, **BidNinja.com**, and **SnipeSwipe.com** are just a few of the alternatives. These services charge a small fee, but the cost is usually well worth the convenience. Amazon's Merchants program can also deliver excellent value and the peace-of-mind that Amazon will intervene in buyer-seller disputes.

If price is your most important criteria, try **Craigslist.com**. It's the best destination for used equipment. Don't limit your search to your local area. Craigslist sellers can often be convinced to ship an item if you pay the charges and you can often get them to negotiate on price. You can also check out local geocaching organizations. Some have classified sections where you can buy from serious geocachers whom you may know personally. This is just another reason to get involved with your local geocaching group (see Chapter 10, "The Social Side"). Your friends in the organization may be willing to give you a special deal.

To get the best prices, buy products one generation out of date. You won't get all the latest features, but prices can be as little as half those of the current models. Some manufacturers will let you upgrade software for free so that your two-year-old model can have many of the latest goodies. This strategy is also a good way to save money on mapping software, which changes relatively little between new releases.

The best way to **conserve battery life** is to turn off the unit or temporarily disable satellite reception. The process of locking onto a satellite signal burns about half the operating battery power of a GPSr, so limiting this function to the times you really need it can save big. Because it can take several minutes to lock onto a satellite signal again, units shouldn't be turned off unless you won't need them for at least 10 minutes.

Manufacturers are doing some clever things to conserve battery life, including putting their units into sleep mode during idle time without losing satellite signals, or enabling you to turn off GPS reception and continue in a simulated navigation mode. We tested a Lowrance unit that had this feature, although that's about the only thing we liked about it. These bells and whistles can save a lot of juice, but be careful about trusting the product maker's claims of battery life. In most cases, they're optimistic. Always carry spare batteries.

Routes—This is a very useful option that a lot of GPSr owners don't use. Some receivers let you specify a sequence of waypoints to visit in the order that you choose. Since this can be arduous to program on a handheld device, you'll probably want to create these paths on a desktop computer and then download the route to your receiver. This can make your caching trip more efficient, which is a plus if you're going for a large number of caches.

When they were planning their record-setting 312-cache, 24-hour run, the team at GeoWoodstock IV used Microsoft Streets & Trips to optimize their route and then loaded the plan into their GPSr (see more on Streets & Trips in Chapter 9). The record run wouldn't have been possible without route optimization.

Routes take up memory and some GPSr devices limit their length and detail. Check the capacity of any unit you plan to buy to be sure it can accommodate several miles of programmed routes.

Sun/moon—Standard fare in outdoor units, this feature tells you the time of sunset, which is useful information when you're out in the wild trying to squeeze in one more find.

Screen—Look for a unit with a bright screen that is large enough to deliver detail without making the receiver bulky. Auto navigation units generally excel in this area, but most aren't waterproof and the screens are easily broken. A resolution of 320×320 pixels is standard on handheld units and should serve most needs pretty well.

Screen brightness varies widely. You'll want a GPSr that can be easily read in bright sunlight, so ask retailers to let you take a few units outdoors and test them. As a rule, you'll want to run battery-powered units at the lowest possible level of brightness in order to conserve battery power, but you need to be able to jack up those lumens when the situation demands it.

Interface—There are lots of options here and your choice is a matter of personal preference. We prefer scroll wheels or touch screens. However, the most popular GPSr with avid cachers—the Garmin 60CSx—has neither. It uses a system of buttons and up/down arrows to control the cursor.

Scroll wheels are ideal for one-handed operation, although they're not very good for entering text. Touch screens are fast and intuitive to use, but they can be a liability when unintended contact with clothing and other objects changes the display. The touch screen electronics also tend to make the units more fragile. For text entry, a small keyboard on a touchscreen unit can't be beat.

Tides—You'll probably never need this information unless you geocache at shorelines where water level is a factor. You don't want to use a handheld unit designed for land navigation when you're out at sea. In that case, invest in a specialized system.

Vendor website—Most vendors do a pretty good job of providing basic documentation and firmware downloads from their websites, but some add special features like downloadable maps, satellite images, and specialized lists of waypoints. Also look for companion software—preferably free—that can extend or add features to your GPSr. You should update your firmware regularly to fix bugs and take advantage of new features. Some vendors also post software written by their customers.

Water resistance—Believe us, you'll need this. GPSr devices get dropped onto wet grass and in mud puddles all the time. A unit labeled "water resistant" can survive a brief dunking or a few minutes in the rain. One labeled "waterproof" can be submerged for several minutes. For most casual cachers, water resistance is sufficient. Note that "waterproof" doesn't mean "floatable." It's a good idea to attach any unit to your body in some way so it doesn't sink down to Davy Jones' Locker.

Area calculation—This feature calculates the area encompassed by a series of waypoints. You won't need it for geocaching.

Music/video—The spacious memory and storage capacity of today's units have enabled many manufacturers to add the ability to play MP3 and video files. We can't imagine why this would be useful for geocaching (unless you're a devotee of the *Podcacher* podcast), but it could be nice to have on long hikes.

Geocaching features—In the early days of handheld GPS navigation, most GPSr manufacturers included a few geocaching features strictly as an afterthought. Cache waypoints were all but indistinguishable from any others and the volume of information that users could capture was limited.

All of that has changed recently. With the release of its Colorado and Oregon line of receivers in 2008, Garmin came out with products that cachers could

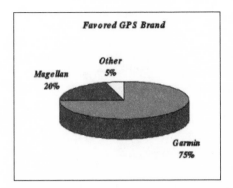

Favored GPS Brand

Magellan 20%

Other 5%

Garmin 75%

Source: Our online survey of 142 geocachers.

truly call their own. These capable but pricey units can store detailed descriptions, log entries, and hints downloaded from the **Geocaching.com** website. They even give users the ability to log and comment on their finds for later upload. Expect Magellan to add similar features.

Memory/Storage—Cheaper and older GPSr units, including the Garman 60 series, come with only 24 MB or less of internal memory. That's enough to hold a few states' worth of maps, which doesn't seem like a big deal until you travel halfway across the country and realize you forgot to load the local maps. Not that we know anything about this.

Most handheld GPSr devices accept plug-in memory modules that use inexpensive "flash" or chip-based storage. These slots are usually used for pre-programmed map modules for non-U.S. territories or for specialized city guides. These add-on memory cards don't solve the storage problem unless the unit can treat them like main memory. Ask the sales rep or check the vendor website.

Chip—The key name to remember here is SiRF, a chipset that makes receivers more accurate. Invest in a SiRF chip. It will save you time in the field.

WAAS (Wide-Area Augmentation System)—Most GPSr support this option, which improves accuracy somewhat, although at the expense of some battery life. You'll want to have it available, though.

Why, After All This, You'll Probably Buy a Garmin or Magellan

Technology markets tend to be dominated by a small number of vendors, and the GPSr receiver market is no exception. Garmin and Magellan are the two most established players with the broadest lines of handheld units. Garmin, in particular, is a favorite of geocache enthusiasts. An overwhelming 75 percent of the cachers we surveyed said they use a Garmin device, with the workhorse 60CSx being the favorite of half of them. Other popular Garmin models include the eTrex and Legend. Magellan users split about evenly between the Explorist, Sportrak, and Meridian models.

Farewell, Old Friend

Geocachers' fondness for the 60CSx was dramatized in a post by Parzival on The Online Geocacher (**onlinegeocacher.com**). Entitled "Mourning the Loss of an Old Friend," it's a eulogy to a favored GPSr that fell out of a truck somewhere between Indiana and North Carolina:

> I wish I could convey just how much that little guy meant to me. He wasn't just a tool for finding geocaches, he was my best friend, and now he is gone. He always gave me great reception even in the densest of tree cover. His compass was always true. I know one day I will have to replace you with another of your kind. I know that in your heart you would want me to move on and be happy. I can only hope I can have the same relationship with my next 60CSx as I have had with you.

As mentioned previously, with the introduction of the Colorado and Oregon lines, Garmin moved the bar higher by improving the display, adding topographic maps, and integrating full GPX support. This makes it possible for a user to load full descriptions, difficulty/terrain ratings, logs, and even hints right into the unit and to overlay that information on maps. These new units are expensive, but the price will come down.

Magellan is more focused on vehicle navigation than outdoor use, but its Triton series offers a good range of capabilities and values, with street prices ranging from under $70 to about $300. Its high-end Triton 2000 has a large, vivid color display as well as a calendar, MP3 player, and voice recorder. A few veteran cachers we talked to liked to keep their daily tallies on their calendars, and the voice recorder could come in handy for documenting your travels as well. The Outlaw usually takes a separate voice recorder with him to note trail details.

Garmin and DeLorme have a couple of advantages over the competitors: a free software utility that **Geocaching.com** users can apply to load GPX files directly from the website into their handheld devices. Several manufacturers support geocache logging in the field with subsequent upload to Geocaching.com. The Geocaching Swiss Army Knife (GSAK) software also supports direct downloads to Garmin and Magellan devices, although some add-on macros have been written to support others. GSAK should be in every serious cacher's toolbag (see Chapter 9, "Software Goodies for Geocachers"), so this compatibility is a plus.

Real Simple

The GPSr market is a features war, with device makers competing to load up their devices with fancy add-ons like music players and digital cameras. These extras play well to the digerati, but what about the technophobes among us who just want to find a geocache?

In the spring of 2009, mobile software maker Apisphere teamed with Groundspeak and outdoor equipment retailer REI to introduce an ultra-simple geocaching device called the **Geomate.jr**. Targeted at kids and families, the **Geomate.jr** carries a list price of $70 and comes preloaded with 250,000 U.S. geocaches. Switch it on and the GPSr points you toward the closest geocache. It also tells you how to get back to where you started. Other than a compass and a couple of simple informational screens, the two-button device has no additional features. An optional update kit enables owners to download new waypoints when they've exhausted nearby options. Kids may be the target audience, but something tells us they'll be the ones showing their parents how this gizmo works.

Other Manufacturers

DeLorme has recently started to make a play for the geocaching market with its Earthmate series. We tested a PN-20 provided by DeLorme and found it to be a serviceable and very compact unit, although it lacked advanced features. The Earthmates do have the advantage of coming with DeLorme's spectacular Topo USA mapping software. This bright, beautiful tool far outstrips the rather basic software that comes with Garmin devices, although its graphics-intensive features make it run slowly on older computers. We also found the route calculation to be quite good. DeLorme now also offers a software plug-in to **Geocaching.com** that makes it simple to download GPX files directly into the device. The vendor ran a major promotion at GeoWoodstock VII, indicating that it's serious about the geocacher market.

Lowrance is another player to consider with its iFinder series. We had a chance to test the iFinder Expedition C, which is targeted at geocachers among other users, and we liked its screen and options, which included a visual "averaging" option for fine-tuning accuracy and a nice power-saving feature. Still, neither the device nor its basemap software supported GPX files—an unpardonable sin in the geocaching world—and there were no features for exchanging data with **Geocaching.com**. We give Lowrance credit for courting the geocaching market, but it still has a ways to go.

This advice isn't meant to deter you from looking seriously at competing products. Some GPSr makers are actively trying to appeal to the caching community and offering giveaways and incentives to compete. Vendors that principally develop auto navigation systems, though, have a lot to learn in understanding the unique needs of geocachers.

Our Recommendations

We always root for the little guy, so it's with some reservations that we advise you to stick with the big brands when buying a GPSr. Software compatibility is an important variable in the decision process and Garmin and Magellan have both been favorites of geocachers since the early days. Their large base of users means that answers to common problems are often only a Google search away. Their products are almost universally supported by software developers and they work seamlessly with **Geocaching.com**.

Don't buy more GPSr than you need. For basic navigation, an $80 unit works just as well as a $400 one, sometimes better. Bells and whistles like a camera and MP3 player add costs and reduce battery life. Chances are you already have other devices that perform these functions better, anyway.

There is a list of online resources at the back of this book to help you hunt for the perfect GPSr for you, your style, and your geocaching preferences.

CACHER PROFILE
MonkeyBrad

Geocaching.com handle: MonkeyBrad
Name: Brad Simmons
Claim to fame: Co-organized GeoWoodstock
   VII in 2009
Location: Chapel Hill, Tennessee
Caching since: August 30, 2002
Total finds: 11,897
Total hides: 183
Preferred GPSr: Garmin Quest

Favorite Cache Types

"I love doing virtuals because they bring you to really neat areas. I'm a huge fan of traditional caches, but I am basically an omnivore, I love them all."

Special equipment

"I carry a 70-foot rope, a harness, and climbing gear. Sometimes it's easier to rappel than to walk around."

Great Caching Stories

- "We were in a park that was closed, but we didn't know it. The cops approached us, so I threw my keys in a mud puddle to stall for time. The officer was very excited to help us find the keys. And while we were searching we found this Tupperware container (the cache we had been looking for). We opened it up and acted surprised: 'Hey, whaddya know, there's a book in here that people have signed.' And then we all signed the book, *including the police officer.*"
- While caching with a group of friends in Jacksonville, Florida, MonkeyBrad retrieved one cache that involved reaching inside the rear end of a kids' horseback ride amusement at a Wal-Mart. "We got there at ten at night and got

the cache," he says. "Suddenly, there were about 50 people milling around the front of the store. There was no way for us to return the cache to this unusual location without being seen. We came up with another tactic. I started yelling at my friend and we walked away across the parking lot shouting and screaming at each other. While we distracted everyone, my wife slipped the cache back in place." Grace under pressure.

Most Memorable Finds

MonkeyBrad tells a good story about the value of extraneous clues. He had given up on searching for one cache in an area with lots of heavy industrial equipment. He remembers, "As I was walking away, I found a piece of plastic with some epoxy on it. I figured it might have blown away while the owner was placing the cache. So I decided to revisit the scene. I discovered that one of bolts on the machinery didn't match the others. The cache turned out to be a hollowed-out nut that had been epoxied to the surface. This is one of the most devious hides we have found." Other favorites are Tube Torcher II (GCWA47), Bradley's Bottom (GC6A02), Old Rag Mountain (GC16H3P), and A Claustrophobic's Nightmare (GCK2AW).

Words of Wisdom

"Always log your DNFs," he advises. "We have an obligation to the person coming after us to tell them if the cache might be missing, or to let the owners know that they fooled us."

CHAPTER NINE
Software Goodies for Geocachers

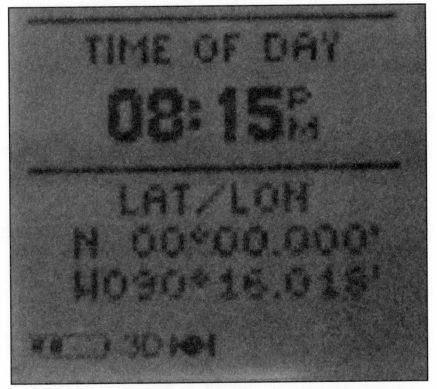

GPS readout at the North Pole. *Photographer unknown*

One of the forces behind geocaching's surging popularity is the bounty of new software and Web-based tools that have emerged to make it possible for players to customize the experience.

A few years ago, there wasn't much you could do except load a few coordinates into your GPSr, print out a stack of descriptions, and head out the door. Today, high-end GPSr units like Garmin's Colorado and Oregon as well as cheap software for the Apple iPod have made geocaching truly paperless. The powerful PC database manager called Geocaching Swiss Army Knife (GSAK) makes it possible to customize an outing to your liking. And everything from routes to favorite caches can now be shared online.

In recent years, a lot of useful software has emerged to help geocachers plan and optimize their outings. The resources page on Geocaching.com lists a few (**Geocaching.com/waypoints/default.aspx**) and enthusiasts swear by the programs described below as essential utilities for serious players. Most of these tools carry modest license fees, but we've found the cost to be well worth it for serious geocaching.

Geocaching Swiss Army Knife

This is by far the most powerful program to store and manipulate caches. It basically takes all the information you find in a geocache description, breaks it up into its component parts, and presents it to you as a series of fields that looks a little like a spreadsheet. If you've ever worked with a database management system, you'll quickly get the hang of it, but if you haven't, it's important simply to know that GSAK can "understand" a lot of the information stored in GPX files and help you look at it in different ways.

Once you start using GSAK, you'll want to keep all your cache information there. Every time you load the results of a new pocket query, the existing information in GSAK is updated. This has value over time. For example, new logs are added to existing ones in GSAK's database, which gives you a richer body of information to mine as time passes. You can also modify or add to listings stored in GSAK, something that's impossible to do on **Geocaching. com**. Any modifications you make are kept on file even as new information is imported.

Sold yet? Head to **GSAK.net** to download the software. We'll wait here for you.

GSAK doesn't require an Internet connection to run. You can load it onto a laptop, import your GPX files, and take them with you on the road. You can even download images from **Geocaching.com** using GSAK's "Database|Grab Images" menu option. This allows you to view full HTML pages, including images, when you're not connected to the Internet. That's especially useful for puzzle caches, which often rely upon images displayed on the descriptions page.

Another very useful feature of GSAK is that you can edit cache listings. For example, say you're seeking a puzzle cache that you solved at home before heading out on the road. Final coordinates for a puzzle cache are never the same as listed coordinates, so you can enter corrected coordinates in a separate field. Right-click on the cache, choose "Corrected Coordinates" and type or paste in the new information. The original coordinates are still stored in the description in case you need to refer back to them. You may also make notes to yourself that you'll want to see when you're in the field. You can't post this information to the website unless you own the cache listing, but you may find it of value later.

Another reason to edit waypoints is to update them with new information. For example, suppose you find the cache has been damaged by water and you've replaced it with a new container. You can write a detailed description of the new container and update your records. You can even share that information later via a log entry on **Geocaching.com**.

Navigating GSAK

Start by loading a GPX file into GSAK using the "File|Load GPX/LOC/ZIP" option or directly from e-mail using the "Get Data Via E-mail" menu (you have to set up the latter to work with your e-mail account).

Here's a basic GSAK startup screen:

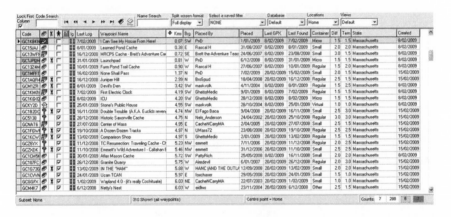

The headings of each column of cells correspond to the information found in a typical geocache description. If you click on a heading, all the geocaches on the list will be sorted by that category. You can choose which columns you want to see by choosing the "View|Add/Delete Columns" option on the menu.

The first thing you want to do is set your home point. This is a little tricky. Open the "Tools|Options" menu or click on the Tools button 🔧. A screen like the one shown on the next page pops up.

Choose the "Locations" tab and type or paste in your home coordinates. Remove the "#" sign to set these as your default. If you frequently geocache from more than one location, you can enter as many sets of coordinates here as you want and then change your home coordinates depending on your location. GSAK will only see the ones that don't have the "#" sign in front of them.

Options   ☒

| General | HTML | Locations | Display | Abbreviations | Keyboard shortcuts | Advanced |

Default action when you double click on a waypoint
Show offline in browser ▼

Method for matching placed (hidden) and found caches
○ Exact match   ○ Wild card match   ○ Owner ID#   ○ RegEx
PnD

Database Folder
C:\Program Files\GSAK\data   🔍 Find

User Sort
Current Value [0]   Increment By [10]

☑ Automatically sort by distance after setting a centre point
☑ Move to first waypoint after column sequence change
☑ Show tips at start up
☐ Suppress "Customize" popup hint
☑ Automatically size status bar to fit
☐ Name/code search beep rather than zero records message
☐ Suppress "Finished OK" messages

Status Attributes
	Colour	Priority
Unavailable/Archived	Pink ▼	1 ▼
Placed	Lime ▼	2 ▼
Found	Yellow ▼	3 ▼
Not found	White ▼	4 ▼
Highlight	○ Code ● First column

Distance calculation
● Kilometres
○ Miles

Calendar Start Day
Sun ▼

Automatic Backup
☑ Enable ☑ Prompt ☐ Include images [1 ▼] Frequency
C:\Program Files\GSAK\backup   🔍 Find

Sort column colour [   ] ... Active row [   ] ...
User flag line color [   ] ...   Grid font ...

Smart Name
Drop words [the;this;a;is]
Length [8 ▼] Keep chars [   ]
Conversions [   ]

✓ OK   ✗ Cancel   ? Help

Upon updating your home coordinates, the main screen will be reset with distances measured from there.

Not all the icons on the main GSAK screen are intuitive, so let's look at two that we find especially useful.

This icon, found in the "lg" column, shows you the status of the last four logged find attempts. Green means found and red means not found. You might want to avoid caches with three or four red squares because there is a high likelihood that they have been lost.

This is called a "user flag" and it's used to mark caches you might want to revisit later. For example, if you're scanning a list and selecting caches that look interesting to you, you can quickly mark them with a user flag and later filter your choices to include only caches you've marked this way. You can set or clear all the user flags in a view by choosing the "User Flags" menu item.

What We Use

Small books could be written about GSAK, and they actually have been, given the tool's voluminous help menus and large FAQ section on **GSAK.net**. You probably will never need to use two-thirds of the choices the program offers, but there are a few core features you will use all the time. In the rest of this section, we'll review the features we find most helpful and help you sort out the sometimes overwhelming number of options.

Waypoint Menu

Double-clicking on any cache name opens a browser window with the cache description. If you're connected to the Internet, you'll see the page on **Geocaching.com**. Otherwise, you'll get an HTML page populated with information from the GPX database. If you've downloaded images using the "Database|Grab Images" option, the off-line page will look pretty much like the online one.

Right-clicking on any item brings up this menu with some useful options. "Custom URL" gives you the option of opening that waypoint in a variety of mapping services, logging your visit, or visiting the cache's photo gallery on **Geocaching.com** if you are online.

"Edit" brings up a summary menu that lists all the information in the GPX record for that waypoint. This is a fast and easy way to learn about the cache and to edit that waypoint if you wish.

"Add/Change/Delete Note" is useful if you're using GSAK in the field. Choosing this option opens a window where you can type comments and notes for your log. These can later be uploaded to **Geocaching.com** directly, although the process is not fully automated (see "Logging Your Finds" on page 186).

"Corrected Coordinates" gives you the option of updating coordinate information so you can share it with others. This is useful if you manage to find a cache but discover that the coordinates are significantly different from the ones listed, or if you want to add solutions to a puzzle cache. You can post the corrected coordinates on **Geocaching.com** as a log entry to help future players. Puzzle solutions, however, should not be published.

"Set This Cache as Centre Point" can be helpful if you want to find other caches in the area or explore the region around the designated cache. This resets the default GSAK view with the selected cache as the center point so you can quickly see what else is nearby.

"Add to locations" automatically adds the designated cache to the box in the "Locations" tab on the Tools|Options menu. Waypoints in this box can easily be set as center points for other views of the list.

"Project waypoint" is an option you probably won't use very much, but it comes in handy in certain situations. Some puzzle caches, for example, don't point you to a specific location but rather "project" the destination as a distance and bearing. Figuring this out without a computer can be difficult, so the "Project waypoint" option can help you pinpoint the destination with greater accuracy.

"Color waypoint" highlights the designated waypoint record in a color of your choice. This is a useful tool for marking geocaches with similar characteristics that you may want to easily find later.

Creating a Filter

The most powerful feature of GSAK is its ability to filter a database of caches by any criteria you supply. You can access this feature with the "Search|Filter" menu option or by simply clicking on the filter button 🔍 on the toolbar. This presents you with a dialog box that looks like this:

This looks pretty daunting at first, but once you start experimenting with the options you'll quickly get the hang of it. Basically, a filter lets you drill down to any field of information in a GPX file and create a customized view based on the criteria you specify.

You can build filters with as many options as you choose, which enables you to plan routes precisely. Here are a couple of examples of how you might put filters to use:

Easy Outing

Suppose you wanted to make it in an easy day. You're going to look only for caches that are of low difficulty and have been found by lots of other people. Starting on the "Set Filter" dialog box in the "General" tab, choose terrain and difficulty that are "Less than or equal to" and select "2.0" from the drop-down box. Then go to the "Other" tab, click the "Clear All" button and select the "Traditional" check box. If you want to make this *really* easy, under "Container size," click the "Clear All" button and then select the "Regular" and "Large" options. This will limit your results to only the largest containers.

Now click the "Logs" tab. This instructs GSAK to find certain kinds of logs filed by previous visitors. Set "Logs to Search" at "Last 5," choose "Include," set "Required Count" to "Greater than or equal to" and "5" and choose "Log Type" of "Found it." Here's what the screen will look like:

To review: We've just told GSAK to find regular or large caches with difficulty and terrain ratings of 2.0 or less that have been found by all of the last five visitors. Click the "Go" button 🦊 Go and check out your results. You can now sort this list the same way you would any other. You can also save your filter for later use.

Complex Filter

Now let's try constructing a really complex filter, probably more complex than you would ever want to create. This simply shows you the range of options that are available to you in GSAK. We're going to look for caches that:

- Are less than 10 km from our home point (you can also ask GSAK to display in miles);
- Have a difficulty rating of less than 4.0;
- And a terrain rating of less than 3.0;
- Are available (in other words, not archived);
- Have travel bugs;
- Were last found and logged after February 1, 2009;
- Are multi or traditional;
- Are east or southeast of our home coordinates; and
- Are small, regular, or large size.

Our filter screens look like this:

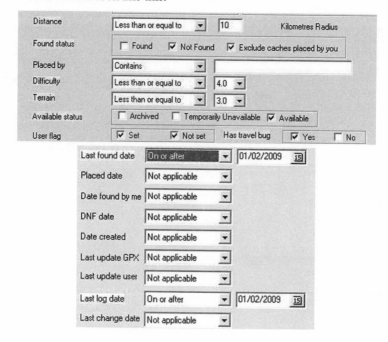

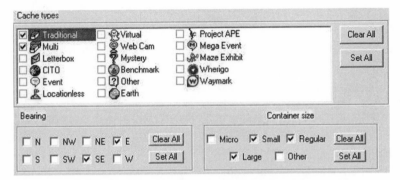

Our filter yields one matching cache working from our home base in eastern Massachusetts: Rhodys & Canoe stop (GCWA0W). Check it out!

Customizing Data

As we mentioned earlier, you can customize the records in a GSAK database to add your own notes and logs. If you look at any individual waypoint record, you'll notice there's a place for "User Data."

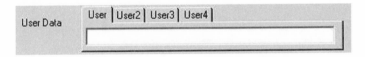

This is a very powerful feature of GSAK that lets you add your own information to any record and filter or sort on that information. For example, say you were browsing a set of geocaches in your area and wanted to mark some for a later visit by your scout troop. You could enter "scouts" in the user data field for the selected caches and later create a filter that lists only waypoints containing that notation. GSAK supports up to four user data fields, which should be enough for anyone.

Where'd the Data Go?

Whenever you create a new filter, the results on your screen usually change. Don't panic; your data is still there. All that's changed is the *view* of the data. You can get your original data set back by clearing all filters (in "Select a Saved Filter," choose "NONE"). However, be aware that if you edited or deleted any individual record, that record is permanently changed. It's a good idea to keep the original GPX files generated by the pocket query if you need to refer back to them.

Okay, I Like My Filter. Now What?

GSAK gives you several nice ways to use the results of your filters. You can print them out in a plain text format that preserves just the most essential information, export them to a spreadsheet, or upload them to a GPSr or mobile device. Chances are you'll want to do the latter at some point.

You can export your selection of caches as a GPX file for upload to any compatible GPSr device. GSAK supports most popular units via the "GPS" menu, and the transfer process is straightforward if you plug the device into your computer's USB port.

However, every GPSr unit is different. The newer breed of devices, with their ample memory space, can store and display entire descriptions, logs, and hints. However, many older devices are more constrained and can display just a few characters. This is where the export options come in handy. By default, most GPSr units identify waypoints by the GC number (for example, GC1MFFT). This code has little utility to a geocacher in the field, though. GSAK lets you modify the identification number so that your GPSr displays useful information about the cache.

Go to the "Export" option, choose "Export GPX/LOC file," uncheck "Use Defaults" and enter new variables in the "Cache Description" field. This will create an alternative code to the GC number that tells you something about the cache.

Waypoint name

You can build the waypoint name using tags (see help)

%con1%dif1%ter1%bug%last4

There is a vast number of variables you can use, ranging from obvious to obscure. Consult GSAK's help screens for a list.

For example, entering the following instructions gives you a code that tells you the container type, difficulty, terrain, whether the cache contains a travel bug, and the results of the last four logs:

This will replace a geocache named GCZENK with the letters R15YFNFF. Why is this useful? Because each letter refers to a different characteristic of the cache:

R = Regular size
1 = Difficulty in one digit (1 = 1, 1.5 = 2, 2 = 3, 2.5 = 4, and so on)
5 = Terrain in one digit (1 = 1, 1.5 = 2, 2 = 3, 2.5 = 4, and so on)
Y = Cache has a travel bug (simple Y/N)
FNFF = Results of last four logs (three "Finds" and one "Did Not Find")

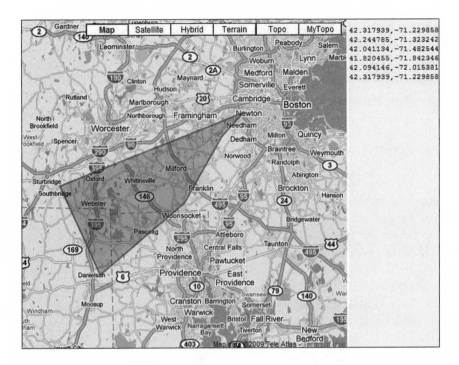

Load this information into a GPSr with limited memory and display capabilities, and you can see much more information about a cache than you would with the standard GC codes. By changing the naming convention, we have turned a relatively meaningless code into five bits of useful information. There are many more options you can build into the file you export, but these are some of the more useful ones.

GSAK also has the ability to create a list of caches along route, similar to the "Create a Route" option on **Geocaching.com**. It's called Arc/Poly, and it's available from the menu you use to filter geocaches. The instructions in GSAK may make your head want to explode, but it's really just a matter of specifying a list of geographic points along the route you're planning to travel. GSAK will filter caches that lie within a specific distance of those points. Fortunately, newer versions of GSAK link to a Google Maps mashup page (**gsak.net/google/ polygoneditor.html**) that makes it pretty simple to generate a list of waypoints. The sample route above generates the coordinates on the right that can be copied and pasted into GSAK.

Logging Your Finds

It would be nice to be able to log your finds by uploading them directly to **Geocaching.com**, but the website doesn't permit this. All is not lost, however. GSAK contains a macro that makes the process almost automatic.

If you carry a laptop running GSAK with you, you can log your finds offline in the program and upload them later one-by-one using a macro. A macro is a little program that plugs into GSAK and performs a small but useful task that isn't included in the main software. Users have written hundreds of macros that you can download from **GSAK.net**. Some are very useful, like Email Log Reader, which automatically grabs e-mails from **Geocaching.com** from your inbox and updates relevant waypoints in GSAK. Most macros are pretty obscure, but if you use an uncommon GPSr or want to load your results into a specialized Web service, chances are someone's written a macro to do that.

Log your finds using the "Add/Change/Delete Note" option in the "Waypoint" menu or by right-clicking on the cache record in the list view. Anything you enter in the "User Notes" field will be kept in your own records. Whatever you enter in the "Logs Section" field will be uploaded to **Geocaching.com**.

When you return from your journey, connect to the Internet and run the macro called "LogCache.gsk." This will pull up the appropriate log page on the website and enter your comments. Just follow the prompts. It isn't perfect, but it's a heck of a lot faster than cutting and pasting everything yourself.

Using Google Maps and Google Earth

Google gave geocachers a gift with its 2005 release of Google Maps and later Google Earth. Not only do these impressive Web services allow you to map nearly any spot on earth, but they're also the foundation for thousands of third-party software applications that ride on top of their basic features. **Geocaching.com**'s "Find with Google Maps" feature is just one example.

As with GSAK, entire books can be written about all you can do with Google Maps, but we'll stick to a few basic features that we find most valuable.

Although many people don't know it, Google Maps can provide you with the precise geographic coordinates of any spot it can map. To find this information, click on the "Print," "Send," or "Link" options. The dialogue box that pops up has the coordinates in both decimal and UTF formats embedded in it, although you may have to hunt around a bit to find them. The string of text looks something like this (we've bolded the coordinates):

http://maps.google.com/maps?f=q&source=s_q&hl=en&geocode=&q=
1+park+ave.,+new+york,+ny&sll=**42.287469,-71.421304**&sspn=0.007588,
0.016565&gl=us&g=4+thurber+st.,+01702&ie=UTF8&ll=**40.746948,
-73.981504**&spn=0.007771,0.016565&z=16&iwloc=addr

Copy and paste this code into a text editor like Notepad and then copy and paste the coordinates into whatever application needs them.

An easier way to find the coordinates for any address is to enter the address into the "Hide & Seek a Cache" page on **Geocaching.com**. The results page provides the coordinates of the address just above the search results.

Alternate Views

Some more recent Google innovations that are interesting to geocachers are the satellite, street, and terrain views. The terrain view (shown below) is useful if you don't have a topographic map and want to get an idea of what kind of climb you may be in for.

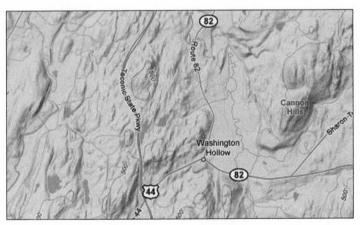

Google Street View gives you an actual photo of the location you searched for with the ability to pan and zoom all around you (see next page). You can also use this view to get an idea of the neighborhood you're going to be entering, or even to scout out potential hiding spots. Street View is a work in progress that Google is building out by laboriously sending teams of photographers into the field to capture images. It works well in major North American cities, but rural and suburban areas are spotty.

And as of this writing, Google Maps can't import GPX files, which gives it limited utility as a way to organize your outing. However, the service is constantly being improved. Google Maps can export a waypoint to a GPSr pretty cleanly.

Choose "Send" and then select the "GPS" option and follow the instructions (although not all GPSr manufacturers are listed in the options box).

If you're interested in the innovative things people are doing with Google Maps, a blog called Google Maps Mania (**googlemapsmania.blogspot.com**) does a fantastic job of keeping up with them all.

Google Earth

A global initiative that seeks to apply satellite imagery to mapping the entire globe, Google Earth is an impressive technical achievement that has modest value to geocachers. As of this writing, Google still requires a software download to display Google Earth's full capabilities. A $400 annual fee gets you the Professional Edition, but that functionality is more appropriate to surveyors and architects than it is to geocachers. Fortunately, what you get for free is pretty amazing.

Google Earth can give you a bird's eye view of any spot on the planet photographed by satellite and made available to the service via Google's network of information providers. You can specify an address or a set of geo-coordinates and zoom in to that exact location to view landmarks and surrounding territory. The quality of the imagery can be quite striking in some cases, although the basic free version does not provide enough detail to enable you to make out features of individual buildings with much clarity. However, Google Earth can give you a pretty good idea of the terrain you might encounter in searching for a geocache. In that respect, it's a capable free alternative to the topographic maps that cost $50 or more.

Google Earth can import GPX files created by **Geocaching.com** or GSAK and show you waypoints on its satellite maps. In our experience, however, this process is somewhat error-prone. Clicking on the waypoint titles on the map delivers the

The White House as seen on Google Earth.

Google Earth image showing a cache site and driving directions.

descriptions downloaded from the Internet. The software also has extensive information about local features such as bridges, dams, and scenic areas. Most of this is gathered from public domain resources and will improve in time. Some of the same features in Google Maps are also available in Google Earth, such as driving directions. The combination can provide you a much richer view of your destination and the surrounding area, which can be helpful in deciding how to prepare for a trip.

What's a Geotag?

Digital picture, video, and audio files have information hidden in them that computers can understand but many people never see. If you've ever clicked the "Properties" or "Info" option on one of these files, you might notice information like dates, shutter speeds, and f-stop settings. These are tags, and there are a lot of things you can do with them.

Tags are used by computers to organize and describe digital media. So if you tag each of your geocaching photos with the word "geocaching," you can easily see all those pictures in one group. In recent years, people have started adding geographic coordinates to photo tags. This means that a computer can automatically associate pictures with places on the map, which is very cool. For example, you can geotag all the pictures of your sister's wedding and share them on a Google Map. Other people can do the same, creating a kind of collage of geotagged images.

For cachers, geotagging is a great way to associate the pictures you take with the places you've been. It's also a good way to show other geocachers what scenery to expect when they go after a cache. Photo-sharing services now make geotagging pretty easy. Upon uploading your photos, you have the option of dragging them onto a map. Sites like Flickr and Google's Picasa automatically tag those photos with the appropriate coordinates based upon where you drag them. You can even tag those photos with a GC number to make it easy to remember what cache you were looking for when you snapped the picture.

For an example of geotagging in action, go to Google Maps and look up Bell Buckle, Tennessee, which was the site of GeoWoodstock VII. Select the "More" option and check the "Photos" box. You'll then to the be able to see geotagged pictures submitted by visitors to GeoWoodstock. Surprisingly, **Geocaching.com** does not support geotagging in its gallery images. Perhaps this is because Groundspeak doesn't want to be in the photo-sharing business. This seems a pity, since features like finding caches along a route would be enhanced by virtual tours.

GeoBuddy tracks and caches superimposed on an aerial map of Orlando, Florida.

Other Software

There are quite a few other applications and utilities for geocaching, with a growing number of them running on Apple's iPod platform. Many of these are free and they do a basic job of managing waypoints and logs. For example, **EasyGPS** is a simple PC tool for managing waypoints and tracks in LOC format and loading them into a GPSr. **GPSBabel** is a free utility (built into GSAK) that addresses the incompatibility problems between different GPSr units by converting waypoints, tracks, and routes between receivers and mapping programs. Use a search engine to find them.

One of the few that carries a license fee is **GeoBuddy**, available from mapmaker Topografix. While some of its features are duplicated by the free Google Maps and Google Earth services, GeoBuddy has some unique characteristics. You can import GPX files and see the waypoints and detailed information about individual caches on maps that download automatically from Topografix's database. Choices include topographic, aerial, and urban maps, which are somewhat more detailed versions of aerial photos. GeoBuddy downloads new maps from the Topografix site whenever they're needed. These topographic maps are mostly hand-drawn and feature excellent detail, but suffer from the limitations of poor scanning and enlargement capabilities. Users also have the option of scanning in their own maps or retrieving them from Microsoft's TerraServer.

GeoBuddy displays cache waypoints and descriptions in a separate window. You can narrow down a list of target caches by flipping between this list and the maps, and then create a GPX file to load into your GPSr. There's also a feature for drawing tracks and routes on a map and another one that makes it easy to geotag photos.

In our tests, GeoBuddy's library of topographic maps was excellent. However, you need to be connected to the Internet to take full advantage. If the topographic map isn't available, GeoBuddy has to download it from a server, which can take several minutes if you need a lot of map segments. In most cases, you're also working with scanned images of paper maps, which have the limitations of weak resolution at high magnifications and fixed labels that don't scale to match your view.

GeoBuddy's collection of urban and satellite maps is weak in rural areas and practically nonexistent outside the United States. While you do have the option of scanning your own maps, it's hard to believe many people will have the patience to do that. Some of GeoBuddy's basic features are becoming irrelevant because of advances in Google Earth. The big advantage of GeoBuddy is that you can save maps locally and take them with you on a laptop. For caching in major metropolitan areas, GeoBuddy is a useful complement to GSAK, but for $50 the software will probably appeal mainly to the most enthusiastic geocachers.

Microsoft Streets & Trips

Microsoft positions this powerful PC application (street price of about $60, including a plug-in GPSr) as an automobile navigation aid. It performs many of the functions of a Garmin Nuvi or Tom Tom on a PC, but also has a rich database of information about local attractions and businesses. When connected to the Internet, Streets & Trips can also update routes with information about construction delays and route you around them. The software comes with a miniature GPS receiver that plugs into a USB port on a laptop, and directions can be delivered by a text-to-speech synthesizer. In our view, it's worth the extra money to invest in a convenient navigational GPSr, but if you want to get away on the cheap or don't always have your auto navigation unit with you, Streets & Trips can fit the bill.

Streets & Trips is not intended for geocaching use. In fact, it doesn't even read GPX or LOC files. It does have one unique geocaching feature, though: the ability to optimize routes. This can save time if you're planning to pick up a lot of geocaches and want to minimize driving.

Creating a route is a bit of a kluge. You need to export your list of target caches in CSV format (GSAK has a special filter for this and there is a macro that automates the process), which basically separates fielded data with commas. You can then import that list into Streets & Trips and display the waypoints on a map. Select the individual caches you want to visit or draw a rectangle around a group of waypoints and Streets & Trips automatically generates an optimized route and detailed driving directions. These routes aren't perfect, and their quality deteriorates with length and complexity, so it's a good idea to reality-check the results. For journeys with multiple stops, though, Streets & Trips can save you a lot of drive time.

The other nice feature of Streets & Trips is its database of information about local attractions. If you want to add a restaurant or a museum to your itinerary, simply include it in the waypoint list.

Geocaching iPhone Application

One of 2009's most eagerly awaited events was the release of Groundspeak's Geocaching iPhone Application. While clearly a work in progress, the $9.95 utility rapidly became an essential tool for iPhone-toting geocachers. A version for Google's Android operating system is planned for release in 2010.

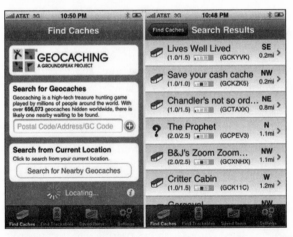

Users can search for caches near any location they specify or near their current location using the iPhone's GPS tracking feature. Results are displayed with all the familiar **Geocaching.com** colors and icons. The query function is somewhat less flexible than that of Geocaching.com's Hide & Seek a Cache page, but it's not bad. The cacher in the field can click through to read a full description (photos aren't supported), hints, and a limited number of logs. Caches can also be saved for later use.

The Groundspeak application can indicate the location of a cache relative to the user's current position and alternatively display results on a topographic map. Field notes can be recorded and submitted wirelessly. Curiously, the application does not enable users to actually log a find from the iPhone. The actual "find/did not find" must be submitted on the website.

The setup screen includes a handy "Basics" option that only returns traditional caches in the result set. There's also an integrated "S and A" page for querying trackable items.

There are a few quirks in the version 2.0 release that we tested. Groundspeak will presumably iron them out over time. One is that geocaches can't be saved in categories. Everything is clumped together in one list and deletions must be made one-by-one. Users also can't save groups of caches, but must store each one individually. The inability to display images is a problem, since many descriptions use them for clues. It's also baffling why logs can't be filed from the field. We have to assume this is just a technical issue.

Recent versions of the iPhone come with a built-in GPSr technology. This can be used with Groundspeak's and other geocaching applications to find caches in the immediate area or to direct you to a location. However, the iPhone's GPS has been criticized as being too imprecise for geocaching. For now, at least, players will continue to need a dedicated GPSr and will have to content themselves with the fact that the iPhone is the up-and-coming platform for paperless caching.

Geosphere

A recent entrant to the iPhone market is Geosphere, a $7.99 application from GBHomeTech. Geosphere appears to address many of the shortcomings of Groundspeak's application, including:

- GPX files can be downloaded directly to the device from a supported e-mail provider;
- Geocache locations can be overlaid on satellite images of an area;
- Caches can be categorized and grouped, addressing a major shortcoming of the Geocaching iPhone Application;
- A simulated compass shows bearing and distance to a destination.

Geosphere's developer doesn't have direct access to the Groundspeak database, so it's unlikely that the application can duplicate Groundspeak's functionality. We tested version 1.1 and found it difficult to use and limited in function. Version 2.0 was due to appear as we went to press. Hopefully, it will give Groundspeak a run for its money and inspire everyone to a higher standard.

CACHER PROFILE
The Genius of GSAK

Helen and Clyde England.

In 2001, Clyde England tried geocaching and found it to be a relaxing antidote to the pressure-cooker world of corporate information technology. The game was an ideal indulgence of England's twin passions for physical fitness and enjoying the countryside of his native Western Australia.

England is a techie by nature and by profession. His day job involved collecting information related to the housing and construction industries and selling cuts of the data to businesses and the public. The job required specialized technical skills. Large databases can become almost unusable if they're poorly designed or if queries (requests for information) aren't well expressed. Database architects are skilled not only at optimizing performance but also at extracting complex combinations of information based upon customer requests. England had soaked up these skills at work, not knowing that they would later come in handy.

A Tinkerer

A proclivity for technology tinkering led England to write some extensions for Ozi Explorer, the mapping software that many geocachers use. He began enhancing his own software with database routines that sorted geocaches by various criteria. He shared these improvements with some friends, who quickly began asking for more. Geocaching Swiss Army Knife (GSAK) was born.

GSAK is to geocachers what Excel is to financial professionals: an indispensable way to organize, track, and record data. Many experienced geocachers carry a laptop running GSAK with them in their cars and constantly filter and sort through its database as they plan their routes. Want to find all caches within a two-mile, west/northwest radius that were placed within the last six months and contain travel bugs? Set a few switches in a GSAK filter and you're there. Want to log your finds on the road and then upload them quickly when connected to the Internet? GSAK does that, too. Want to see full geocaching Web pages, including images, when you're 20 miles from the closest Internet connection? GSAK can download and store the information needed to serve that need as well.

Early versions of GSAK managed only a few variables, such as location and name, but requests from customers caused England to quickly expand the criteria. Today, users can filter caches by nearly any combination of characteristics listed in **Geocaching.com** descriptions, and even by some that aren't. Clyde England doesn't claim to understand why anyone would want that level of granularity. "I'm a fairly simplistic geocacher. I don't use half the capabilities of my own program," he laughs. He just aims to give customers what they want.

From Hobby to Career

England gave away GSAK for free, until a takeover and reorganization at his company in 2003 left him jobless. Uncertain what he would do next, he started charging a licensing fee for GSAK to see if there was a market. There was. Since then, GSAK has been a career for Clyde England.

And, maintaining and enhancing GSAK is certainly a full-time job. In fact, as of mid-2009, Clyde England (ClydeE) has only logged a couple of hundred finds himself. The demands of supporting thousands of other geocachers takes up too much of his time to enable him to get out into the field.

Each morning, he finds his mailbox stuffed with questions, requests, and suggestions submitted by his tens of thousands of registered customers. The forums on **GSAK.net** bristle with more than 1,000 requests for new features.

Clyde England will be the first to admit that there's plenty more he could do with the software. Flexibility is somewhat limited by an underlying third-party database engine that is "getting long in the tooth" and the need to smoothly integrate new features without disrupting existing customers.

The task of improving the program has been made easier by GSAK's support for macros, or small programs that users can write to automate common tasks. Customers have submitted hundreds of their favorite macros to **GSAK.net** that they freely share with each other. Some, like the macro that inserts a collection of waypoints into a Google map that can be displayed on a geocacher's blog or website, have thousands of fans.

The constantly expanding range of geography-based services on the Internet also present an opportunity. England admits he's only scratched the surface of what can be done with Google Maps, for example.

But then again, he's just one man. England has declined opportunities to build a company around GSAK or to expand the program into non-geocaching applications: "I've been tormented about whether I should expand my horizons, but geocaching is the main use of GSAK and it will probably stay that way." He is grateful to an active and generous group of forum members who answer many of the day-to-day questions and leave him time to focus on new features.

England has plenty of ideas for what he wants those features to be, but asked to reveal them, he politely declines. "Some features I would rather make a surprise," he says. "I want to give my customers something to look forward to."

SECTION IV

Beyond the Game

CHAPTER TEN
The Social Side

More than 5,000 people gathered in Bell Buckle, Tennessee, for GeoWoodstock VII in May 2009. Can you spot us? *Daniel Johnson (JDAN150)*

Geocachers instinctively connect with each other, so it's not surprising that there are geocaching organizations in every state of the United States, as well as in scores of foreign countries. While we're not aware of any perfect list of them all, you can find pretty good links here:

- **cacheopedia.com/wiki/List_of_Regional_Organizations/Groups**
- **forums.groundspeak.com/GC/index.php?showtopic=198818**

Veterans say groups are a great way to learn the fine points of caching. "To ramp up your knowledge quickly, cache with someone more experienced than you and learn from their methods," says WE4NCS. Ventura_kids says new cachers should go to an event to connect with people who can help with a new GPSr, advise on tactics or strategy, and explain the best caches in the area. He adds that one of the most valuable resources is a player's lifelines: other people to call for help.

So where do you meet these people, these lifelines, these future geocaching companions? At geocaching events. Events have many faces, but all of them are caches in their own right. Players can log events the same way they log caches, and events have their own page, just like any traditional geocache.

Types of Events

There are many types of events, but the most common are Meet and Greets (or Meet and Eats), at which geocachers meet at a restaurant or park and share a meal and stories. But events aren't about simply breaking bread. Groups organize all types of outings: river rafting trips, hiking or camping trips, weekend tournaments, pig roasts, picnics, mass park caching trips (where the group clears out all the geocaches in a given park together), night-caching expeditions, and competitions. Event organizers look for any excuse to arrange a get-together. Occasions like a change of seasons, days starting in T, eclipses, planetary alignment, a group member's wedding, a visitor to the area, holidays, blockbuster movie premieres, first or last days of school, and more can be celebrated with a geocaching event. As with any type of cache, the limitations are only the owner's imagination.

Cache In Trash Out (CITO) events have their own designation on **Geocaching. com**. These events take place when a group of geocachers gets together to clean up trash or debris from a park or other public place.

Mega events—those with attendance of 500 or more geocachers—are another animal altogether and also get their own listing on **Geocaching.com**. Megas usually involve educational seminars, vendor sponsorship, and/or giveaways. Regular events sometimes becomes mega events after attendance is tallied, but organizers usually know how many people to expect.

GeoWoodstock

The largest international annual mega event is GeoWoodstock, which is located in a different part of the United States each year. The first GeoWoodstock, held in 2003, was attended by just 86 souls. By 2009, between 4,000 to 5,000 geocaching enthusiasts swarmed Bell Buckle, Tennessee, for a day of educational sessions, auctions, and giveaways. Vendors like Garmin and DeLorme rubbed shoulders with niche retailers like Cache Advance and Crazy Caches! in the exhibit area. The collaborative, meet-and-greet atmosphere allows cachers to meet the people behind the online handles and to pick up a lesson or two. Veterans use the event to reunite with friends. And, of course, there's a fair amount of geocaching, too. Veterans like to use GeoWoodstock as a platform for extraordinary achievements. Remember our discussion of one group nabbing a record 312 finds in 24 hours at GeoWoodstock IV?

Tips for Event-Goers

- Before you attend an event, be sure to log your intent on the event cache page. This gives the organizers a much-needed expectation of attendee numbers.
- Read the event description carefully. Some events are "come as you are" gigs, while others request that you bring food, and still others are geocoin-swapping forums where visitors furiously trade trackables. That being said, if you show up empty-handed at a party where everyone else has brought something, chances are good that fellow cachers will share what they have. Even events that suggest bringing food become more potluck than private stores. Such is the sharing nature of the geocache community.
- Chat it up with as many people as you can. Geocachers are open to having their conversations interrupted by a stranger or newbie.
- Don't be afraid to admit that you're new to the game, the area, or the group. This is often an ice-breaker among even the most tightly-knit organizations. Admitting you'd like to learn more about the area or brush up on a skill or even learn more about your new GPSr will usually get you lots of helpful advice.
- Don't be afraid to ask people for their phone numbers and offer your own. Building a database of lifelines can prove invaluable if you find yourself in the woods looking unsuccessfully for the same prize for an hour.

Tips for Event Planners

- Meet and Greets are easy to plan and usually attract a good number of players. Conversations strengthen bonds and also help educate the group as a whole. These types of events usually run themselves and require little hands-on interaction from the organizer once they begin.
- However, don't limit yourself to Meet and Greets. An event cache is defined as any group of cachers who meet at a certain place at a certain time. Like any other kind of cache, let yourself be creative about timing, location, and theme.
- If you see a park that needs to be cleaned up, why not organize a CITO event, where players come with trash bags and—voila!—clean up the park?

- If you see something that needs to be celebrated, get people together to do just that. One Pennsylvania group celebrates the first day of school by asking cachers to bring their senior yearbooks or pictures.
- New to an area or visiting for a few days? Organize your own event to get to know people. Traveling internationally to a place with very few caches? "You're guaranteed a smiley if you host an event," says Mrs. Captain Picard.
- If you're visiting and don't have the time or local knowledge to take up the task, find a contact in the local organization and ask what local caches shouldn't be missed. Geocachers love to share their area with visitors and they may just host an event for your visit. Local organizers love any excuse to get their friends together.

Born to Entertain

The most creative event planner we met is Mrs. Captain Picard, whose imagination is unmatched. We met her Austin, Texas-area friends one night at a Meet and Greet arranged in honor of our 100-cache run (we told you cachers don't need much of an excuse) and discovered people who have a special kind of camaraderie.

Mrs. Captain Picard arranged one event called "Bon Voyage Funky Bus." She rented a renovated school bus, complete with fuzzy seats and decorated ceiling, and got attendees to group-cache around Austin in it. She has also organized bike caching trips and the GPS Olympics, in which she arranged games like the following (feel free to steal these ideas and create others; Mrs. Captain Picard would be flattered):

- **Track Log Writing:** Mrs. Captain Picard assigned a word that teams had to write by walking out the letters in an open field and producing a track log that looked like the cursive spelling of that word. She got a kick out of the different techniques teams used. She downloaded the logs, printed them out, and judged whose "foot-writing" was the best.
- **Waypoint Speed Entering:** How fast can you enter a waypoint in your GPSr? Mrs. Captain Picard gave each pair of Olympiads a waypoint. Not only did they have to enter it quickly, but they had to be the first to shout out how far it was from where they were standing. A bracket system similar to the one used in college basketball championships tracked the teams' progress. What contestants didn't know when they entered this game was that there was a stunt they had to do while they shouted out the distance to the waypoint. These included wearing a piece of someone else's clothing, dangling from the top of a jungle gym, and having a piece of toilet paper stuck to their shoe. The finalists had to shout the distance while sitting on Mrs. Captain Picard's

lap. This would have been simple enough—though rather intimate—if the organizer hadn't hidden herself in the crowd so as not to be easily found.

- **Fear Factor:** One of Mrs. Captain Picard's events required attendees to pick a stranger from the crowd as a partner. She then gave participants a sequence of games that favored large contestants. A few events later, she again told players to pick a partner. People naturally gravitated to the biggest people in the group, but this particular event was a string-gobbling contest that ended with partners kissing, something like the famous scene from *Lady and the Tramp*. Size mattered not a bit.

What if you aren't an "event" person? Go anyway, says ventura_kids: "Just walk up to anyone and say you're new to geocaching." Almost everyone is there not only to regroup with their local buddies, but also to meet new friends. One of the most wonderful things about geocaching is that the people you meet are approachable, friendly, and honest. The magic words, "I'm new. Can you help me figure this out?," are an invitation for geocachers to start a conversation.

Caching with Friends

Whether it's sharing a 12-mile hike with someone or taking a long weekend with a group, geocaching friends are hard to beat. Even top power cachers told us the secret to maintaining their frantic pace is, "We don't get tired because we're laughing all the time and having so much fun." Ask prolific cachers about their most memorable days and their stories always begin with a list of the people who shared the experience. Members of each local geocaching community enrich each other.

Events are a great way to build a database of lifelines. WE4NCS publishes his cell phone number on all of his caches. He just wants to help. And help he does: Plenty of geocachers call him every week and ask not only about his own caches, but also about others that he's found. He's always willing to give a hint that gets a fellow player closer to the target. And he finds value in the calls, too: Each caller goes into his phone book, becoming one more player to call when WE4NCS gets stuck himself.

EMC of Northridge, CA, climbed the 14,000-foot White Mountain in California with other geocachers in a 10-hour trek. Even though one fellow geocacher had to stop because of altitude sickness, she made it to the top. Elin never would have accomplished this feat without her geo-buddies. And yes, there was a virtual at the top of the mountain.

On his 50th birthday, mondou2's brother took him on a caching trip to Spain. There they came upon a cache with a business card that said, "If you bring this card to Budapest, I'll put you and your family up for a week and feed you homemade meals."

A year later, mondou2 traded in frequent flyer miles and headed to Hungary. He had e-mailed the business card owner to arrange the visit. His new geocaching friends treated him to four nights' accommodations and meals, as well as a ride to and from the airport. Where else can you find instant companions like that? In the world of geocaching, it's just part of the game.

Critter Encounters

This moose waylaid Gary & Vicky for more than an hour (see below). *Gary Hobgood*

When crashing through the woods or hiking through the desert, you aren't on your own turf anymore. The local fauna found the ammo can long ago and couldn't care less about your search. They've been known to protest intrusions by geocachers with sometimes frightening ferocity. Here are a few stories to learn from.

When In Texas ...

Total deafness hasn't stopped Richard and Natalie North (Deafdillos) of Dripping Springs, Texas, from amassing a count of more than 5,400 geocaches, but one West Texas hide was particularly memorable. "We were about 50 feet away when we realized we were coming from the wrong side of the river," Richard writes. "As we moved around to the other side, Natalie heard something, thanks to her cochlear implant, that she hadn't heard before. But it was gone quickly and we dismissed it. We found the ammo can in good shape. Later, when we visited the Monahans Sandhills State Park, we learned that Natalie had heard a rattlesnake for the first time!"

... Or Florida

InfiniteMPG can relate: "Once while caching and hiking on vacation with Cathy (Paddler Found), we set out on the Big Oak Trail at Suwanee River State Park. There is a spot on the map labeled 'Big Oak,' so I was walking with my GPSr in one hand and trail map in the other, looking up at the trees to find which oak was THE big oak. Suddenly Cathy yelled, 'You just stepped on that!' and pointed at a large snake that was sunning on the path and looking at me, wondering what the heck I was doing. Luckily, we all went our own ways." Snakes are one more hazard that teaches us all to watch where we're walking!

Who Tastes Like Chicken Now?

MonkeyBrad remembers caching in Florida in 40-degree January weather. "We were 150 feet from the cache site when we found a creek. I said it was no big deal; I'd take off my jeans and cross. As I was removing my pants, my wife asked, 'What are those two little reflecting lights in front of you?' Turns out it was an alligator. My friends freaked out and some wanted to turn back. But I said, 'Hey, we just came a half mile through knee-deep water. I'm not turning around just because of some alligator!'"

Bearly Made It!

Dutch Sanders (Linuxxpert) came face-to-face with a cacher's worst nightmare on one search. The area of rural Pennsylvania where he was hunting was filled with old coal mines that are gradually being turned into state parks. While pursuing a challenging cache, he and a buddy were poking their heads into the abandoned mines along the way. "We hiked down into a gully and there's a mineshaft held up by one of those old beam supports," he says. "I ducked down with my flashlight, stepped into the hole, and shined my flashlight into the eyes of a bear. It was bigger than I was. I didn't even have a chance to think. I turned around and ran screaming 'Bear!' My buddy and I were halfway up the hill before we peeked back to see the bear hadn't followed us."

Snakes and Ivy and Bears, Oh My!

Peasinapod has a friend who is a game warden in Canada: "'Rattlesnakes are for wimps,' he tells me. He's got grizzly bears where he lives." A tip for caching in grizzly bear territory: Don't scare them. Make plenty of noise so they can get away from you in time. Know what the dangers are in the area you're caching, especially if you are not in your home region. Poison ivy, poison oak, rattlesnakes, and any number of strange critters can land a cacher in a hospital, as Peasinapod knows all too well. He's landed in the hospital to get steroid treatment from a reaction to poison ivy.

Elks Club

Gary and Vicky Hobgood (Gary & Vicky) are at a point in their geocaching career where they're looking for challenges. The DeLorme Challenge is a great one. It involves finding a cache (or placing one if none yet exists) in the region covered by each page of the DeLorme atlas for a particular region or state. Gary and Vicky live in California, so they were involved in achieving the goal for that state. There is only one cache on page 62 of their state's atlas and that prize involves driving three miles on a dirt road, then hiking a few more miles to the cache through lovely coastal wilderness and wildlife areas. The couple saw "Danger—Wild Elk. Do not approach on foot" signs on the path to the cache, but they noticed no unusual wildlife. And they had to admit they were kind of disappointed. They reached the cache and took in the great views. They signed the log and wrote that they wished they had seen some of the famous elk, and they were hopeful they would spot some on the way back out.

Sometimes people's logs tell the best story, so we'll let Gary and Vicky take it from here:

> We were about 15 minutes into our return. As we were going around a blind corner we came face-to-face with a 1000-pound bull elk. The elk immediately charged at us. I don't normally carry a walking stick, but I'm sure glad I did that day. I swung it wildly at the great beast while yelling at the top of my voice to 'Get Back!' The huge elk stepped off the trail a few feet but started displaying the aggressive behavior of clanging its antlers on a nearby tree. A few moments later, it vocalized its displeasure by bugling. All the time it stood between us and our only way back to our car. He continued to stare us down for 20 minutes or so. To one side of us was a steep ravine, to the other side a thick forest. With no way around the bull, we hoped he would move up the trail so we could slip by.

> We've been hiking in the wilderness for decades and have come across all manner of wildlife before. They're mainly interested in getting away from us. Not this time. The bull elk stayed just down the trail from us. Slowly, we would tip-toe down the trail, only to see it there. After about an hour of this game, we moved down the trail a little farther. We peeked around a blind corner, only to come in full view of the elk again. Once again, it came charging at us. We backed off the trail and stood behind some short manzanita bushes while I swung my hiking stick and yelled. Finally, I threw a rock at the animal's rear-end. That moved it in the right direction. I tossed another and we moved up the hill and away from the trail. Finally, we saw an opening and ran as quickly as we could down the trail.

> That was the last we would see of that particular animal. We walked cautiously and quickly for the next mile and a quarter. We came to a ravine that we needed to cross. On the other side was another bull elk.

Fortunately, it wasn't startled by our presence. For the rest of the hike, we announced ourselves loudly at every corner. When we saw the Needle Rock Visitor Center, it was a sight for sore eyes. Took only pictures. Left with our lives.

Not a Bad Dinner Substitute

Ventura_kids were walking along a fire road and came across a mountain lion with a squirrel under his paw. When the lion stood up, the squirrel ran away and the lion looked at VK as if to say, "You just cost me my dinner, but you look yummy, too…." Upon further inspection, the mountain lion decided they'd be too much work and trotted off into the brush.

Get the Point?

Shortly after Deafdillos had divided up at ground zero (GZ) to search for the container, Richard yelled "Found!" Natalie signed back to him "Shhh! There's a porcupine up in the tree!" Sure enough, in a branch right above the decon container was a porcupine sleeping on a branch. To make sure it was real, Richard tossed a tiny stone toward it. The animal woke up bleary-eyed and climbed a little higher up the tree. Afraid the animal would start tossing its quills at them, the Deafdillos had to log a DNF for this one.

CACHER PROFILE
Mrs. Captain Picard

Geocaching.com handle: Mrs. Captain Picard
Name: Julie Perinne
Claim to fame: Master power cacher and the most creative event planner we know
Location: Austin, Texas
Caching since: August 3, 2002
Total finds: 17,957
Total hides: 100
Preferred GPSr: Garmin 60 CSx

Favorite Cache Types

Anything that makes her smile, whether that means creative containers or memorable events.

Special Equipment

She takes a cell phone to call a friend if she needs help. She clips a pen to her GPSr so she always has it with her. She also keeps a laptop in the car, but usually caches with other geeks who bring the real gadgetry.

Great Caching Story

Texas cachers have an annual statewide caching competition. To pay for it, each region has a silent auction fundraiser. One year, Mrs. Captain Picard donated a custom 100-find power caching trip that she would design for the highest bidder. She mapped out the route, brought home-baked snacks, filled the cooler, and told all of her wonderful caching stories to the winners, who actually weren't as interested in finding 100 caches in a day as much as caching with an expert.

Mrs. Captain Picard made the day extra special for the winners. She arranged for some of her celebrity cacher friends to call her cell phone during the day of the adventure: EMC of Northridge, CA and mondou2 called and shared their fun stories. Then Captain Picard himself called the cachers, saying he was sorry he couldn't be home to meet them at the end of the day, but that he was out in the Delta Quadrant. (Okay, it wasn't really Captain Picard: Julie got an actor friend to play the part, complete with the Patrick Stewart accent.)

Most Memorable Hide

You're cordially invited to the nuptials of Captain Picard and his Mrs. The ceremony is being held today in a park near Austin, Texas. If you miss it, though, you can still take part in the festivities—there is birdseed to toss, a wedding registry book to sign (the logbook), and a flower bouquet and veil to wear. The cache is called The Picard Nuptials (GCJG9B) and if you're in the Austin area, it's a can't-miss. And there really is birdseed inside!

Words of Wisdom

"Stay on the trail until you have to get off of it. It prevents a lot of unnecessary bushwhacking." This one simple tip has saved us miles of thorny and tick-infested hikes through raw woods.

A blushing Paul logs The Picard Nuptials.

Mrs. Captain Picard also advises players to make online logs mean something. Most cache owners love the stories and messages that finders leave behind. If you sign "TNLN, TFTC," you miss an opportunity to tell about your adventure and even share a joke or make someone smile. Entries don't even have to be about the cache. Mrs. Captain Picard was caching on the day her dad died (he was a fellow geocacher) and the logs she wrote that day are especially poignant: "Share your thoughts or feelings or the funny story on the trail with the cache owner and others in your online log."

CHAPTER ELEVEN
Geocaching in Education and Business

Deborah Goodman, an educator from Edenton, North Carolina, has a cool job. She gets to experiment with new technologies and figure out ways to apply them in education. She's an instructional technology facilitator for a local elementary school and she also provides training to other schools in the state on ways to integrate technology with the curriculum.

Deborah has been playing with a lot of new technology in recent years, including blogs, wikis, and the Internet phone system called Skype. But one of her favorite new tools is a Garmin ETrex. She uses it in a workshop to train teachers how to help students identify animal tracks and trees, using the GPSr as a locator tool.

The program, funded by a grant from the state's nonprofit Golden LEAF foundation, has the teachers hiding pictures of animal tracks in geocaches on school grounds. Students carry a book that helps them identify which animals made the tracks. Another exercise involves students classifying trees by locating their coordinates and then taking a series of measurements.

For a unit on rocks, fourth-grade students used GPSr devices to find rocks hidden around campus and then consulted field guides to identify the type of rocks they found. "Students took more ownership in the learning process knowing the information was needed to be successful in the geocache activity," she says.

Earlier, a group of academically gifted elementary students was given the task of identifying a location for a frog pond to be built on their school campus. Teachers chose four possible spots, divided the kids into groups, and gave each a set of coordinates. The students had to find the designated locations and perform a series of tests to determine if each area had the right kind of soil, water absorption rate, and other characteristics. Each team then had to create a persuasive PowerPoint presentation to argue their case.

Geocaching "gets students out of the classroom and addresses their various learning styles and personality types," Deborah says. "There is something in this game that all learners can identify with, like reading, writing, math, and geography." Deborah Goodman doesn't get to geocache as much as she'd like. She's too busy introducing the concept to eager educators across the Tar Heel State.

Social Exercise

Geocaching exercises muscles, brain cells, and social skills. That makes it useful for more than just gaming. From educators to corporate marketers to team-building consultants, professionals are figuring out innovative ways to apply geocaching to other disciplines.

Educators led the way because geocaching can be applied to so many classroom tasks. It's great for learning geography, of course, but puzzle caches may require students to look up historical facts, solve mathematical puzzles, or untangle logic problems in order to find the treasure. Geocaching can also be an exercise in problem-solving. Students may each be given a portion of a clue and required to collaborate to complete the puzzle.

Former Arizona State University President Alice Christie posted a series of sample lesson plans on the Internet detailing how geocaching could be incorporated into curricula ranging from elementary to high school. In one example, students retrieved objects from caches to place around campus and then sorted, grouped, and analyzed them using Microsoft Excel. The exercise teaches the concept of sets while also introducing students to spreadsheet software.

Another lesson aimed at sixth-graders involves geocaches filled with information about national parks. Students are instructed to plan a family vacation using the materials. In the process, they learn about the National Park System as well as the geographic diversity of the United States. (Ironically, as noted previously, the National Park System doesn't permit the placement of physical geocaches on its properties.)

Geocaching is a fun way to teach adults, too. Reid Smalley (Pirates Be Here), director of continuing education and workforce development at Fulton-Montgomery Community College in Johnstown, New York, uses it to teach outdoor navigation to would-be campers and backpackers.

"They don't come to my class to learn how to geocache. They come to learn how to navigate and come back alive," he says. But a multi-cache at the end of the five- to six-hour class helps to cement lessons learned. Students plan and follow a route that simulates an outdoor adventure. For those who want to tack on the multi-cache, there's a temporary container full of chocolate bars.

Pirates Be Here sees multiple dimensions of geocaching to organizational development. "For personal development, it's a good confidence builder in the satisfaction of 'I found it,'" he says. "For goal-oriented people, there are hundreds of thousands of geocaches out there to get."

Promotion on a Budget

Government agencies and even corporations have also caught the geobug, enticed by the game's openness and relatively low cost.

Because geocaching doesn't require extensive facilities, equipment, or staff supervision, it's a natural for cash-strapped municipalities.

The California county of Amador organized a fund-raising event around geocaching in March 2009. Participants paid $10 to get a list of clues that took them through historic downtown districts and nearby attractions like the Preston Castle in Ione and the Kennedy Mine in Jackson. Each downtown selected a theme and prepared appropriate clues around it. Players mingled with locals dressed in period costumes. In one town, participants took part in a murder mystery.

The Arkansas State Parks system is one of a growing list of recreational agencies throughout the United States that has found geocaching to be a low-risk, high-return way to entice citizens out into the woods. In 2008, Arkansas placed 52 geocaches—one in each of its parks—and invited geocachers to visit them all. Visitors could pick up clues that add up to the coordinates of a bonus fifty-third cache, which contains a series of geocoins that Arkansas minted specifically for this promotion.

The campaign was intended to attract tourists to Arkansas, says Joe Jacobs, marketing and revenue manager, and it quickly bore fruit. "We've got about 125 finds in the first week and a lot of great comments about the parks and how much they appreciate what we're doing for the geocachers," he says. It took less than a month for someone to run the entire gauntlet. The project was an outgrowth of a program launched by the state's Department of Parks and Tourism one year earlier to honor of the 70th anniversary of the state's National Great River Road. The agency placed a series of geocaches in the ten counties that bordered the byway.

Maryland's passport.

The Arkansas Parks system built a special page devoted to geocaching, including a worksheet to track finds. The state has supported caching in its parks for years and even offers geocaching instruction as a core program. State organizations swap GPSr units among each other. Jacobs sees geocaching as a way to get people off the couch and out into nature. "Put a screen in front of my 12-year-old and she'll go anywhere," he laughs.

Not to be outdone, the state of Maryland created the Maryland Municipal League Geocache Trail, which is comprised of 78 caches located in the league's

11 district regions throughout the state. Geocachers have to pick up or download a "passport" to carry with them on their journey and stamp each page with a unique rubber stamp at locations along the trail. Each location also houses a code word. The first 500 geocachers who logged at least 22 finds got a special geocoin.

Strictly Business

There's corporate action, too. PPL Corp. (PPLPreserves), a Pennsylvania-based utility, has had geocaches on its properties in Pennsylvania, Maine, and Montana since 2001. The treasure entices people to come visit the company's wildlife refuges. "This is part of getting across the message about generating electricity in a safe and environmentally responsible way," says Meg Welker, education relations director. "Commitment to the environment is part of our philosophy."

PPL currently has six containers stashed, one on each of its six preserves. About 2,500 finds have been logged in the last two years, says Welker: "It's been pretty successful."

There's also a company devoted to building business teamwork using geocaching. Geoteaming is a Groundspeak-sponsored venture headed by a former Microsoft executive that arranges one-day offsites where business colleagues "balance competition and collaboration in this unique business simulation." The exercises require players to both collaborate within teams and compete across teams, as well to come up with inventive solutions to problems. Communication, strategy, and leadership skills all come into play.

Putting Geocaching to Work

There are nearly endless possibilities for incorporating geocaching into a classroom or business promotion. Here are some ideas we came up with:

Education

- Kids don't want to read? Have them complete sentences plucked from books you've assigned them in order to figure out coordinates. The number of letters in the missing word corresponds to digits in the coordinates. Or, make the coordinates correspond to pages in a book where certain lessons can be found.
- Make a geocache a reward for students (or your own kids, for that matter) for completing a certain number of homework assignments or achieving a des-

ignated grade point average. Stash a few geocoins in the container to reward the most ambitious students.

- Make the coordinates the outcome of whatever math you're teaching. Sites like Calculate for Free (**Calculateforfree.com/**) can perform just about any kind of conversion you can imagine.

- Want to be devious? Choose the most likely mistakes students will make and place dummy caches at those locations. Instead of a geocoin, give them a "Nice Try!" message.

- For history lessons, correlate coordinates to facts and figures. For instance, students have to find out what year the Civil War ended into order to learn key numbers.

- Along that vein, there are already lots of puzzlers who have conveniently created puzzles that require research, whether it be astronomical, historical, or local. Find a creative puzzle cache in your area and set your students loose in the library to research the answer. Or, contact a puzzle owner in your area, tell her what your class is going to be learning about this year, and have the cacher make a puzzle especially for your class. Most puzzlers are usually just waiting for their next inspiration to strike and would welcome the challenge to give back to their community.

- Take students on a virtual tour of your area by hiding caches containing facts and artifacts about locations on the tour. Students compete to fill out a questionnaire with answers that can only be found in the geocaches.

- Teach geography by placing caches that are at opposite ends of the compass. Or, make it harder by requiring searchers to navigate with a compass from a central point.

- Have teams compete to find a sequence of geocaches within the shortest time period. Challenge players by requiring members to solve a puzzle at each stop.

Promotion

Geocaching can be used to liven up a fair, festival, or business event. You can place caches specially designed for an occasion or hide a cache on your property with the goal of drawing visitors who may later become customers. Many restaurant owners find this to be an inexpensive way to draw hungry players around lunchtime!

Be aware that Groundspeak rigorously enforces provisions against the use of **Geocaching.com** specifically for commercial purposes. However, there's no provision against hiding a cache on private property as long as the owner grants permission. Just don't try to promote your business on the Geocaching.com site. Here are some ideas for incorporating caching into business operations and marketing:

- Create a geocache challenge. Players must visit all the caches in a series to collect clues that lead them to the final destination. The first ten visitors to the final get a special prize.
- Use a prize hidden in a geocache as a reward for volunteers who achieve the most success signing up new volunteers or donors.
- Attract visitors to your retail store by hiding a cache nearby. Caches hidden on private property are rare, so why not welcome searchers to your location? Toss in some discount coupons to promote word-of-mouth awareness.
- Sponsor a series of puzzle caches with clues that relate to the cause your organization supports. Charge a tax-deductible entry fee and offer prizes for the competitors who complete the circuit most quickly.
- Promote your town or region by placing caches that relate to items of local history.

Team-Building

Geoteaming creates competitions to build business teams, but there's no reason you can't do this yourself. Here are some ideas:

- Place caches that require teams to figure out creative solutions to retrieve them. For example, a container placed well out of arm's reach would necessitate team members to cooperate on a solution.
- Challenge teams to retrieve a designated number of caches in a limited time frame.
- Using available placements in your area, challenge players to retrieve a cache of each type (for example, traditional, multi, puzzle, virtual, Wherigo) in the shortest time.
- Require team members to learn little-known facts about each other or about your organization in order to find coordinates.
- Challenge teams to take photos of items in the vicinity of caches that you place.

Geocaching's flexibility and low cost lends itself to lots of business and organizational uses. It's great for building teamwork, stimulating creative thinking, and inspiring leadership. It balances personal accomplishment with shared goals. By fine-tuning the rules of the game, you can make it as cooperative or as competitive as you want. As the population of geocachers grows, expect more organizations to unlock its potential.

CACHER PROFILE
Ecorangers

Photo by Bill Taves (Mister Greenthumb)

Geocaching.com handle: Ecorangers
Name: Tami and Wade Mauland (with their kids, Dane and Tait)
Claim to fame: Have taken their kids on every single caching experience, dragging them in a sled or carrying them piggyback when they were small
Location: West Bend/Brookfield, WI
Caching since: October 10, 2003
Total finds: 19,374
Total hides: 277
Preferred GPSr: Magellan Meridian Gold

Favorite Cache Types

Any cache with $100 bills in them! There are a few caches in their area that have been visited by retired veterinarians from Illinois who randomly place $100 bills in the caches they find.

When that's not an option, the family likes caches that bring them to places they never would have seen: a spectacular waterfall in a park, Johnny Cash's grave, a sculpture to honor the Navajo windtalkers, the bell from the warship *Arizona* from Pearl Harbor, and monuments to firefighters and war heroes.

The Ecorangers also like events, where they can put faces to the names they see in online logs and share funny stories. They also lead some workshops for geocaching newbies.

Special Equipment

- Palm PDA
- Hiking gear
- Window scraper brush to get rid of soft snow
- Tackle boxes with goodies for the kids

- Compasses
- Extra batteries
- Hiking stick to knock aside bushes or spider webs
- Flashlights for night caching
- Water
- Travel bugs
- Gloves for reaching into holes
- DVD player in the family van for when kids get tired of doing so many caches in a day.

Great Caching Stories

While Tami ran ahead on one cache hunt, Wade decided to explore some unusual ice formations on Lake Michigan. Suddenly, he crashed through the ice. Standing in freezing water up to his armpits and with no help in sight, his life flashed before his eyes. Thank goodness for his walking stick. Wade pried himself loose and managed to struggle out of the water, but his snow pants and heavy boots were soaked and freezing. He slogged 500 yards back to the car. Luckily, there were extra pants and boots there.

One of the most memorable finds of the Ecorangers was a series called "Manitowoc's WWII Submarines," which involved finding 30 actual submarines (all separate caches) in a number of Wisconsin counties. Pulling these together provided coordinates to a park honoring Civil War veterans. A puzzle there led them to a three-foot submarine that the cache owner had made and submerged. Ecorangers brought up the model sub and signed the logbook inside. Due to maintenance problems, the final cache has been archived along with most of the individual parts of the series. But the whole idea shows how ingenuity and creativity can lead to a summer's worth of fun for cachers in an area.

Most Memorable Hides

Tami likes a cache she hid inside a fake doorbell button. Frequently, people put their hands on it without realizing it. She also created a magnetic "Waste Management" sign with a log on the back to slap on the side of a dumpster. She's also pretty proud of her "Colors of a Rainbow" series. The final cache is a puzzle that requires coordinates from the other colors in the series.

Wade wrote a story for his daughter in "The Princess and the Hedgehog," which sets up a hunt for three friendly animals (parts of the multi) who were lost in a storm. It's a lovely little fable that gets kids of all ages involved in the cache. Wade also likes his Evil Monkey series, an idea he imported from Florida, where tree-climbing or "monkey caches" are popular. All the cache containers in that series involve climbing trees.

Words of Wisdom

"Take your kids along. They get an appreciation of outdoors and nature, but also the importance of being with family, of accomplishment, and team values. Dane is also getting pretty accurate with his compass skills. The kids also learn a fun way of keeping physically fit."

APPENDICES

APPENDIX A
Glossary

Adapted from GeoLex, the Lexicon of Geocaching (geolex.locusprime.net). Used by permission. Copyright GeoLex

1/1—Cache difficulty/terrain rating shorthand. The difficulty number is always presented first, followed by the terrain rating. Each number can range from 1 to 5 in 0.5 increments. A 1/1 cache is the easiest to find and reach. A terrain rating of 1 indicates that it's handicapped accessible, while a terrain rating of 5 indicates extreme terrain, or that specialized equipment (climbing gear, boat, scuba gear, etc.) is required.

Additional Logging Requirement (ALR)—Conditions that must be met to log a cache as found beyond simply finding the cache. The owner reserves the right to delete logs that do not follow the requirements. While cache owners are allowed to set logging requirements, the more outlandish requirements are not looked upon favorably by the caching community. The requirements may be listed on the cache page or in the cache container.

Approver—See Reviewer.

ATCF—As The Crow Flies. Point-to-point mileage, irrespective of roads or barriers. This is not a *true* point-to-point distance, as the distance calculated by a GPS is actually measured using a mathematical model of the curvature of the Earth.

Beach Tube—Lightweight, plastic, water-tight cylindrical container, typically used to hold car keys and money while swimming, boating, or surfing. Can be used for micro caches.

Bee Dance—See Drunken Bee Dance.

Bison Tube—Small, metal, water-tight cylindrical container that can be used for micro caches. Small enough to fit on a keychain, and normally used to hold pills. The name is derived from the company which manufactures most of these types of tubes, Bison Design.

Blinky—Often used as another word for *Nano*, this is a small light that uses a button battery and micro LEDs. It comes with a powerful base magnet and a separate removable magnet that allow the device to be attached to clothing without puncturing the fabric. The electronics and battery can be removed to create a magnetic nano cache.

Bookcrossing—A book exchange network in which players register books online and then share them by leaving them in designated places to be found by other members.

Bookmark—A premium feature of **Geocaching.com** that enables members to store links to caches in their own lists.

Bookmark List—A collection of Bookmarks. Each Bookmark List has its own owner-defined title and descriptive text. An automatic e-mail function can be set for each list. When active, an e-mail will be sent to the list's owner whenever a log is posted to a cache on the list. Similar to the Watchlist, but doesn't alter the listing of the number of people watching a cache. Bookmark Lists can also be either "Private" (the default) or "Public."

Breeder Cache—A cache that has an **Additional Logging Requirement** that requires finders to place a new cache of their own before being allowed to log a find. A breeder cache may contain smaller cache containers inside for the finders to use.

Bug—See Travel Bug.

BYOP—Bring Your Own Pen.

Cache Machine—When a number of cachers form a group for the purpose of finding a large number of caches in a relatively short period of time for the purposes of increasing their find count, a method also referred to as power caching.

Cacher—A person who engages in geocaching.

CITO—Cache In, Trash Out. The act of removing and disposing of trash one finds while searching for a cache. CITO is also a special type of Event Cache in which players gather to clean up a park or public space.

CO—Cache Owner.

Codeword Cache—A variation on a virtual cache, a codeword cache has no log book, but rather requires the finder to e-mail a code or password to the owner. Briefly allowed on **Geocaching.com**, they are now banned because codeword caches gave rise to a large number of worthless and uninteresting caches. Sometimes called a Password Cache.

Constellation—The configuration of GPS satellites overhead at any specific time. Some constellation configurations are better than others for calculating your position.

Decon Kit—U.S. military decontamination kit box, approximately 2.5" × 3.5" × 1.5", sold by military surplus stores and often used as a small cache container.

Digitalfish—A type of signature item, each digitalfish has a unique identifier that enables it to be tracked online at **Geofish.net**.

Dipping—The act of logging a Travel Bug or Geocoin into a cache, and immediately logging it back into one's possession. Someone might "dip" a Travel Bug or GeoCoin in order to register miles traveled before physically handing off the trackable to someone else.

DNF—Did Not Find. This type of log indicates that a cache was not found. DNFs can be important (to admit) because a string of them can mean that the cache has disappeared.

DPM—Including these letters in a cache log was once a secret way to indicate the cache was of low quality. DPM is an abbreviation for "des palourdes mortes," which is French for "the dead clams." Rarely used today, as the meaning quickly spread through the geocaching community and secrecy was lost.

Drunken Bee Dance—The movements of a geocacher, trying to pinpoint Ground Zero, chasing the directional arrow first in one direction and then in another. Drunken Bee Dances produce a zigzagging track log.

Film Can—35-mm film container, the archetypal container for small caches.

Force, The—Sixth sense gained from experience finding geocaches. From the *Star Wars* movies. Also called Geosense.

Frisbee Rule—A guideline proposed by a geocacher in an online forum that suggests that one should not be required to ask permission to place a geocache anywhere that one wouldn't need permission to play Frisbee. While an interesting guideline, this is not **Geocaching.com**'s official position.

FTF—First to Find. The first person to locate a cache after it has been placed. There is sometimes an FTF prize in the cache, which is an item of slightly higher value than the usual cache contents and which the FTF gets to keep.

FTL—First to Log. Sometimes the second or third cacher to find a new cache gets online before the FTF logs their cache.

GC.com—Geocaching.com.

GCxxxx—The GCxxxx waypoint identifier has little significance other than as a unique ID. Originally limited to six characters or less to accommodate the limitations of GPSr units, the first two characters are always "GC" and the following characters are calculated based upon a conversion algorithm in base-31 format. The six-character limit was later scrapped because there were more caches being created than digits to represent them and many newer GPSr units could accommodate longer waypoint names. Also known as GC ID or GC number.

Geocachers' Creed—A voluntary set of guiding principles for geocacher behavior. It was developed by 60 cachers in open forums to orient new players to the ethos of the community. The full creed and background are at **Ageocreed.info**.

Geocoin—Coin-size tokens especially made for individual cachers or caching groups. Some may be very elaborate metal coins with tracking numbers stamped on them and encased in plastic. On the other end of the scale are homemade coins made from a wooden disk and handmarked with an ink stamp. Some coins use the same tracking system as travel bugs. The same general rules that apply to travel bugs apply to these geocoins. Geocoins started as collectibles and some cachers still collect them like baseball cards or stamps, but coins have in recent years also become basically travel bugs.

Geomuggle—See Muggle.

Geomuggled—See Muggled.

Geopath—A path, usually in the woods or through vegetation, stamped down by previous geocachers. Also called a Geotrack.

Geosense—Sixth sense gained from experience finding geocaches. Also called *The Force*, from the Star Wars movies.

Geostripes—Refers to the arm and/or leg scratches received while geocaching.

GJTB—Green Jeep Travel Bugs (see YJTB). The third (2006) Jeep contest used green Jeeps.

Gladware—A generically used term for cheap, disposable plastic food containers. Compared to reusable containers, they make poor cache boxes, as they don't seal as well, and don't stand up as well to the environment.

GPS—Stands for Global Positioning System. It is comprised of three parts: The Space Segment, which is comprised of the orbiting satellites (SVs); the Control Segment, which are the ground based monitoring facilities; and the User Segment, the actual receivers.

GPSr—A GPS receiver. The "r" refers to "receiver," to differentiate the unit from the entire GPS system.

GPX—A cache database file format. Files in the GPX format are available only to Premium Members. This format contains virtually all the information available on a cache page, plus the last 5 logs made to the cache, as well as any logs the person requesting the file may have made to the cache. GPX files can be requested from a cache page, or via Pocket Queries. See also LOC.

Ground Zero—The point where the coordinates displayed on your GPSr exactly match the coordinates given for a cache. Sometimes abbreviated as "GZ."

GSAK—Geocaching Swiss Army Knife. The most useful software program for organizing any number of geocaches.

Guidelines—The rules for cache placement. They can be found at **Geocaching. com/about/guidelines.aspx**

GZ—See Ground Zero.

Huckle-Buckle-Beanstalk—A method of group caching, which takes its name from a classic children's game. When a member of the group spots the cache, they walk elsewhere (to not give away the cache's location), then call out, "huckle-buckle-beanstalk!" (or whatever word or phrase the group has decided on). This continues until everyone in the group has either spotted the cache, or given up, after which the cache is retrieved and logged. Contrast this to the Three Musketeers method.

Hula Wave—Some GPS receivers (mostly Magellan units) automatically engage a location-averaging function when it detects that the unit is moving slower than a certain speed. To avoid this, the "hula wave" is used. This involves holding the unit to your extreme right, then quickly moving it to your extreme left (or vice-versa). The unit will detect this as movement greater than the prescribed speed limit for averaging and will temporarily turn averaging off.

IBTL—In Before The Lockdown. Forum usage only. Indicates that the poster thinks the forum thread will soon be forced closed. Not exclusive to geocaching.

LEO—Law Enforcement Officer.

LN—Left Nothing. Sometimes paired with TN.

LOC—A cache database file format. The LOC format is available to all members. Only the most basic cache information is included in a LOC file. LOC files can be requested from a cache page, a Pocket Query (for Premium Members), or from a search list. See also **GPX**.

Lock & Lock—A food-storage system that features a recessed, soft-rubber gasket in the lid and a hinged latching mechanism on each edge of the lid, which snaps into the container's sides. A excellent choice for a geocache container, it comes in a variety of sizes, can be opened and closed more easily than an ammo box, and remains waterproof over time. Its downside is that its plastic surface can be difficult to paint, if it requires camouflage. The name "Lock & Lock" is often applied to similar locking storage products, such as Snapware.

LPC—Lamp Post Cache or Light Pole Cover. A very common hiding place for micro caches, this exploits the fact that the shroud (or "skirt") on lamp posts that cover the anchor bolts are usually not secured, and can be lifted up to provide a hiding place. The term LPC is sometimes intended to be a derogatory reference, since LPC hides are generally all the same and require little skill or imagination.

Maggots—Also called Pirates.

Markwell—Used in the forums only. To "Markwell" is to respond to a message with a link to another thread where the posted question has already been answered. Named after the geocacher Markwell.

McToys—Originally referred to the toy give-aways that come with a Happy Meal. In geocaching terms, it now refers to any cheap trinket that may be found in a cache box. McToys are now mainly fun for children to take and swap between caches.

MEFF—Most Esteemed First Finder. Also called FTF.

Member—Technically, anyone with a **Geocaching.com** account is a member. But the term "Member" usually refers to those with a paid Premium Membership. Premium Members can have more caches on their watchlist, can run Pocket Queries, and have access to caches that have been designated for Premium Members only (see MOC). Members who subscribed during the first year that subscriptions were available are designated Charter Members. Other than the name, there is no difference between a Premium and Charter membership.

Micro-spew—A usually derogatory term for the proliferation of micro caches placed in obvious and uninteresting locales. The classic example of this is the LPC.

Mini-Cache—The long-time "missing" cache size. For a time, there was not an official cache size category for cache containers that are larger than a "micro" but smaller than a "regular." So the geocaching community invented the "mini-cache." Mini-caches have room for a limited number of small trade items and may be big enough to hold a small pen (see Shorty Pen). The classic mini-container is the military Decon Kit. In the fall of 2004, the cache size "small" was finally added to handle the mini-cache size. The term "small" was chosen over "mini" to give it a unique, single-letter abbreviation (avoiding confusion with "micro").

Mitsuko—Geocaching's most famous Sock Puppet. Created by Choberiba, the Mitsuko persona was that of a young, attractive Asian-American female. Images of the Japanese model Akane Souma were used to complete the deception.

MKH—Magnetic Key Holder. The hide-a-key box, usually intended to conceal a car or house key, can be utilized as a ready-made micro container. Since they are usually not watertight, logs need to be placed within small zip-lock baggies, if the container is going to be out in the elements.

MOC—Members Only Cache. An MOC is one that's reserved for Premium Members (see Member). MOCs are designated with a icon. Only Premium Members can display an MOC page, and consequently, only Premium Members can log an MOC.

Muggle—A non-geocacher (taken from the *Harry Potter* series of books). Also called Geomuggle.

Muggled—The discovery of a cache by a non-geocacher. Also called Geomuggled. Although non-cachers are encouraged to "play along" should they come across a cache, when someone refers to a cache as having been muggled, it almost always means it was stolen or vandalized.

Nano—An unofficial cache size. A nano cache is usually considerably smaller than the typical micro. One popular container is approximately the size of a pencil eraser. They usually have a magnetic base to keep them in place. A nano container is sometimes referred to as a Blinky, because some do have small LED lights in them.

NIAH—Needle In A Haystack. A small cache placed in an area where there are a great number of possible hiding locations.

OCB—Original Can of Beans. One of the items placed in the very first geocache (actually called a "stash" at the time), the can was later made into a Travel Bug, and occasionally makes appearances at various geocaching get-togethers.

P & G—Park and Grab. A easy-to-find cache that you can get very close to by car. Sometimes written as P-n-G or PNG.

PAF—Phone A Friend. Usually done in the field via cellphone. This may take one of two forms. If the cacher is hunting a cache without the cache page information, he or she may call someone who will look up the cache page and relay the description and the hint. Most often, though, the cacher may phone someone who has already found the cache or the cache owner, in hopes of receiving additional information about its location.

Password Cache—See Codeword Cache.

PI—Poison Ivy. Used generically to include poison oak and poison sumac.

Pirates—A short-lived phenomenon where rogue geocachers would steal caches, and then either: a) destroy the cache; b) hold it for ransom; or c) move it to another location, leaving only a note behind to indicate the new location. A number of minor variations were also used. A late attempt was made by some pirates to legitimize the practice by making it an opt-in, non-destructive activity. But by that time, pirates had generated so much ill-will among mainstream geocachers (which still exists) that they were drummed out of the sport.

Plunder—Similar to muggled. A plundered cache is one that has been stolen or vandalized. However, there is a slight difference in meaning. Saying a cache has been plundered leaves open the possibility that the act was not done by accidental finders. See also Pirates.

PNG—Park and Grab. See P & G.

Pocket Cache—A pocket cache is a cache carried on one's person, usually to geocaching events. Often, these are actual caches that the owner has moved from their assigned location. Since **Geocaching.com** no longer supports Traveling Caches, and the removal of active caches can cause confusion for those seeking them in their posted location, Pocket Caches are not condoned. Using a cache in this manner may cause it to be permanently archived and locked.

Pocket Lint—See Pocket Cache.

Pocket Query—(PQ) A cache query engine available only to Premium Members. A wide variety of search and filter parameters are available. The resulting query is e-mailed to you in either GPX or LOC format, on whatever schedule you set. The term "Pocket Query" is often used to reference the actual zipped file that the query generates.

Podcache—A puzzle or multi-cache which utilizes spoken or aural clues that the cache-finder listens to on-site via a portable MP3 player. The finder downloads the audio file from a link on the cache page, uses the GPSr to navigate to the starting point, and then uses the instructions from the audio player to locate the cache. There may be additional puzzles and GPS navigation required along the way.

Podcacher—One of several podcasts about geocaching. Hosted by Sonny and Sandy Portacio.

Power Trail—A path with a large number of easy, traditional caches placed every one-tenth of a mile. Like a Cache Machine, it's another way for people to easily increase their find count. As such, it is looked down upon by some. Also called Power Cluster.

PQ—See Pocket Query.

Preform—A micro container resembling a wide test-tube, made of transparent plastic (usually clear, but sometimes tinted) with a screw-on cap. Preforms are actually the "blanks" that are heated and blown into a form to create soda bottles. They are very durable and waterproof, making them a good choice for a micro-size cache container. The main downside to preforms is that they generally have to be purchased in bulk quantities, rather than individually.

Premium Member—See Member.

Project A.P.E.—A promotional tie-in with Twentieth Century Fox to publicize its remake of the movie *Planet of the Apes* in 2001. Twelve caches were placed around the world and stocked with promotional items from the movie. Two of these caches still exist (one in Washington state; one in Brazil) and now function as traditional caches. For the curious, A.P.E. stood for Alternative Primate Evolution.

Reviewer—A local volunteer who validates a cache submission prior to the cache being posted. Sometimes referred to as an Approver, but Reviewer is the preferred term. Reviewers do not personally visit a cache site, but confirm that the cache, as presented in the submission, adheres to the posted *Cache Placement Guidelines*.

ROT-13—A simple encryption scheme where each letter is rotated 13 characters up or down the alphabet. Based on one of the world's oldest encryption schemes, ROT-13 came into common use in the 1970s on early bulletin board systems, and later on Usenet. In geocaching, cache location hints are often encoded using ROT-13.

ROW—Right Of Way. Often, the area between a street and the sidewalk.

SBA—Should Be Archived. Log type indicating that there is a severe problem with a cache (missing, destroyed, inaccessible, or on private property without permission). When a SBA log is made to a cache, a copy of it is automatically sent to the **Geocaching.com** administration, who then routes it to a local reviewer. The official log type is "Needs Archived" but the term "Should Be Archived" came first and has stuck.

Seed Cache—See Breeder Cache.

Shorty Pen—An ink pen that has been shortened enough to fit into a small cache container. There are companies that sell them ready-made (**ShortyPen.com**) or you can make your own in any size you want for 15¢ to 20¢ each. See **TexasGeocaching. com/mini_pens.asp** for a tutorial on how to transform a pen into a shorty pen.

Signal—Signal is the official mascot of **Geocaching.com**. Designed by artist Koko, Signal is a frog with an GPS antenna on his (her?) head.

Signature Item—An object used as a trade item in caches that is meant to be identified with a specific geocacher (or group of geocachers). Some signature items, like some Geocoins, digital fish, or pathtags have unique identifiers that allow them to be tracked online.

SL—Signed Log.

Sock Puppet—A false account used in a forum or chat room account in order to hide the true owner's identity.

Spoiler—An online log entry (or photo attached to an online log) that may give away the location of a cache or in some other way "spoil" the caching experience for others.

STF—Second To Find. The second person to locate a cache after it has been placed.

SV—Space Vehicle. In GPS terms, SV refers to the satellites comprising the Space Segment of the GPS system.

Swag—Not exclusive to geocaching. Contrary to popular thought, swag is not an acronym, nor is it a recently invented term. The word has been around for several centuries. It has a number of meanings, but the one utilized in geocaching stems from "swag" as referring to stolen or plundered loot. In more modern times, it's come to mean free promotional items, like those you might get at a trade fair or an expo. Because of this, in a bit of creative reverse-etymology, people have come to say that it's an acronym for "Stuff We All Get," which is clever, but wrong. In geocaching, "swag" just means the trade items found in a cache or things that could be used as trade items.

Tadpole—New forum users are given the avatar title of Tadpole until they have posted at least 10 messages, at which time their title changes to Geocacher. The Tadpole is a reference to the **Geocaching.com** mascot, Signal. Those who are Premium Members have the option of changing their avatar title at any time.

TB—See Travel Bug.

TB Jail—See Travel Bug Prison.

TB Prison—See Travel Bug Prison.

TFTC—Thanks For The Cache. Occasionally written as T4TC or TFT$.

TFTH—Thanks For The Hunt (or Hide). Occasionally written as T4TH.

The Creed—See Geocachers' Creed.

Three Musketeers—A method of group cache hunting, which takes its name from the Musketeer motto, "All for one and one for all." Unlike the *Huckle-Buckle-Beanstalk* method, as soon as one person in the group finds the cache, the hunt is over, and all members of the group log their find.

TN—Took Nothing. Often paired with LN.

TNLN—Took Nothing, Left Nothing.

TNLNSL—Took Nothing, Left Nothing, Signed Log.

TNX4GC—Thanks For The Geocache. Similar to TFTC.

TOTT—Tool Of The Trade. This generally indicates that some type of tool or instrument may be required to retrieve or gain access to a cache. The nature of the tool is usually not specified, but there may be hints within the cache page. It could be an actual tool, such as a screwdriver, or something as simple as a long stick to retrieve a cache from a high perch.

TPTB—The Powers That Be. Refers to the upper echelon of the **Geocaching. com** administrative hierarchy.

Travel Bug (TB)—An item that travels from cache to cache. Each item has a unique tracking number (assigned by **Geocaching.com**), which allows you to follow its journey. A travel bug is *not* a trade item, and you are not required to leave anything in the cache when you pick up a travel bug, though you are expected to place it in a different cache in a reasonable amount of time. Some travel bugs may have a specific goal, such as to reach a certain location. If a travel bug has a goal, and you are unable to help it reach that goal, even in a small way, it is customary that you leave it for someone who can assist it in that goal.

Travel Bug Hotel—A geocache with the intended purpose of acting as an exchange point for travel bugs. These are almost always regular or large containers.

Travel Bug Prison—A Travel Bug Hotel that requires that you leave as many travel bugs as you take, and/or that you do not take more than a certain number of travel bugs. They are called prisons (or jails) because travel bugs can get "stuck" in them for an extended period of time, as people who find the cache don't move any of the bugs on, because they don't have a bug to leave. In fact, only the travel bug owner, not the cache owner, has the right to apply any kind of movement restrictions on a travel bug. Because of this, any movement restrictions placed by the cache owner may be ignored by the cache finder.

Traveling Cache—A cache whose purpose is to change locations with every find. When someone finds a traveling cache, they can place it in a new location and post that location in their find log. Due to numerous problems with this type of cache (showing up in off-limit areas, disappearing for extended periods of time, failure to log new locations, etc.), traveling caches are no longer published on **Geocaching.com,** but there are still a small number of them that were grandfathered.

UPR—See UPS.

UPS—Unnatural Pile of Sticks. A common telltale sign of a hidden cache. Sometimes UPR (Unnatural Pile of Rocks) or URP (Unnatural Rock Pile) is used.

URP—See UPS.

US—Use Stealth. Commonly used in a place with a high muggle-to-geocacher ratio.

Virtual cache—A containerless geocache in which the reward is visiting a location rather than finding a container. Visitors are usually asked to send the cache owner answers to questions in order to log the visit. Virtual caches are now called Waymarks and tracked on a Groundspeak site called **Waymarking.com.**

Watchlist—A list of caches for which the member receives, via e-mail, a copy of any logs made for those caches. The number of caches on a watchlist is dependent upon the type of membership the geocacher has.

Wherigo—A variation of geocaching in which players interact with objects and characters—both real and virtual—as directed by a software program. Wherigo doesn't necessarily involve the use of a GPSr or even coordinates. However, a variation called a "Wherigo Cache" includes conventional geocaching.

WG—Refers to either a Where's George dollar bill or the Where's George website (**Wheresgeorge.com**).

WJTB—White Jeep Travel Bugs (see YJTB). The second (2005) Jeep contest used larger, white Jeeps.

WOFM—Watch Out For Muggles. Since Muggles are blamed for caches that have disappeared, cachers often try to be as inconspicuous as possible, which takes practice if you're trying to look under a bench on which someone is sitting.

XNSL—eXchanged Nothing, Signed Log. Equivalent to TNLNSL.

YACIDKA—Yet Another Cemetery I Didn't Know About.

YAPIDKA—Yet Another Park I Didn't Know About.

YJTB—Yellow Jeep Travel Bugs. A contest held in conjunction with Jeep. The logs and pictures for the Jeep Travel Bugs were judged for creativity and originality in order to win Jeep gear. See also Travel Bug.

APPENDIX B
Resource Lists

The Basics

- Your GPS manual.
- *Outdoor Navigation with GPS*—Stephen W. Hinch, Annadel Press, 2nd ed., 2007.
- *The Complete Idiot's Guide to Geocaching*—Editors and Staff of **Geocaching. com**, Penguin Group, 2009.
- *GPS Outdoors—A Practical Guide for Outdoor Enthusiasts*—Russell Helms, Menasha Ridge Press, 2006.
- *Basic Essentials Using GPS* (Falcon Guide)—Bruce Grubbs, Morris Book Publishing, 2005.
- *GPS Made Easy*—Lawrence Letham, The Mountaineers Books, 3rd ed., 2001.
- *The GPS Handbook*—Robert Egbert and Joseph King, Burford Books, 2008.
- *GPS for Dummies*—Joel McNamara, Wiley Publishing, Inc., 2004.
- *Fun with GPS*—Donald Cooke, ESRI Press, 2005.
- *Geocaching—Hide and Seek With Your GPS*—Erik Sherman, Apress Books, 2004.
- Picture of poison oak, ivy and sumac (**myhealth.ucsd.edu/library/healthguide/ en-us/support/topic.asp?hwid=aa83178** or **tinyurl.com/nxa9m2**)

Online Resources

- Geocacher University (**geocacher-u.com**)
- List of regional geocaching organizations: **cacheopedia.com/wiki/ List_of_Regional_Organizations/Groups**
- It's Not About the Numbers, organizes geocaching statistics, has map capability, too. (**itsnotaboutthenumbers.com**)

- World66.com, to make maps of places (states, countries, counties, etc.) where you have cached
- Wherigo (wherigo.com)
- CacherStats.com, created by Grand High Poobah, Brady Nellis
  - Top 1000 geocachers ranked by number of finds (zinnware.com/HighAdv/Geocaching/most_caches_found.php)
- Debbie Does Decals (debbiedoesdecals.com/DebbiesRide.html)
- Earthcache.org
- Extreme-caching.com
- Gcinfo.no
- Navicache.com
- TerraCaching.com
- GPSgames.org
- GeoChecker.com, to verify that the answer to a puzzle cache is correct (only for puzzles that use the service)

Sites that Help You Choose a GPS

- GPSReview.net is an excellent and exhaustive source of reviews and news on GPSr devices.
- GPSrInformation.net has a large library of reviews contributed by enthusiasts. However, many are dated, so be sure you aren't making a decision based upon opinions of early generations of a product.
- Maps-gps-info.com has some very good advice on buying the right GPSr for your needs, as well as a nice list of free software and online services.
- Engadget.com is a popular news site about consumer electronics and a very good source of news, although it does not publish many reviews.
- GPSMagazine.com is stronger on auto navigation units, but has a very useful *Consumer Reports*-like grid for viewing the strengths and weaknesses of various models.
- CNET.com houses more than 100 reviews of handheld units, dating back several years. CNET is known for the quality and comprehensiveness of its professional reviews.

Geocoin Sites

- 3geeks.ca
- cacheaddict.com
- cachezone.de
- chqualitycoins.com
- coinsandpins.com
- coinswag.com
- crakeproductions.com
- dorkfishcoins.com
- dwprods.com
- geocachingshop.com
- geocachingshop.cz
- geocachingshop.de
- geocoin.no
- geocoin.se
- geocoins.biz
- geocoins.net
- geocoinshop.com
- geocoinshop.de
- geocoinstore.com
- geoswag.com

- hogwildstuff.org
- k2coins.nl
- landsharkz.ca
- lillysue.com
- montereycompany.com
- mygeocoin.de
- oakcoins.com
- personalgeocoins.com
- socalgeocoins.com
- thecachingplace.com
- TnTGeocoins.com
- tsunrisebey.com
- ukgeocachers.co.uk
- usageocoins.com
- we-belong.com
- worldcaching.com

Other Trackables Sites

- geofish.com (geofish.net)
- geogems.com (geogems.us)
- pathtags.com (pathtags.com)

APPENDIX C
Great Geocaches by State

Here are the caches we've discussed in this book, plus some other really interesting ones not in the book. In our estimation, these are must-visit caches if you're in the area. This list is also saved as one of our public bookmark lists on **Geocaching.com**.

AL
The Mountie Cache: GC7D75
Higher Than a Hawk: GCG37P

CA
100 Movies, 100 Quotes, 100 Numbers: GC133VK
Angelina's Ink: GC134XA
ANX: The Angle of Eternity: GCK1CC
Assume Nothing #7: WoW's 45th Birthday Micro-Multi: GCMDN5
   (rest of Assume Nothing series is located in description)
The Basilisk: GCPX5Q
Coca-Cola Cache: GCG2CC
Date With Insanity: GC13Y0G
The dragonfly scroll: GC7F3A
Edendale in the Golden Age of Silent Film: GCGX16
Found 50 States, I'm Going to Disneyland!: GCRFNN
Kwvers'! Nano Cache! (archived): GC1F1R0
Looking Into the Whale's Mouth: GCKE5K
Looking within myself: GC11TCJ
Radio Central: GCMB4Q
Snakes and Ladders: GCJG08
West Lake Bus Stop: GCKK3W
White top : GCADC9

FL

Alfred's Birds: GC1DHMA
None Shall Pass: GC1351F
Nowhere In Sight: GCT75R

HI

The Other Way To Hanalei: GCHH2F
Tunnel #1: GC146Q9

IL

BoB 99: GCKMBQ
A Mule, a Shovel, and a Golden Dream: GCZDG5

KY

Ben and Grace 1,000th Find Golden Ammo Box: GC1CZHM
Deja Vu: GCBAA5

LA

Vieux Carar: GCE02C

MA

Curling Cache: GCJV4B
Evil Framingham Tour: GC1PA2T
Knot Up Here!: GC1Q8N7
Nobscot Cagers: GC108B0
Rhodys & Canoe stop: GCWA0W
Whitin 'Tree' Park: GCVF7A

NC

101 Dalmatians series (bookmark list): http://tinyurl.com/ygklopp
A Claustrophobic's Nightmare/Just Say NO to Crack: GCK2AW
Bradley's Bottom: GC6A02
Cache, Cacher, Cache! (now archived): GCQC5A
Daniel Ridge Loop: GC1HRWV
Dawn of Aviation: GCB57D
High Water! (now archived): GCK9YD
Holy Wastewater! (She It?) (now archived): GCKTF2

Holy Wastewater II: GC11EPJ
The Mile high series of Geocache's...Hangover: GCVZ2W
Old Rag Mountain: GC16H3P
So Easy Even A Caveman Can Find It!: GC11ARM
Tube Torcher II: GCWA47
Wildlife: GCMXA2

NY
1776 Phase 1 Gathering Storm - Revolutionary War: GC12GQ4

OH
The Rickety Old "Skull Splitter" Bridge: GCZFA3
The "RockWood" Pirate Prison: GCZETP
Up On The Trail: GCTPFV

OR
Dr. Who: GCW6EM
The Stairmaster: GCJ4N1

PA
Conquer Your Fears: GC17VAR
Impossible?—Nah! The Sisters of Slatington: GC1F925
Impossible?—Nah! II Lonely In The Gorge: GC1G86E
The Gauntlet: GC1NEPJ
National Treasure I: GCNV5A
Noah's Ark: GCZGCJ
Those Olden School Days (event): GC1T4H8
Too Difficult, Too Dangerous and Just Too Crazy!: GC1812Z
White Noise: GCRFZB

TX
Barney Smith's Toilet Seat Museum: GCB6A8
Bon Voyage Funky Bus! (event): GC1DJ48
Cattle Pens: GC1KN57
Kirk vs. Picard: GC18433
Mrs. Captain Picard's 3rd Four Digit Smiley Event! (event) aka, GPS Olympics:
   GCQHEV

My Latitude Attitude: GCW6D5
Our First Hide: GC1A2PM
The Picard Nuptials: GCJG9B
The Round Rock: GCA219
Spinning Wheel: GCGNP4
Spring Creek Headwaters II: GCNZ3Y
You Gotta Be *&^%* Kidding Me! (now archived): GC1BWVN

UT
Arches National Park—Delicate Arch: GCJG49
Depth Perception: GCG62F

WA
Mission 9: Tunnel of Light (Project A.P.E. Cache): GC1169

WI
The Princess and the Hedgehog: GCNM5D
Rainbow's End...Pot-of-Gold: GCJE16
Super Sized!: GCND98
USS Geocache (SS-379)—Manitowoc's Final Submarine (now archived):
    GCJXJK
Submarine series (most are archived): http://bit.ly/subseries

Other Countries

Ghana
G.G.friendship (now archived): GCZH49

Mexico
Los Ebanos Ferry: GCT8HK

Portugal
Rainbow Hydrothermal Vents: GCG822

Tanzania
Karibu! You made it!: GCGETW

Acknowledgments

When we started researching his book, we had fewer than 100 found caches to our name and the security of knowing what we didn't know, which was nearly everything. We had to rely upon the generosity of the veterans we interviewed and they never ceased to amaze us with their responses. Many spent hours with us on the phone, in one case returning our call while they were in the 16th day of a grueling power caching run.

Listed here are the people who made our year-long learning experience fruitful and fun. We are proud to call them our new friends. But trying to recognize everyone who helped us with this book would be nearly impossible. We know that we have probably omitted some people, and they have our deepest apologies.

We contacted most of the 50 most prolific cachers in the world for interviews, and all but a handful consented. In addition, we had enthusiastic response from people in the education, government, commercial, and public service fields who are finding innovative new uses for geocaching.

We are particularly indebted to the Austin, Texas-based team of Wayne and Candy Lind (The Outlaw and Moosiegirl), Trey Bielefeld (TreyB), and Julie Perrine (Mrs. Captain Picard). Not only did they spend hours with us on the phone, but they invited us to Austin and spent two days of their time demonstrating the finer points of the game. The Outlaw organized a 15-hour power caching run and TreyB donated his time, expertise, geosense, and several hundred miles on his Toyota FJ Cruiser to the effort. The group also organized an event cache that introduced us to several other remarkable people, including Richard and Natalie Norton (Deafdillos), whose pluck and good humor in the face of deafness is inspiring. Mrs. Captain Picard spent a fun-filled day caching with us in San Antonio, and also helped us immensely with promotion ideas for this book: We were happy to have her incredibly creative mind at work for us.

The creator of GeoLex (**geolex.locusprime.net**), who chose to be known to us only as Prime Suspect, agreed to let us adapt that fine resource for publication as our glossary. Many thanks.

Several geocachers dug into their personal photo albums to share memories and several of their contributions grace these pages. We are particularly indebted to Mark Wilcoxson (Deermark), Scott Veix (InfiniteMPG), Dave Grenewetzki (dgreno), and Dutch Sanders (Linuxxpert) for their prowess with the camera. Other geocachers who agreed to extended interviews and follow-ups included Lee van der Bokke (Alamogul), Elin Carlson (EMC of Northridge, CA), Tami & Wade Mauland (ecorangers), Bill Lopez (mondou2), Steve O'Gara and Sandy Gude (ventura_kids), Bert Carter (WE4NCS), Ray King (Peasinapod), Darrell and Marcia Smith (Show Me the Cache), Clyde England, Brad Simmons (Monkeybrad), Graeme McGufficke (OzGuff), Larry Lemelin (Stressmaster), Ed Manley (TheAlabamaRambler), and Benjamin Thomas (bthomas).

TheAlabamaRambler was particularly forthcoming in helping to promote our efforts to contact veteran geocachers after Groundspeak declined our request to help. Many of these people not only expended considerable time on the phone with us, but also submitted lengthy written responses to a questionnaire. Our only regret is that we couldn't share more of their stories. Fortunately, we recorded nearly every interview and will be making many of them available on JoyOfGeocaching. com as audio diaries.

Other geocachers who spent time answering our many questions included Paul & Dot Bunn (Geo13); Jim and Denice Moody (kwvers!); Karin Claus (Greasepot); Gary & Vicky Hobgood (Gary&Vicky); Aurelia Taylor (meri-adoc2003); Lynn Wilcoxson (daggy); Reid Smalley (Pirates Be Here); MacKenzie Martin (CachingBox); Meg Welker; Kim Gorenflo (KimbyJ); Kathy Markham; Deborah Goodman; Michael Jacobus; Joe Jacobs; Ken Alexander (Granpa Alex); Tom and Anna Mary Bowers (SerenityNow); Michael Babcock (Ether Bunny); Kandy and Dann McWilliams (WheelerDealers); Lee, Cookie and Bethy Campbell (Bikely, Wifely and Psychly, respectively) and Bethy's fiance, Casey (Trekly); George Merenich (keoki_eme); and David & Nancy Tabuchi (DavidT21 & Fisherwoman). We are also grateful to the more than 140 geocach-ers who responded to our online survey, in many cases contributing thoughtful essays about why they love the game.

Several technology providers contributed evaluation units of their equipment and software, including DeLorme, Lowrance, Bushnell, Microsoft, and Topografx. We are grateful for the attention and we hope we didn't mess up the GPSr units too much.

Neil Salkind of the StudioB literary agency has represented us through three books with diligence and encouragement. And we will always have a special place in our hearts for Kent Sorsky and Steve Mettee of Linden Publishing. When our original publisher backed out of its contract due to financial problems, Kent and Steve agreed to take on the project at a moment's notice and with little justification. They then managed to shoehorn us into an already packed production schedule to deliver in 2010.

Finally, we are grateful to our family for putting up with us as we hopscotched across America, attempting to cache in as many new places as possible, and then burned nights and weekends documenting our experiences. While they didn't always understand the appeal of geocaching, they understood our passion for the project and for the people who made this experience so rewarding.

Index

E

Earthcache 16, 34
EasyGPS 191
eBay 166
ecorangers 74, 76, 80, 87, 219, 220
Edenton, North Carolina 213
Eisenbraun, Mark 77
elmbaek 42
Email Log Reader 186
EMC of Northridge, CA 58, 60, 87,
    115, 126-128, 133, 205, 212
England 147, 148
England, Clyde 83, 84, 195, 196
England, Helen 195
Equator 148
Ether Bunny 7, 71
Europe 120
event cache 33
Evil Framingham Tour 31
evil hide 83
Evil Monkey series 221
extreme cachers 128
Eyre, Doug 2
EZSniper 166

F

f0t0m0m 126, 128, 129
Facebook 127
fake leaf 81
fanny pack 64
fantasy factor 9
film canisters 29, 81, 83, 103, 135,
    137, 138, 139, 140, 143
Find Caches Along A Route 42
first aid equipment 61, 73
first-to-find (FTF). See FTF
Fisherwoman 16
fishing line 84
fishing vest 64
FishPOET 6
flashlights 62, 73, 89, 130, 164, 220
Flickr 190

Florida 11, 106, 116, 120, 125, 191, 221
Florida Geocaching Association 117
forums.groundspeak.com 201
Found 50 States 65, 131
FPS (Friend Positioning System) 137
Framingham 32, 71
Framingham, Massachusetts 70
France 88
Franklin, Benjamin 46
Fraygirls 114
FTF 31, 66, 97
Fulton-Montgomery Community
    College 214

G

gadget appeal 9
Galileo 155
Garmin 22, 23, 78, 202
Garmin 60 CSx 16, 65, 116, 143, 168
Garmin ETrex 213
Garmin GPSMAP 60CS 161
Garmin Nuvi 192
Garmin's Colorado and Oregon 175
Garmin's MapSource 143, 164
Garmin Tom Tom 192
Gary & Vicky 35, 98, 207, 208
Gauntlet, The 122
GBHomeTech 194
GCStatistic (www.macdefender.org/
    products/GCStatistic/) 26
geoadventure 41
geo-buddies 205
GeoBuddy 191
Geocacher's Creed 76
Geocachers of the Bay Area 47
Geocacher University (geocacher-u.com/
    content/blogsection/8/54/) 109
Geocaching.com 2, 21-24, 26-29,
    32-34, 36, 37, 40-42, 48, 50,
    52-56, 58, 63, 65, 74, 75, 89,
    92-95, 98, 99, 100, 101, 109,
    110, 127, 147, 149, 154, 155,

About the Authors

Paul and Dana Gillin are professional communicators who caught the geocaching bug a few years back and wanted to tell more people about it.

The Joy of Geocaching is the result of scores of interviews with avid geocachers and people who use geocaching in their classrooms, communities and businesses. The authors also crisscrossed the country to geocache in different environments, meet with local groups and even go power caching in Texas.

Paul's been in technology publishing for 25 years and is the author of two books about social media: *The New Influencers* and *Secrets of Social Media Marketing*. He speaks, trains and consults with businesses about how to use social media in their marketing programs. He blogs about this topic at paulgillin.com and writes about changes in the media industry at newspaperdeathwatch.com.

Dana has been a technology editor for nine years, most recently at Internet companies. She blogs about house rabbits at BunnyBlab.com, which attracts hundreds of other bunny lovers each month. She's also a professional crafter who runs FramesByDana.com.

The couple lives in Framingham, MA, where winter makes geocaching a challenge about five months a year. They migrate south whenever possible. They've made most of the mistakes geocachers can make but still love the game.